VIRGINIA & MARYLAND
50 HIKES WITH KIDS
WITH DELAWARE, WEST VIRGINIA AND WASHINGTON DC

VIRGINIA
& MARYLAND
50 HIKES
WITH KIDS

WITH DELAWARE, WEST VIRGINIA
AND WASHINGTON DC

**ALISON HUMPHREYS
AND WENDY GORTON**

Timber Press · Portland, Oregon

Timber Press
Workman Publishing
Hachette Book Group, Inc.
1290 Avenue of the Americas
New York, New York 10104
timberpress.com

Timber Press is an imprint of Workman Publishing, a division of Hachette Book Group, Inc. The Timber Press name and logo are registered trademarks of Hachette Book Group, Inc.

Printed in China on responsibly sourced paper

Series design by Hillary Caudle
Cover design and illustration by Always With Honor
All maps by Bart Wright

The publisher is not responsible for websites (or their content) that are not owned by the publisher.

The Hachette Speakers Bureau provides a wide range of authors for speaking events. To find out more, go to hachettespeakersbureau.com or email hachettespeakers@hbgusa.com.

ISBN: 978-1-64326-162-1

A catalog record for this book is available from the Library of Congress.

To Ronnie, my partner in life, love, and adventure, thank you for your endless support and for never saying no to an adventure. And to our five mavericks—Izzy, Teagen, Willow, Weston, and Stone—may you always live a great story and go where there is no path and leave your own trail.
—AH

To Riley, every hike and adventure I've embarked on my whole life prepared me for you, and I'm so lucky to get to enjoy the trails with you now.
—WG

CONTENTS

PREFACE

This slice of the mid-Atlantic region is a collection of five amazing states filled with rich history and diverse geography that provides endless opportunities for adventures. Its landscape is defined by coastal plains along the East Coast, rolling hills heading west, and the Appalachian Mountains farther inland. Unique rock formations and water features, combined with one-of-a-kind plant and animal species, along with the local pride of adventuring in nature throughout all four distinct seasons, makes hiking in the mid-Atlantic region a special experience for families all year long.

This guide aims to provide kids of all ages a curated selection of some of the most varied and interesting destinations in the mid-Atlantic, while reassuring busy adults about what exactly to expect from any given trail, the features they will see when they arrive, and the logistics that can make or break an outdoor excursion with kids. We hope you get a sense of the love steeped in these pages—the love for outdoors, the love for adventure, the love for planning and preparation, and the love for family and community. The mid-Atlantic's number of "kid-friendly" hikes is almost staggering, so choosing which adventures to include was no easy task. Alison's husband and four children were her co-adventurers on every single hike, often squeezing in up to three hikes a day, several days in a row in order to test and find just the right hikes for this guide. We carefully selected hikes that included fun features kids will look forward to seeing and places parents will feel comfortable navigating to and exploring with their children.

The driving question behind this book is this: How can we design experiences that inspire wonder in our children? If we—as educators, caregivers, aunties and uncles, grandparents, and parents—can provide a fun environment and the initial sparks of curiosity, we can help children discover and explore the world around them, creating a generation of

resilient, curious kids who appreciate natural beauty even from a young age. This book is designed to give adults some tools to help ignite questions on the trail, to teach kids that it's great to stop and look at things instead of just rushing from point A to point B, and to begin to introduce a broader understanding of just how many unique places surround us in this mountainous land. By simply venturing out and interacting with kids along the trail, we are building their skills in questioning things they see around them—everywhere—and encouraging them to look for answers.

It is our belief that not all classrooms have four walls and that there is no better way to learn about the world than to experience it. As you explore the outdoors with your own crew, please keep in mind that while the scavenger hunt items called out on each hike might help you to add excitement or teachable moments, finding them all need not be the main goal of your outing. We wrote this guide to help you get outside, spend time with your family, and have fun in the great outdoors.

It has been found that one-quarter of kids have never climbed a tree—ever. What was once a staple of childhood is starting to disappear. We understand it can be hard to watch your children take risks like climbing a tree or hiking a mountain, but allowing children to engage in risk-taking activities enables them to test their abilities and develop strength and confidence that can be applied to activities far beyond that tree or hill. Many of us have seen the copious amounts of research about the benefits of getting kids outdoors more and interacting with the world in an open-ended way. We also know that kids today lead more structured lives than ever before. We think you will be pleasantly surprised when you see how much your children enjoy simply being set loose in wide-open spaces. And unstructured time outdoors is very important for children's development. It has been found that children who spend time learning outdoors develop higher confidence, greater independence, increased creativity, and better decision-making skills.

Children also grow when they face challenges. This is why hiking and spending time in nature is such a powerful tool for children. Many children do not think about hiking a mountain and might assume they could never

Challenging hikes offer times for power-up stops and contemplation of the surrounding beauty

make it to the top. But they can. And when they do, they are filled with such joy and pride at this accomplishment that it spills into other areas of their lives. When you spend time with your children outdoors, you will notice that they begin to show more initiative, are more likely to be up for a challenge, and persevere more during hard times.

In our families, we think of ourselves more as forest wanderers than hikers. We find being outside in nature to be extremely calming while also invigorating. When you hear the term "hiker," sometimes the image that comes to mind is of a fit young adult with technical gear going up very steep mountains at a fast pace. But that is not what hiking, or this book, is all about. This is about getting out in nature, reconnecting with the natural world, and getting our bodies moving. It's about going at your own pace, stopping to smell the flowers, and enjoying time with your family away from everyday distractions. No matter what you call it—hiking, tramping, walking, exploring, or our favorite, forest wandering—amazing things happen when you get out of the house, off your phone, and into nature.

But please keep in mind that not all adventures go as planned. On our first official hike for this book, we were halfway through the hike when Alison suddenly heard her children crying. They were a little ahead of her on the trail and had unknowingly walked right past a huge hornet's nest. Her four young children got stung a total of fifteen times. She walked them a safe distance away from the nest, and they evaluated the damage. The kids cried, drank some water, and had a snack. And then you know what happened? They continued on their adventure. These amazingly brave and resilient children regrouped, comforted each other, and then calmly continued to hike back to the trailhead. You will be amazed at how your children are able to overcome obstacles and challenges on the trails and have an amazing experience, even when the adventure does not go as planned.

Time spent in nature is never wasted time, and it is a truly wondrous thing to see how the wild calms the child. It is important that children have an outlet for their energy, their creativity, and their passions. Giving children unstructured time outdoors allows them this much-needed time and freedom. And playtime outdoors isn't just for preschoolers; children of all ages benefit when given the freedom to freely explore the great outdoors.

Alison's family motto is to never give up and to live a great story. We believe that life, just like adventure, is not just about the destination but also about enjoying the journey. We refuse to follow the script that enjoying life is a goal only for the future—we don't believe you should have to wait until the kids are older or until you retire to go on adventures and start enjoying life. We also believe in raising mavericks—independent-minded people who want to achieve what has never been achieved before. People who are daring, innovative, influential, and willing to take chances. In a world that often encourages children to follow along with what the crowd is doing, we feel it is important that children develop the confidence to take their own path and follow their own dreams. We want our children to think for themselves, dream big, be courageous, do things their own way, and take a path in life that makes them happy. Our wish is that you also choose to raise mavericks.

We hope this guide will help you foster curiosity and a love of nature in the kids in your life, and that it helps to raise our next generation of naturalists by putting the guidebook in their hands. Experiencing the wonders all around us creates lifelong habits of seeking out adventure, appreciating the gifts nature gives us every day, and caring about keeping our natural resources clean, beautiful, and accessible for many generations to come. Our wish is that this guide serves a good foundation for you and your family in getting outside and getting more active. And we hope, just as naturalist and conservationist John Muir did one hundred years ago, that of the paths you take in life, "a few of them are dirt."

CHOOSING YOUR ADVENTURE

This guide is designed to help children become co-adventurers with you across this diverse portion of mid-Atlantic landscape, so build excitement by involving them in the planning process from the beginning. Let them flip through and mark the pages of the adventures they want to go on. Ask your children what features they love to see and experience outside. Ask them how long they want to hike and how hard they want to work on their next adventure. The following tables can help you and your children choose which adventure you want to go on next. For maximum success with young explorers, no hike is over 5 miles long or gains much more than 1,000 feet, perfectly attainable for most little legs. This means that there can be plenty of time for exploration, rest stops, snacks, and just taking in the sights and sounds around you.

ADVENTURES IN DELAWARE

ADVENTURE	HUB	LENGTH (MILES)	DIFFICULTY/ ELEVATION	HIGHLIGHTS
① **Alapocas Run** PAGE 64	Wilmington	2.7	Easy 246'	Blue granite cliffs, waterfall, dam
② **Bombay Hook** PAGE 68	Smyrna	1.3	Easy 10'	Tidal salt marsh, migratory birds, history
③ **Cape Henlopen** PAGE 72	Lewes	3.6	Moderate 102'	Maritime forests, salt marsh wetlands, dunes, and history
④ **Trap Pond** PAGE 75	Laurel	3.9	Moderate 43'	Pond, history, flora and fauna

ADVENTURES IN MARYLAND

ADVENTURE	HUB	LENGTH (MILES)	DIFFICULTY/ ELEVATION	HIGHLIGHTS
⑤ **Turkey Point Lighthouse** PAGE 84	North East	2.0	Easy 154'	Lighthouse, beach, fauna, views of Chesapeake Bay
⑥ **Otter Point Creek** PAGE 88	Edgewood	1.8	Moderate 180'	Flora and fauna, water views, stairs
⑦ **King and Queen Seat** PAGE 92	Street	2.9	Moderate 469'	Geology, rock scrambles, flora and fauna
⑧ **Kilgore Falls** PAGE 96	Catonsville	0.9	Easy 85'	Waterfall, boulders, river exploration

ADVENTURE	HUB	LENGTH (MILES)	DIFFICULTY/ ELEVATION	HIGHLIGHTS
9 **Hemlock Gorge** PAGE 100	Manchester	2.7	Moderate 453'	Hemlock gorge, river exploration, geology, flora and fauna
10 **Patapsco Valley** PAGE 104	Elkridge	2.1	Moderate 305'	Waterfall, river exploration
11 **Wye Island** PAGE 108	Queenstown	1.5	Easy 26'	Beach, tunnel of trees, flora and fauna
12 **Calvert Cliffs** PAGE 112	Lusby	3.7	Moderate 98'	Cliffs, beach, fossils, shark teeth, boardwalk, marsh
13 **Underground Railroad Experience Trail** PAGE 116	Sandy Spring	3.9	Moderate 207'	Historical experience, footbridge, flora and fauna
14 **Sugarloaf Mountain** PAGE 120	Dickerson	2.0	Challenging 489'	Mountain views, boulders, geology, rock stairs
15 **Washington Monument State Park** PAGE 124	Middletown	4.3	Challenging 925'	Monument, history, flora and fauna, part of Appalachian Trail
16 **Cunningham Falls** PAGE 128	Thurmont	1.3	Easy 157'	Waterfall, flora and fauna
17 **Paw Paw Tunnel** PAGE 132	Oldtown	1.2	Easy 33'	Tunnel, canal, history
18 **High Rock** PAGE 136	Grantsville	2.0	Moderate 456'	Summit, flora and fauna, history, fire tower
19 **Swallow Falls** PAGE 140	Oakland	1.3	Moderate 108'	Four waterfalls, 300-year-old hemlocks, history, sandstone cliffs

ADVENTURES IN DC

ADVENTURE	HUB	LENGTH (MILES)	DIFFICULTY/ ELEVATION	HIGHLIGHTS
20 **Dumbarton Oaks** PAGE 146	Washington, DC	1.4	Easy 157'	History, waterfall, flora and fauna
21 **Theodore Roosevelt Island** PAGE 150	Washington, DC	1.9	Easy 56'	History, flora and fauna, tidal marsh, forest, swamp

ADVENTURES IN VIRGINIA

ADVENTURE	HUB	LENGTH (MILES)	DIFFICULTY/ ELEVATION	HIGHLIGHTS
22 **Great Falls** PAGE 158	McLean	1.6	Easy 30'	Waterfall, geology, ruins, history
23 **Government Island** PAGE 162	Stafford	1.75	Easy 56'	Geology, history, marshland, river, flora and fauna
24 **Stony Man** PAGE 166	Luray	1.5	Moderate 318'	Summit, views, geology
25 **Dark Hollow Falls** PAGE 170	Luray	1.9	Challenging 584'	Falls, lush foliage
26 **Blackrock Summit** PAGE 174	Luray	1.1	Moderate 162'	Geology, summit
27 **Blue Ridge Tunnel** PAGE 178	Afton	3.5	Moderate 367'	Tunnel, history, fauna

ADVENTURE	HUB	LENGTH (MILES)	DIFFICULTY/ ELEVATION	HIGHLIGHTS
28 **Humpback Rocks** PAGE 182	Lyndhurst	2.4	Challenging 817'	Summit, geology, flora and fauna
29 **Crabtree Falls** PAGE 186	Montebello	3.7	Challenging 1086'	Waterfall, summit, wooden stairs, bridge, flora and fauna
30 **Blackwater Creek** PAGE 190	Lynchburg	5.6	Moderate 279'	Suspension bridge, high railroad bridge, flora and fauna
31 **Bear Creek Lake** PAGE 194	Cumberland	3.8	Moderate 174'	Lake, beach area, flora and fauna, river exploration
32 **Pocahontas State Park** PAGE 198	Chesterfield	2.8	Moderate 177'	Lake, flora and fauna
33 **Taskinas Creek** PAGE 202	Williamsburg	2.3	Moderate 171'	Marsh, creek, marsh overlooks, flora and fauna
34 **First Landing State Park** PAGE 206	Virginia Beach	1.8	Easy 30'	Bald cypress, other flora and fauna
35 **Chincoteague Island** PAGE 210	Chincoteague	2.4	Easy 16'	Feral ponies, marsh, beach area, flora and fauna
36 **Occoneechee State Park** PAGE 214	Clarksville	1.4	Easy 112'	History, flora and fauna
37 **Devil's Den** PAGE 218	Fancy Gap	1.0	Moderate 272'	Cave, geology, flora and fauna

ADVENTURE	HUB	LENGTH (MILES)	DIFFICULTY/ ELEVATION	HIGHLIGHTS
38 **Stiles Falls** *PAGE 222*	Shawsville	4.0	Challenging 348'	Waterfall, rock scrambles, river exploration, flora and fauna
39 **Roaring Run** *PAGE 226*	Eagle Rock	1.6	Easy 276'	Waterfalls, historical furnace, geology, history, natural waterslide
40 **Cascades Falls** *PAGE 230*	Pembroke	5.1	Challenging 663'	Waterfall, river exploration, geology, flora and fauna
41 **New River Trail** *PAGE 234*	Gambetta	4.3	Moderate 223'	Tunnel, river, flora and fauna, rail trail
42 **Grayson Highlands** *PAGE 238*	Mouth of Wilson	2.3	Moderate 325'	Feral ponies, mountain views, geology, flora and fauna
43 **Big Falls** *PAGE 242*	Honaker	3.9	Moderate 308'	Waterfalls, The Pinnacle rock formation

ADVENTURES IN
WEST VIRGINIA

ADVENTURE	HUB	LENGTH (MILES)	DIFFICULTY/ ELEVATION	HIGHLIGHTS
44 Hanging Rock *PAGE 250*	Waiteville	2.1	Moderate 436'	Summit, observation tower, hanging rocks, flora and fauna
45 Long Point Trail *PAGE 254*	Fayetteville	3.1	Moderate 141'	View, historical bridge
46 High Knob Tower *PAGE 258*	Brandywine	2.9	Challenging 689'	Fire tower, summit, flora and fauna
47 Seneca Rocks *PAGE 262*	Seneca Rocks	2.9	Challenging 758'	Summit, bridge, platform, geology, flora and fauna
48 Blackwater Falls *PAGE 266*	Davis	2.6	Moderate 299'	Waterfall, geology, flora and fauna
49 Valley Falls *PAGE 270*	Fairmont	4.5	Challenging 548'	Waterfall, geology, flora and fauna, working railroad, history
50 Harpers Ferry *PAGE 274*	Harpers Ferry	2.2	Easy 72'	History, geology, flora and fauna

Young adventurers getting ready to explore inside the Blue Ridge Tunnel

ADVENTURES BY FEATURE

Can you remember the first cave you explored? The first waterfall that misted your face? Each of these adventures includes a destination or item of particular interest to motivate young legs and reward hard work. Encourage kids, as co-adventurers, to talk about which types of natural features tickle them the most and why.

FEATURE	ADVENTURE
Lakes and ponds	(2) Shearness Pool at Bombay Hook
	(4) Trap Pond
	(31) Bear Creek Lake
	(32) Beaver Lake at Pocahontas State Park
	(34) Cypress Swamp at First Landing State Park
Waterfalls	(1) Alapocas Run
	(8) Kilgore Falls
	(10) Cascade Falls at Patapsco Valley
	(16) Cunningham Falls
	(19) Swallow Falls
	(22) Great Falls
	(25) Dark Hollow Falls
	(29) Crabtree Falls
	(38) Stiles Falls
	(39) Roaring Run Waterfall
	(40) Cascades Falls
	(43) Big Falls
	(48) Blackwater Falls
	(49) Valley Falls
History	(1) Historical dam at Alapocas Run
	(2) WWII headquarters building at Bombay Hook
	(3) WWII bunkers at Cape Henlopen
	(4) Church at Trap Pond
	(9) Cemetery at Hemlock Gorge
	(13) Underground Railroad Experience Trail
	(15) Washington Monument State Park

FEATURE	ADVENTURE
History *(cont'd)*	**17** Paw Paw Tunnel
	18 Fire tower at High Rock
	19 300-year-old hemlocks at Swallow Falls
	20 Beatrix Farrand garden at Dumbarton Oaks
	22 Canal ruins at Great Falls
	23 Quarry at Government Island
	27 Blue Ridge Tunnel
	29 Cemetery at Crabtree Falls
	36 Chimney ruins at Occoneechee State Park
	39 Iron furnace at Roaring Run
	40 Old boiler at Cascades Falls
	46 High Knob Tower
	49 Grist mill ruins and B&O Railroad at Valley Falls
	50 Factory and mill ruins at Harpers Ferry
Flora and fauna	**1** Pawpaw trees and northern copperheads at Alapocas Run
	2 Bird-watching at Bombay Hook
	4 Bald cypress trees at Trap Pond
	5 Hawk-watching at Turkey Point Lighthouse
	6 Otters and birds at Otter Point Creek
	9 Hemlocks at Hemlock Gorge
	11 Osage orange trees at Wye Island
	13 American persimmons and milkweed on the Underground Railroad Experience Trail
	14 Southern flying squirrels at Sugarloaf Mountain
	15 Eagle-spotting at Washington Monument State Park
	20 Wild and formal gardens at Dumbarton Oaks

FEATURE	ADVENTURE
Flora and fauna *(cont'd)*	**21** Shorebirds and mallards at Theodore Roosevelt Island
	22 Virginia pines at Great Falls
	23 Ospreys at Government Island
	24 Wild turkeys at Stony Man
	27 Turtles, crayfish, and bats at Blue Ridge Tunnel
	28 Black bears at Humpback Rocks
	29 Wood ferns at Crabtree Falls
	30 Sycamore trees and inky caps at Blackwater Creek
	31 Beavers and bass at Bear Creek Lake
	32 Water lilies and opossums at Pocahontas State Park
	33 Pine trees at Taskinas Creek
	34 Bald cypress trees at First Landing State Park
	35 Feral ponies at Chincoteague Island
	36 Sweetgum trees and raccoons at Occoneechee State Park
	37 Red foxes and ruffed grouse at Devil's Den
	40 Salamanders at Cascades Falls
	41 Chestnut oaks and walking ferns at New River Trail
	42 Feral ponies at Grayson Highland State Park
	43 Swamp chestnut oaks and orange jelly fungi at Big Falls
	44 Raptor-watching at Hanging Rock
	46 Wildflowers and mushrooms at High Knob Tower
	48 Apple trees at Blackwater Falls
	49 Mushrooms at Valley Falls
	49 Boulders at Valley Falls
	50 Great blue herons at Harpers Ferry

FEATURE	ADVENTURE
Geology	**1** Blue granite cliffs at Alapocas Run
	7 King and Queen Seat
	9 Rock formations at Hemlock Gorge
	12 Shark tooth fossils at Calvert Cliffs
	14 Sugarloaf Mountain
	15 Tower at Washington Monument State Park
	18 Sandstone boulders at High Rock
	19 Cross-bedded sandstone, siltstones, and shales at Swallow Falls
	23 Quarry at Government Island
	24 Stony Man
	26 Quartzite at Blackrock Summit
	27 Stone-lined arch at Blue Ridge Tunnel
	28 Greenstone outcroppings at Humpback Rocks
	29 Rock cliffs at Crabtree Falls
	37 Metamorphic schist, quartz, and granite stone with depositions of mica and pyrites at Devil's Den
	39 Limestone at Roaring Run
	40 Stone steps at Cascades Falls
	42 Boulders and outcroppings at Grayson Highlands
	43 The Pinnacle at Big Falls
	44 Sandstone at Hanging Rock
	47 Sedimentary rock at Seneca Rocks
	48 Balanced Rock at Blackwater Falls

FEATURE	ADVENTURE
Caves/Tunnels	(9) Hemlock Gorge
	(10) Patapsco Valley
	(17) Paw Paw Tunnel
	(27) Blue Ridge Tunnel
	(40) Cascades Falls
	(41) New River Trail
	(47) Seneca Rocks
Summits and peaks	(7) King and Queen Seat
	(14) Sugarloaf Mountain
	(15) Washington Monument State Park
	(18) High Rock
	(24) Stony Man
	(26) Blackrock Summit
	(28) Humpback Rocks
	(29) Crabtree Falls
	(42) Grayson Highlands
	(44) Hanging Rock
	(46) High Knob Tower
River exploration	(7) King and Queen Seat
	(8) Kilgore Falls
	(9) Hemlock Gorge
	(10) Patapsco Valley
	(30) Blackwater Creek
	(31) Bear Creek Lake
	(39) Roaring Run
	(40) Cascades Falls
	(41) New River Trail
	(43) Big Falls

FEATURE	ADVENTURE
Beach fun	**3** Cape Henlopen
	5 Turkey Point Lighthouse
	11 Wye Island
	12 Calvert Cliffs
	31 Bear Creek Lake
	35 Chincoteague Island
Campground by trailhead	**3** Cape Henlopen State Park
	4 Trap Pond State Park
	5 Elk Neck State Park Campground at Turkey Point Lighthouse
	10 Hollofield Campground at Patapsco Valley State Park
	15 Little Bennett Campground near Washington Monument State Park
	16 William Houck Campground at Cunningham Falls
	17 Paw Paw Tunnel
	19 Swallow Falls State Park
	24 Big Meadows Campground near Stony Man Trailhead
	25 Big Meadow Campground near Dark Hollow Falls
	26 Loft Mountain Campground near Blackrock Summit
	31 Bear Creek Lake State Park
	32 Pocahontas State Park
	34 First Landing State Park
	36 Occoneechee State Park
	38 Alta Mons campground at Stiles Falls

FEATURE	ADVENTURE
Campground by trailhead *(cont'd)*	**41** Cliffview Campground near New River Trail trailhead
	42 Grayson Highlands State Park
	45 Babcock State Park near Long Point Trail
	46 Brandywine Campground near High Knob Tower
	47 Seneca Shadows Campground near Seneca Rocks trailhead
	48 Blackwater Falls State Park
	50 Harpers Ferry Campground near Harper's Ferry trailhead

ADVENTURES BY SEASON

Many trails are available year round for your adventuring pleasure, yet some really shine during particular moments of the year. Spring is often a great time for wildflower blooms and trails with waterfalls at maximum flow, but for some trails it is also mud season, so always check trail conditions beforehand and be prepared with proper footwear and a hiking stick. Summer is best for higher-elevation trails—which might be snowed in during winter—and for special higher-elevation wildflowers. However, it also comes with copious amounts of flies and ticks, so be sure to bring repellent and always do tick checks at the end of a hike. In autumn, many trails erupt with beautiful colors and mushrooms, but some trails go near areas that allow hunting, so always check trail signs and consider bringing orange shirts and hats in your adventure bags. Winter can be a great time to escape crowds and enjoy lower-elevation trails, but be sure to bring snowshoes or tracks for your shoes, in case they are needed. Keep in mind that any prime season (summer for hikes near swimming areas or autumn for the foliage hikes) means you might encounter crowds, so consider visiting early or late in the day or try exploring off season. Allow your children to understand the seasons by returning to a favorite hike throughout the year and asking them what has changed since their last visit.

Young explorers take in the fall foliage atop a summit

PEAK SEASON	ADVENTURE
Winter	(13) Underground Railroad Experience
	(17) Paw Paw Tunnel
	(27) Blue Ridge Tunnel
Spring	(1) Alapocas Run
	(2) Bombay Hook
	(3) Cape Henlopen
	(4) Trap Pond
	(6) Otter Point Creek
	(9) Hemlock Gorge
	(10) Patapsco Valley
	(16) Cunningham Falls
	(20) Dumbarton Oaks
	(21) Theodore Roosevelt Island
	(22) Great Falls
	(23) Government Island
	(33) Taskinas Creek
	(49) Valley Falls
	(32) Pocahontas State Park
	(34) First Landing State Park
	(35) Chincoteague Island
	(36) Occoneechee State Park
	(38) Stiles Falls
	(43) Big Falls

PEAK SEASON	ADVENTURE
Summer	**11** Wye Island
	12 Calvert Cliffs
	31 Bear Creek Lake
	33 Taskinas Creek
	37 Devil's Den
	39 Roaring Run
	40 Cascades Falls
Fall	**5** Turkey Point Lighthouse
	7 King and Queen Seat
	8 Kilgore Falls
	14 Sugarloaf Mountain
	15 Washington Monument State Park
	18 High Rock
	19 Swallow Falls
	24 Stony Man
	25 Dark Hollow
	26 Blackrock
	28 Humpback Rocks
	29 Crabtree Falls
	30 Blackwater Creek
	41 New River Trail
	42 Grayson Highlands
	44 Hanging Rock
	45 Long Point
	46 High Knob Tower
	47 Seneca Rocks
	48 Blackwater Falls
	50 Harpers Ferry

PREPARING FOR YOUR ADVENTURE

This guide is a starter pack to a life full of adventure with your young ones. One day, your adventurers could be calling you to ask if you want to join them in thru-hiking the 2,181 miles of the Appalachian Trail from Mount Katahdin, Maine, through the mid-Atlantic region and down to Springer Mountain, Georgia. In the meantime, work together to see what each spectacularly diverse region in the mid-Atlantic has to offer and note which ones you want to return to in the future.

INDIVIDUAL ADVENTURE PROFILES

Each of the fifty adventure profiles includes a basic trail map and information on the species of plants and wildlife, points of historical interest, and geological features that you may see on the trail. By allowing children to use the maps and elevation guides to navigate, read the hike and species descriptions, and look for each featured item like a scavenger hunt, you are laying down the foundation for a life of adventure. Marking journeys on the map with points of interest gives relevance and context to kids' surroundings, so encourage them to note anything that stood out to them, even if it is not featured in the book. You will burst with pride when kids start to teach *you* what a lollipop loop is versus an out and back, are able to gauge whether they feel like just kicking it on a hike with 200 feet of elevation gain or tackling 1,000 feet, and make decisions about their own adventure. Each description is written for both you and the kids, so encourage them to read to themselves or out loud to you.

Elevation profile, length, type of trail, and time

An elevation profile is a line that sketches the general arch of the up and down during a hike. You'll notice a few are almost completely flat, and some are nearly a triangle. The elevation gain is how many feet you'll gain from start to finish; so even if it rolls up and then down again, if it says 300 feet, that will be the total number of feet you'll have to walk up from the trailhead to the summit. No adventure is less than half a mile (too short to call a real excursion) or more than 5 miles (inaccessible for many of our younger or newer adventurers). The length of these hikes should give you plenty of time to enjoy the outing before anyone gets too tired. Embracing shorter trails translates into more time to savor them. Some of the routes are shorter versions of a longer route and modified for kids—be sure to check out the map from the land agency of whichever area you're visiting, in case you want to explore more. Along with the length of the trail, we note whether the adventure is an out and back, a loop, or a lollipop loop, and whether we recommend a clockwise or counterclockwise route.

An out and back has a clear final destination and turnaround point, and you'll cross back over what you've already discovered.

A loop provides brand-new territory the whole way around.

A lollipop is a straight line with a mini loop at the end, like reaching a lake, circling it, and heading back.

There are variations on these basic shapes, like a figure eight or a Y-shaped out and back, and discussing shape classification can be a fun way to get kids thinking about the route. Talking about the type of trail you're planning to hike helps young adventurers know what to expect. Our estimated hike time includes time for exploration, but each adventurer's mileage may vary. Always give yourselves the delight of a relaxing hike with plenty of time to stop and play with a pile of fun-looking rocks, have leaf-boat races on a stream, or sketch a cool plant or animal in a nature journal.

Level of difficulty

This rating system was designed to facilitate a good time. It's important to note that these are kid-centric ratings; what's labeled as a "challenging" trail in this guide may not appear to be so challenging for a seasoned adult hiker. It can be fun to create your own rating for a trail when you're finished. "Did that feel like a level one, two, or three to you? Why?" Talking about it can help you understand your particular kid's adventure limits or help them seek new challenges. None of the trails in this book are paved (at least not all the way). Some are level and smooth, but due to the geological history of the mid-Atlantic region, most have some combination of rocks and roots. There will be notes if there are exposed ledges or viewpoints where you will want to hold smaller hands. Rockier terrain requires sturdy shoes, and you'll want to be aware of how wet, muddy, or snowy it may be to decide which footwear will be best for your little adventurers. Check reviews on AllTrails.com or Instagram to get recent conditions and different families' opinions of the difficulty. You can also call the office of a nearby ranger station. Use the information here to make your own informed decisions—every lead adventurer is different.

The adventures are rated as follows:

- **EASY** These trails are typically short (under 2 miles), have low elevation gain, have even, non-rocky terrain, and do not have too many exposed, hand-holding edges.

- **MODERATE** These adventures have a bit more elevation gain (300 to 450 feet) and are likely to have a few hand-holding spots for the youngest hikers near exposed areas like cliffs or hillsides. The path itself may also be rockier or rootier.

- **CHALLENGING** These will give your little adventurers the biggest sense of accomplishment. These have the most elevation gain (500 to 1,000 feet) or include sections where you will probably want kids to stay close as they take in an exposed view. However, if the trial is steeper, it will also be shorter—more than doable with the right attitude and by taking advantage of power-up stops and the adrenaline-inducing rush of finding special scavenger hunt items.

Season

This section lists the season when the adventure is possible; in many cases, the trails can be hiked year round. Also noted are the seasons when features of special interest can be seen, such as wildflowers or rushing waterfalls. Phenology is the study of how plants change across the seasons, and hikers are often the first to notice when leaves change colors or when a certain flower starts to bloom. Try taking the same hike in several seasons to teach your little adventurers about differences, particularly for flora and fauna. The more often you go, the more likely you are to find something you may have missed the last time. As Andrew Philpott, park manager at Hungry Mother State Park, notes, "If you just hike in the summertime you will miss out on the amazing adventures that happen the rest of the year. Early spring wildflowers are amazingly beautiful and spotting a deer or fox in a snow-covered woodland or meadow makes a memory you'll never forget. Different seasons bring new adventures on the trail, each one exciting in its own way. Winter air is crisp and the lack of foliage makes spotting some wildlife easier, while in spring the search is on for spring wildflowers, mushrooms, and migrating birds. Summer is the best time to head out at dusk to see some bats and hear owls, while fall brings the best weather and pretty autumn colors. State parks offer tons of programming to show you the way or provide the space to have an adventure with your kids or all to yourself."

In winter and early spring, check with the local agency listed for each hike to make sure the trail and access road is actually open. In general, the higher up you go, the more likely you could be closed out by snow on either side of summer. Some adventures lend themselves to snow exploration without any gear, while others provide an opportunity to try snowshoes or snow tracks.

"Our family likes to get out and explore our favorite trails multiple times throughout the year. You never know what new experiences await in each season . . . a frozen waterfall, spring ephemeral wildflowers, basking turtles in the summer, or ripe pawpaw fruit in fall. Mother Nature is never boring."

—Cassandra McCreer, Maryland mom of three

Get there

The mid-Atlantic region is large—over 81,000 square miles. This guide is meant to be a sampling of the diverse and beautiful areas all over the region, which call to be explored. One of the unique aspects of this region is that you can be hiking by the Atlantic Ocean in Virginia Beach and then climbing the mountains in Jefferson National Forest in less than five hours, just by taking a road trip between the two.

Car rides are a necessity to reach the amazing plethora of hikes available to you in this region. Embracing the special family time that road trips can offer your crew is an added bonus.

Instead of looking at a screen, consider a few fun ways to make the hours fly by fast, such as riddles, the A–Z game (you claim every time you see something that starts with the next letter of the alphabet), audiobooks about the areas you are visiting, call-and-response–type camp songs (bit.ly/TimberSongs), nature journaling, and just good ol'-fashioned conversation. Always be ready to roll down windows for fresh air and encourage your little riders to talk about the sights they are seeing while driving. Oftentimes, while you are headed to a verified awesome spot to explore, there is even more in the area to check out. We encourage you to always stop by visitor centers and make the most of every trip, including considering camping nearby so you can enjoy each area for longer.

> "Our family loves hiking in the mid-Atlantic. So many beautiful places to explore. Plus, you can go from the beach to the mountains within a few hours!"
>
> —Jessica Human, mom to three boys, and local hike guide and adventure photographer

Basic longhand directions to the trailhead are listed with each adventure, along with a case-sensitive link to Google Maps that you can drop directly into your smartphone browser. Be sure to do it before you head out, while you are still certain to have coverage. You also can download offline maps at Google Maps and the AllTrails app for free, which will allow you to follow your GPS dot and ensure you are staying on the trail or road you want to be on. You also can

Young explorers beginning a hike

get free highway maps mailed to you or printed, which can be helpful and educational for your co-pilot in the car (check the tourism website for each state). Before leaving home, you and your co-adventurers can check out the area on Google Earth or turn on satellite view in Google Maps to see your driving route (and sometimes even the trail) step-by-step.

There's something magical about maps, and each map in this guide was carefully designed with kids in mind to be touched, traced, and held out in front of them to understand their surroundings. Encourage your kids to understand the difference between roads, highways, and interstate freeways. We have simplified the maps so kids can focus on the land agencies they will be visiting, the closest towns with grub stops, and the larger adventure hub cities nearby. Hopefully while they adventure with you, they start to build a good understanding of how to navigate using maps. Ask them navigation questions such as: How long do you think this adventure will take? Where does that river start, and how is it related to the ocean? How many turns will we need to make? What's our next highway? Any cities nearby? Just by asking questions, you can encourage curiosity and leadership with your young adventurers.

Restrooms

We cannot have a hiking book for kids without chatting about bathrooms. Many of the trails have pit toilets or developed toilets right at the parking lot. If not, plan on a restroom stop in the nearest town or gas station on your way in and on your way out. Discuss appropriate trail bathroom etiquette with your kids as well, such as heading safely off the trail, away from water, and properly covering it should the need arise. Bring what you need to be comfortable in your adventure bag, such as a zip-top bag with toilet paper or wet wipes. Do not leave any toilet paper behind to spoil someone else's experience. Always be sure to pack out whatever you bring in.

Parking and fees

Your main goal, lead adventurers, is to get out on the trail. If thinking about how to park gets your boot laces knotted up, rest assured that all the trailheads listed here have a parking lot or pullout and some sort of trail sign indicating where you are and whether you need a parking pass or permit. For some, you'll need to plan ahead and get a day pass or annual pass before you get to the trailhead. Others have self-service pay stations at the trailhead—either those accepting credit cards or an "iron ranger" with a slot in it for a fee envelope with cash or check—and you'll affix the pass to your car. Several parking lots are free, though, and each is noted. Many are free for in-state residents but have a fee for out-of-state visitors (residency is usually determined by your car's license plate). There are several "fee-free days," including National Public Lands Day in September and many holidays.

Treat yourself

The guide lists nearby cafes and restaurants for good, quick bites to reward yourselves, in part so you can plan whether you need to pack substantial snacks or just a few for sustenance on the trail. These are road-tested yummy bakeries, ice cream shops, and burger joints with notable items or

Freshly made donuts from Chesapeake Bay Coffee
Co. perk up young adventurers after a hike

spaces that your kids will enjoy. The mid-Atlantic's bounty of homemade
ice cream, donuts, crab cakes, popcorn shrimp, hush puppies, pepperoni
rolls, burgers, pies, crab dip, and more beckon after many hikes.

Managing agencies

We've listed the name of the agency that manages each hiking trail, along
with its telephone number and social media handles. Before heading out,
it's a good idea to check on current conditions, including weather, roads,
wildlife sightings, and any hazards that haven't been cleared or fixed. The
folks on the other end are often rangers and are generally thrilled to share
information about their trails. They can also connect you to botanists,
geologists, historians, and other experts. We received fast and enthusiastic
responses from many of the rangers behind the Facebook pages of these
parks—involve your kids and encourage them to say hello and ask about
conditions or a lingering question from the trail.

Blazes mark the way on many trails

Following the trail

In the mid-Atlantic, your family needs to keep a keen eye because color blazes guide the way on many trails. While we have made every effort to pick trails that are straightforward and hard to get lost on, it is a good habit to have your children always looking for the next blaze and question your path if you have not seen one in a while. Another good habit to encourage is to take a moment at each power-up stop to note landmarks and check to see what comes next on the map. These skills will help kids out when they get older and graduate from this guide to more difficult trails. Give a hug to one of the trees with blazes on it, and send a mental thank you to the land agencies who maintain these blazes and make outdoor adventure possible for us all.

Scavenger hunts

The scavenger hunt included with each adventure invites you to look for specific fungi, plants, animals, minerals, and historical items of interest. You will find descriptions and photos of trees, leaves, flowers, seeds, cones, bark, nuts, feathers, rocks and geological features, historically significant landmarks or artifacts, natural features such as lakes, rivers, and waterfalls, or culturally significant spots that appear on each trail. Each entry has a question to ponder or an activity to try, and when applicable, you can dig into the scientific genus and species and learn why the plant or animal is called what it is. Encourage kids to "preview" what they might see on the trail and if they think they have found it, take out the guide to see if it matches. Take it up a notch and encourage them to make their *own* scavenger hunt—write down five things they think they might see on the trail, from very basic (at least five trees) to the very specific (five eastern pine cones on the ground).

IDENTIFYING WHAT YOU FIND

Over half of the mid-Atlantic region is covered by forests full of plants, fungi, mammals, invertebrates, and more! Identifying these species in the wild involves using clues from size, leaves, bark, flowers, and the habitat. Work with kids to ask questions that will move them from general identification (Is it a conifer or a deciduous tree?) to the specifics (What shape are the leaves? What species is this?). The species of trees, shrubs, mushrooms, wildflowers, and animals listed in the scavenger hunts were chosen because you should be able to find them with ease or because there is something interesting about them that might appeal to children. However, you may not find every species on the trail every time. It is best to adopt the attitude of considering it a win when you do find one, and to present those you cannot find as something to look forward to the next time.

A young explorer gets a close-up view of a plant along the trail

"Look at the things you encounter from different scales and different angles and different parts. Say a tree—you have a really large organism and you might need to stand really far away to see a picture of it. But look closer, and find the fruit on the ground, look at the bark, look at the leaves. Think of all of the different characteristics that can help you learn what it is, why it lives where it is. Start recognizing all of the pieces of an organism, and thinking how to capture those photographically if you want to share that record with the world. Try to find the part of the thing that is most unique-looking and try to fill the frame with that with a nice, clear photo."

—**Carrie Seltzer, iNaturalist**

Tristan Gooley, British author of *The Natural Navigator*, encourages kids to look for "keys" as they walk on trails. "Keys are small families of clues and signs; if we focus on them repeatedly, it can give us a sixth sense." Start noticing which way the sun is when you start and when you end and where the natural features (hills, mountains) are around you. Use a compass (there is probably one on your smartphone) to start understanding direction and building this natural sixth sense Gooley speaks of.

When you find a particularly interesting species on the trail that is not mentioned in the scavenger hunt, have children either sketch it or take a photo. Remind them to look it up later, either in a printed field guide to the region or on a specialty website such as WildflowerSearch.org or iNaturalist.org. Including basic descriptions and the name of the region in your search will help children find their treasure in online field guides. Apps like LeafSnap and the Seek app by iNaturalist are also great for creating species treasure hunts while still on the trail.

If you are ready to level up everyone's identification skills, join the Native Plant Trust or your state's botanical or native plant society. All have great Facebook groups, newsletters, or online forums where you can share photos of a species you cannot identify or confirm that a certain species is growing or blooming where you hiked. The USA National Phenology Network (usanpn.org) allows children to contribute to science by entering their observations of seasonal changes into a nationwide database, and it has a cool junior phrenologist program and kid-friendly resources. Joining your local chapter of societies and organizations also means getting invited to their fun themed group hikes on topics such as wildflowers, fungi, and everything in between. Plus, you are exposing your children to the power of a community resource where everyone is passionate about nature and science and wants to help one another.

In addition to identifying the plants you see along the trail, you will also notice many rock formations throughout your adventures. Geology is the study of the Earth and the nonliving things it is made of, namely rocks and minerals. The mid-Atlantic region has a diverse landscape that ranges from lowlands along the Atlantic Ocean coastline, to rolling foothills and river valleys, to high rocky summits along the Appalachian Mountains in the west. Rocks exposed throughout this region tell the story of continents colliding and splitting apart. These continental movements were a result of volcanic eruptions, earthquakes, and mountains building over billions of years.

There are three types of rocks—igneous, sedimentary, and metamorphic. Igneous rocks form when molten rock called magma cools and hardens. When magma reaches the Earth's surface, probably through a volcano, it is called lava. Magma can also cool deep below the Earth's surface and form an igneous rock called granite. Geologist Philip Prince (and thru-hiker of the Appalachian Trail in 2006) explains that "everything in geology is an 'expression of process,' meaning nothing is an accident. Looking at patterns and asking 'why?' is an important part of geology. Geologists learn to see the patterns and read the stories that help us interact with our home planet." For example just about all the sedimentary rock in the Appalachian

Mountains formed in an ancient ocean or lake from sand and mud in the water. Look for little rounded "jelly bean" pebbles that are visible in many sandstone or conglomerate layers. Their smoothness is a cool hallmark of how they formed. Metamorphic rocks, on the other hand, are like cakes; they start with a specific batter (other rocks) which then "cooks" deep in the Earth to become metamorphic rock. Just like a brown batter cooks to become a chocolate cake, basalt lava batter cooks to greenstone. Mudrock (shale) batter cooks to schist or gneiss. Limestone batter cooks to marble. And while none of these "cakes" would be very good to eat, they are helpful to remember when examining all the rock formations you will see along your adventures.

The mid-Atlantic region is a great area to explore rocks and geology. When you encounter interesting rock colors, folds, and structures, encourage children to think about the rock cycle—a rock's evolution from igneous to sedimentary to metamorphic—and how rocks build up in formations over time. Use the scavenger hunt items to build a familiarity with rocks and landscapes so your children can start to find them and notice the subtle differences. Ask questions: What does the texture of the rock look like? What color is it? Does it feel heavy or light? Is it hard or soft? Does it break easily? Join a regional geological organization like the Geological Society of Maryland (mdgeosociety.org), Virginia (geology.blogs.wm.edu), West Virginia (wvgs.wvnet.edu), Delaware (dgs.udel.edu), and Washington, DC (gswweb.org) for newsletters, group hikes, and community opportunities. You can even join the National Speleological Society if you are interested in caves.

Historical items

The mid-Atlantic region has a long and rich history. From the first permanent English colony being established in Jamestown, Virginia, in 1607 to Francis Scott Key writing "The Star-Spangled Banner" during the War of 1812 at Fort McHenry in Baltimore, Maryland, this region is steeped with historical significance. Many of the trails in this book include historical landmarks and historical areas that tell the stories of the families and

Captain John Smith's 1612 map of the Chesapeake Bay region. How does it look different from a map of today?

people who once lived there. Learning this history helps children better understand the areas they are exploring and helps them build connections to these areas and their community at large. This in turn helps children to feel more connected to the past and will hopefully inspire them to help build a better future. As David Armenti, the Vice President of Education at the Maryland Center for History and Culture explains, "Historical societies, archives, and historical sites provide a valuable service to communities, sharing credible and authentic information for the public. Historians and educators serve as storytellers who can point to primary source material to spark curiosity in learners of all ages. In addition, visiting historical locations in your local community brings an extra level of connection, as children can truly see how history is relevant to their own lived experience."

Along the trails, you will pass tunnels, canals, railroads, ruins, and historical buildings, each telling a story of the region's past. As humans, it is natural to want to know more about who we are and where we come from, and just reading about these past events will not always give children the same thrill as getting to experience them firsthand. For instance, walking through historical ruins gives children the opportunity to imagine what life might have been like there a hundred or more years ago. Experiences like this can have a long-lasting impact on children. As Edward Richi of the Delaware Historical Society notes, "The more you know about your community's past, the better you can hike the trail ahead." With that in mind, consider joining a local historical society that can assist you in identifying items of historical interest on the mid-Atlantic's trails. Each state, and sometimes even regions of each state, has its own historical society with resources and an email and phone number to ask questions: Maryland (mdhistory.org), Virginia (virginiahistory.org), West Virginia (wvculture.org), Delaware (dehistory.org), and Washington, DC (dchistory.org). While joining a local historical society can help to foster a love of local history, please remember that parents can also foster inquiry on each hike by pointing out the historically significant places and raising thought-provoking questions.

POWER-UP STOPS

Liz Thomas has hiked over 20,000 miles and is a former speed record holder for the Appalachian Trail. Her biggest tip for young adventurers to build stamina is, "Understand your body. Kids are just figuring out how to read their bodies. You can think of your body as having gauges and you're the pilot at the front of the plane. Your goal is to keep your gauges (hydration, exposure, food) in the happy zone." She even sets reminders on her watch to drink and eat as she walks from sunrise to sunset. As lead adventurers, you will be keeping a close eye on these gauges but also helping little ones recognize them, anticipate them, and power through them.

Each hike will suggest a great boulder, bench, or summit to stop and snack at

For each adventure, key places are noted that serve as mini-milestones, or power-up stops. Be sure to pack snacks for kids to eat at these stops to keep blood sugar, energy levels, and mood high. Remember that this amount of physical activity may be challenging for little ones. Often, these power-up stops are at points of interest: fun bridges, switchbacks before a small hill, or overlooking a viewpoint. Stopping for a moment can fuel you up, give you a chance to listen to the wind or animals around you, watch what is going on in the woods, and prepare you for the larger goal of finishing the adventure itself.

Power-up stops can also be great for a nursing mom, a bottle-feeding parent, or for tending to little ones' other needs, as well as for question-based games like "I Spy." As the lead adventurer, use these stops for inspiration, play, questions, and games, and encourage your children to do the same. Do not underestimate the power of choosing a special snack to serve as a particular motivator on tough ascents or rainy days.

ADVENTURE BAG, SUPPLIES, AND SAFETY

Start your kids on a lifelong habit of packing an adventure bag, whether it's the smallest satchel or the largest consumer-grade backpack they can actually hold. The art of having everything you need with you without being too burdened is key to having a good time on the trail. All of these adventures are short enough that even if you did pack too much, its weight won't jeopardize your enjoyment levels too heavily.

- **NAVIGATION** In addition to the maps in this book, consider investing in a compass and full trail map of the area (Appalachian Mountain Club maps are the gold standard). Make sure your smartphone is fully charged, with offline maps available and the compass feature handy. Bringing an extra portable battery charger is also a good idea.

- **HYDRATION** Bring plenty of water for everyone, and remember to drink along the way.

- **NUTRITION** Consider the length of the trail and the amount and type of snacks you will need to keep everyone going.

- **FIRE** Pack a lighter or matchbook for emergencies.

- **FIRST AID KIT** This can range from a mini first aid kit with essentials such as bandages and aspirin to much heftier options with space blankets. Consider what you want your car stocked with and what you want on the trail with you.

- **TOOLS** A small pocket knife or multi-tool goes a long way in the woods.

- **ILLUMINATION** Did you explore just a wee bit too long and dusk is approaching? A simple headlamp, flashlight, or even your phone's flashlight can help lead the way.

SUN AND INSECT PROTECTION If it is an exposed trail, consider sunglasses and sunscreen or hats for you and your little adventurers. In summer, many trails may have mosquitoes, so be prepared with your favorite method of repelling them.

SHELTER You may want a space blanket or small tarp in your adventure bag in case of an emergency on the trail.

INSULATION Check the weather together and decide the type of protection and warmth you want to bring. A second layer is always a good idea—breezes can chill even the warmest of days, and the mid-Atlantic's weather is famously hard to predict, especially in the mountains.

Other fun items to have on hand might include a nature journal and pen or pencil, hand lens, binoculars, a bug jar for capturing and releasing spiders and insects, a camera, a super-special treat for when you reach the top of something, a container for a special mushroom or pinecone, and even a favorite figurine or toy that your littles are currently enamored with, which they can use to interact with that tree stump up ahead. Wet wipes, toilet paper, and zip-top bags are also recommended. First-timer? Consider joining the local chapter of a hiking group like Outgrown (formerly Hike it Baby) or the Appalachian Mountain Club to hike with your peers and learn the ropes of packing and hiking.

While it may be handy for you to navigate to trailheads using your smartphone, remember that many wilderness areas have spotty cell service. As a general safety practice for hiking with kids, always tell a third party where you're going and when you expect to be back, and remember to tell anyone who may need to get ahold of you that you're not certain of cell coverage in the area. If you

"I've seen so many kids have a great hike ruined because they didn't have the gear they needed. Hiking can be the most wonderful thing in the world, but if you don't have the right socks, trail snacks, water, first aid kit, suntan lotion, bug spray . . . it can be awful! The Boy Scout motto is Be Prepared, and it should also be a hiker's motto."

—Adam Raderer, Scout Master in Virginia

To build independence, let your kids pack and hold everything they'll need for adventures

adventure a lot, you might want to consider an affordable satellite GPS, like those made by Garmin, that allows you to send texts from areas that don't have cell service. On the trail itself, every lead adventurer will have their own comfort level with safety, and you'll determine when your children will need handholding or reminders to stay close as you get near tricky terrain, exposed edges, or water.

It is a given in the diversity of climates in the mid-Atlantic region that you can come across adverse weather conditions arriving seemingly out of nowhere. Teaching awareness and common sense, and fostering an attitude of "there's no bad weather, only the wrong clothing," in these situations will go a long way toward creating an adventurous and resilient child. You can model this "love the unlovable" attitude by remaining upbeat and playful as lead adventurer, and you will be amazed at how quickly their attention will turn back to the trail and its wonders.

Lenore Skenazy, president of Let Grow (a nonprofit promoting independence as a critical part of childhood) and founder of the Free-Range Kids movement, has this reply about handling the inevitable fear of shepherding your family. "I'm often asked, 'What if something goes wrong?' I love to ask back, 'Can anyone remember something that went wrong when you were a kid, playing with other kids?' People often look back so fondly on that time when things went wrong. There's even a word for the way

we treasure imperfect things and moments: *wabi sabi* . . . because the imperfection is what makes it beautiful. The outdoors is never without some surprises and even minor risks, but neither is the indoors. My guess is all adults can remember when something went wrong, and it is a treasured (if only in retrospect) memory. Imperfection is inevitable and valuable. Embrace it!"

Poison ivy (*Toxicodendron radicans*)

In addition to weather, poison ivy is another common hazard lurking in mid-Atlantic woods, but once you can identify it, you will be able to spot it with almost infrared vision. Touching this plant will cause a blistering rash in most people. Remember the warning "Leaves of three, let it be." Although the plant can grow as a spreading vine or a low or upright shrub, its groups of three leaflets make it easy to identify. New leaves start out red, then fade to a yellowy bronze before turning fully green in summer and bright red, orange, or yellow in late summer and fall.

Aside from deer on the road, the mid-Atlantic does not have much in the way of large dangerous animals. Northern Copperhead (*Agkistrodon contortrix*), black bears (*Ursus americanus*), and bobcats (*Lynx rufus*) are shy of humans, and you are unlikely to encounter them on hikes. Copperheads are likely hanging out by their dens and will not want to bother you, so give a wide berth as you walk around and do not poke your hands into rocks. If you see a bear, try not to panic—simply hold your ground and slowly back up—as they are not aggressive unless provoked. If it is a possibility, trailheads will often provide information on animals in the area and reminders on how to take precautions. By helping children be aware on the trail, looking for signs of wildlife, and understanding what to do during an encounter, you can create a lifelong safety skill set for adventuring. Please also be aware of all trailhead signs in fall and winter, as hunting is permitted in some parks. If it is hunting season, you will want to wear bright orange on your head and body. Parks that allow hunting will be noted, but it is always good practice to research which parks allow hunting before heading out to the trails during hunting season.

The most dangerous critter in the mid-Atlantic is arguably *Ixodes scapularis*, the deer tick, which can spread Lyme disease. Knowledge of ticks, tickborne diseases, and tick prevention

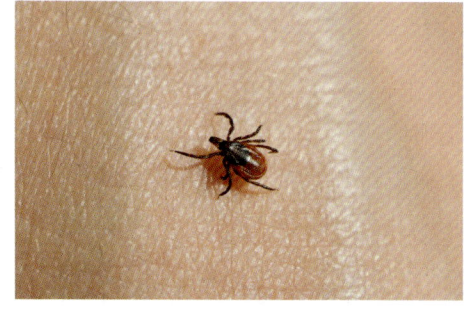

Ticks are small; be sure to check for them carefully

and safety is essential and goes hand-in-hand with hiking. Ticks do not fly or jump—they attach to animals who come into direct contact with them and then feed on the blood of you, your dog, or other mammals on the trail. They love shrubby, grassy areas, so be sure to stick to the center of the trail and do not go off-trail. Before a hike, consider wearing light clothing so you can quickly spot check. Consider treating your clothes with 0.5 percent permethrin or 20–30 percent DEET (be sure to apply for your children, avoiding eyes, nose, and mouth). Make full-body tick checks a part of your hiking routine when you get back to the car. Be sure to check under your arms, behind your knees and ears, and between your toes. Shower or bath time at home provides another chance for a full-body check. If you find a tick, remove it with tweezers or a tick removal kit as close to your skin as possible. Don't handle it with your bare hands. Clean the area with soap and water, and call your doctor. Ticks can be found in almost any season, so it's best to always perform checks.

A young adventurer sketches in his nature journal

NATURE JOURNALING

Nature journals are a great addition to any outdoor adventure. They provide children with an opportunity to record what they have seen during their hike and foster learning in a fun, hands-on way. Consider picking out a small blank journal for kids to bring along in their adventure bags. At power-up stops, when you stop for lunch at the destination, on the ride home, or later that night, encourage your little adventurers to create drawings of things they saw, or document their observations of trees, leaves, flowers, or animals.

Catherine Hughes, retired head of the *National Geographic Kids* magazine education team, suggests a few key maxims for nature journaling:

- **MAKE QUICK, MESSY FIELD NOTES.** You can add details later when you have free time, like the drive home. You don't have to be a great artist to sketch something you see.

- **SKETCH THE MAP OF THE ADVENTURE THAT DAY.** Include special things that made you smile.

- **PERSONALIZE IT.** Did someone say something funny? What was the most unique thing that happened on the adventure?

- **USE IT LIKE A SCRAPBOOK.** Add any trail brochure or ticket to your journal to remember your adventure.

A great trail is a story—it has a beginning, a true climax or crux, then an end, whether that's back the way you came or finishing a loop. As you review your outings with young adventurers, encourage them to feel the story of the trail. How did they like the beginning? What was the climax? How did it end? What characters (plants, rock formations, animals) stood out to them? A fun after-hike activity is taking your nature journal and writing a fictional account of what happened on the trail, making the landscape come alive in a whole new way.

DIGITAL CONNECTIONS

The social media accounts of many of the agencies that manage public lands in the mid-Atlantic region are quite active, and they can be a great way for little explorers to use technology to enhance their experience in nature. Together, you can ask pre- or post-adventure questions about conditions or flora and fauna, and the forums can be wonderful vehicles for sharing images you snapped—for both you and your little adventurer. Search the location on Instagram for recent photos, and be sure to geo-tag yours to contribute to other hikers' searches as well. Enhance the journey and encourage children to define what really stood out to them about the experience with a co-authored trip report on one of these sites:

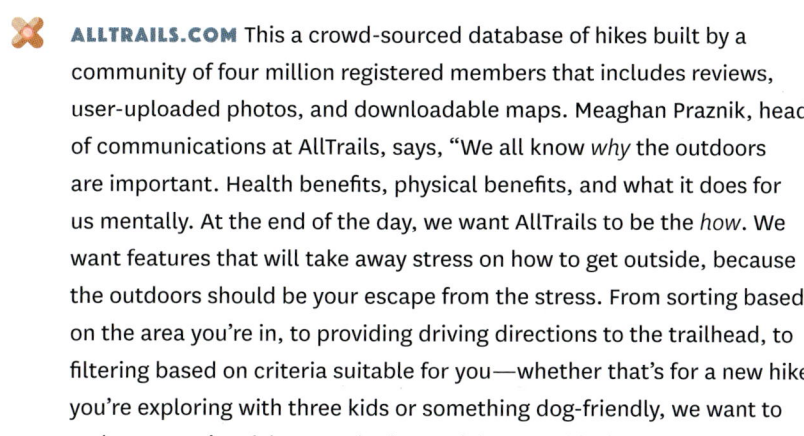

ALLTRAILS.COM This a crowd-sourced database of hikes built by a community of four million registered members that includes reviews, user-uploaded photos, and downloadable maps. Meaghan Praznik, head of communications at AllTrails, says, "We all know *why* the outdoors are important. Health benefits, physical benefits, and what it does for us mentally. At the end of the day, we want AllTrails to be the *how*. We want features that will take away stress on how to get outside, because the outdoors should be your escape from the stress. From sorting based on the area you're in, to providing driving directions to the trailhead, to filtering based on criteria suitable for you—whether that's for a new hike you're exploring with three kids or something dog-friendly, we want to make sure we're giving people the confidence to hit the trail."

AVENZAMAPS.COM The Avenza Maps store has a collection of nearly one million high-quality geospatial PDF maps from professional map publishers around the world. You can use these maps on your mobile devices and locate yourself while out on the trail without the need for the internet or network connections. A blue dot follows you wherever you go, so you always know where you are on the map. You can zoom in and out, navigate from place to place, mark points of interest, and easily attach photos exactly where they were taken.

WILDFLOWERSEARCH.ORG This site has many good tools for identifying flowers. It also has up-to-date lists of species in bloom.

INATURALIST.ORG and **SEEK BY INATURALIST** This web- and app-based online community allows you to share your species observations with other naturalists around the world. It's also a great place to post a question if you can't identify something you found.

GEOCACHING.COM or **THE GEOCACHING APP** Geocaches are treasures hidden by other people with GPS coordinates posted online. If you're heading out on one of the adventures, check the website or app to see if anyone has hidden a treasure along the trail. If they have, you can use your phone to navigate to it, find it, exchange a treasure item or sign the log, and re-hide it where you found it.

SMARTPHONES

You may have picked up this book to find ways of distracting kids from their phones. Not using a phone at all during your adventures can be fun and appropriate, and you probably already know where you stand on the issue of screen time. But if you want to try a balance, letting kids use their phone on the trail to take a picture of an interesting flower, navigate with a digital compass app, use the audio app to capture a birdsong, or share their pictures of the hike on the state forest's Instagram can be a conscientious way to bridge technology and outdoor time (just be sure the phone is put away more than it's out).

Young adventurer using a smartphone to identify the treasures she has found along the trail

SHOWING RESPECT FOR NATURE

The mid-Atlantic has eighteen million lovely people who enjoy the eighty-one thousand square miles that make up this region, so protecting its land will be key to conserving its beauty for generations to come. We hope to inspire stewards—the more we are out there understanding and delighting in the natural world with our families, the more we and our little adventurers

"Every man in his heart revolts at civilization and will revert back to [nature] if given half a chance . . . We don't live long enough to find out what life is all about, but we know what civilization is—it is a mere veneer that keeps on getting thicker, but never too thick to pierce . . . It will be 15,000 years I think, before man will reach such a high point of civilization where he cannot and will not want to go back to [reconnect with nature]."

—Thomas Edison at Muddy Creek Falls (one of the hikes in the book), Maryland, July 1921

want to take care of it in the future. Some of the beautiful areas in this guide are also the most remote and precious. You're doing the most important thing you can to keep the state beautiful—taking your kids outside.

When you and your children are on top of a fire tower overlooking the fall colors or standing in a cave formed thousands of years ago, you cannot help but feel part of something larger. By simply noticing and beginning to identify features, flora, and fauna in nature you are creating a sense of respect and appreciation. Model and embrace the "Leave No Trace" ethos (see LNT.org for more great ideas) on every trail. Be diligent with snack wrappers, always stay on the trail, and avoid trampling vegetation and disturbing wildlife to ensure that everyone and everything can share the adventure.

The scavenger hunts will be asking kids to act as young naturalists, to notice, touch, and play with nature around them in a safe and gentle way. For the most part, do not take a leaf or flower off a growing plant, but rather collect and play with items that are already on the ground. Manipulate them, stack them, create art with them, trace them in journals—but then leave them to be used by other creatures in the area, from the fungi decomposing a leaf to another kid walking down the trail tomorrow. Invite your adventurers to see if they can help with citizen science by reporting observations back to ranger stations, cleaning up trash, and volunteering to maintain trails. Many of these wilderness areas and public lands were created with the help of state leaders, and you're creating the next generation of conservationists simply by getting kids out in them.

ADVENTURES IN
DELAWARE

Adventurers, let's begin in the northern part of the Diamond State at its highest point and slope downward toward the ocean as we hike our way through it. The state of Delaware, which became the first official state of the United States in 1787, gets its name from the Delaware River, which was named for the governor of Virginia, Thomas West, Lord De La Warr. Delaware shares the Delmarva Peninsula with parts of Maryland and Virginia. It is the second-smallest state and is only one hundred miles long and thirty miles wide, but offers plenty of places to explore along the flat Atlantic Coastal Plain. During your adventures, you will explore the blue granite cliffs of Alapocas Run, walk around a tidal salt marsh—one of thirty thousand acres of swamp in the state—at Bombay Hook, climb sand dunes along the Atlantic Ocean at Cape Henlopen, and circle around a pond filled with bald cypress trees at Trap Pond. Celebrate the state's motto of "liberty and independence" as you hike. Let's go!

1

EXPLORE THE BLUE GRANITE CLIFFS OF ALAPOCAS RUN

N

0   1000 ft.

trailhead

P

• *turn right*

Alapocas Woods Trail

ALAPOCAS DRIVE

ALAPOCAS RUN STATE PARK

Northern Delaw Greenway Trail

stay straight

Upper Reach Trail

PawPaw Loop

Brandywine Creek

turn right •

Alapocas Run

turn left

turn left

Wilmington

waterfall •• *blue granite cliffs*

old mill dam

Northern Delaware Greenway

Bancroft Trail

YOUR ADVENTURE

Adventurers, today you'll explore Delaware's beautiful blue granite cliffs in the historical land of the Lenni-Lenape. To start, hike over a bridge and turn right onto Alapocas Woods Trail. Stay straight, passing the Pawpaw Trail. Wind along the packed-earth path through beautiful pawpaw trees and pass the other end of the Pawpaw Trail. Keep going straight. Pass the

These cliffs are made of gneiss, more commonly known as blue rock or blue granite →

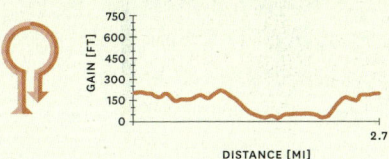

LENGTH 2.7-mile lollipop loop

ELEVATION GAIN 246 ft.

HIKE TIME + EXPLORE 2 hours

DIFFICULTY Easy—packed-earth and paved paths with mild elevation

SEASON Year-round; best in spring when the pawpaw trees are blooming.

GET THERE Take I-95 North from Christiana to DE-141 South / Foulk Road. Take Exit 8 to DE-141 South for 10 miles. Turn left onto Alapocas Drive. Look for an Alapocas ball field sign at the east entrance to the DuPont Experimental Station. Parking lot and trail located next to the ball fields.

Google Maps: bit.ly/timberalapocas

RESTROOM At parking lot

FEE None

TREAT YOURSELF Enjoy waffles and ice cream 3 miles north at Sweet Nel's off US-202 North.

Alapocas Run State Park
(302) 577-1164
Facebook @ARSP.WSP

Upper Reach Trail on your left, the Unnamed Trail on your right, and the Upper Reach Trail on your left again, continually going straight. Finally, turn right onto the Northern Delaware Greenway, then take another immediate right. Leave the woods and start on a paved path. The Brandywine Creek Dam will appear on the right and a small waterfall on the left. Soon you will see the massive Blue Rock Cliff on the left. It's the only natural-rock climbing wall in the state. Many people call these huge rocks "blue rock" because when it is broken, the freshly exposed rock is blue. These formations are found only in northern Delaware. Power up at the picnic tables and look up to try and spot rock climbers! Return to the Northern Delaware Greenway Trail, traveling past the way you entered, and turn left on the Bancroft Trail past more granite cliffs. In many places, you can see water pouring out of the rocks like a mini waterfall. Continue along Brandywine Creek before turning left on the Bancroft Trail, then turn right on the Unnamed Trail before turning left back onto the Alapocas Woods Trail. Turn left and go over the bridge to return to the trailhead.

SCAVENGER HUNT

Pawpaw trees

Pawpaw trees are North America's largest native fruit-bearing tree, with large drooping leaves. They produce purple flowers in spring and a yellow-greenish fruit in fall that's sweet, with a custard-like flavor similar to a mix of mango and bananas. While they can be eaten raw, they can also be used to make desserts. Would you try pawpaw ice cream?

Asimina triloba

Waterfall

Although small, the waterfall along Alapocas Run is a sight to be seen. Runs are streams that "run" downhill. This run flows into 20-mile-long Brandywine Creek, which pours into the 31-mile Christina River, which flows into the 301-mile-long Delaware River, which drains into Delaware Bay and the Atlantic Ocean. Drop a leaf and imagine where it might go!

This small cascade is one of Delaware's only waterfalls

White oak acorns

You will see many types of oaks today. Look up to see if you can tell the difference between them based on their leaf shape. Then look on the path to see the different acorns, especially in fall. Collect some from the ground as you hike and make nature artwork. Remember: it is important to leave no trace, so when you finish, always return nature to where you found it.

Quercus alba acorns are a great source of food for wildlife

Brandywine Creek

The first dam on Brandywine Creek (also called Wauwaset River) was built in the early 1700s. Over time, ten more were added to generate water power for mills. Today, conservationists are trying to change the dams to allow migratory fish like American shad to return to their ancestral spawning grounds. Can you see any fish swimming in the water?

Dams like this still allow fish to swim upstream

2

HANG WITH THE BIRDS AT BOMBAY HOOK

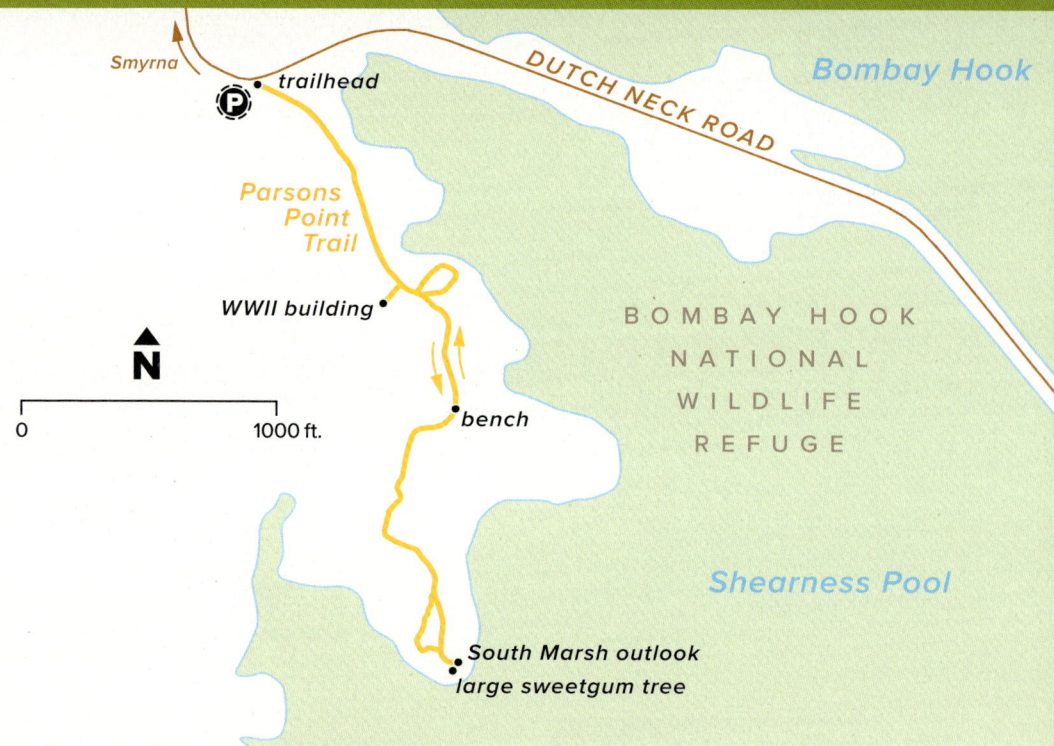

Smyrna · **P** · *trailhead*

DUTCH NECK ROAD

Bombay Hook

Parsons Point Trail

WWII building ·

N

BOMBAY HOOK NATIONAL WILDLIFE REFUGE

0 — 1000 ft.

· *bench*

Shearness Pool

· *South Marsh outlook*
large sweetgum tree

YOUR ADVENTURE

Adventurers, today you will explore a wildlife refuge especially known for the thousands of migratory shorebirds that stop here on their way north in spring and on their way south in late summer and early fall. You will have an amazing 365-degree view of a tidal salt marsh, but first you must walk through a wooded area on a path on the historical homeland of the

Bombay Hook National Wildlife Refuge is known for having one of the largest tidal salt marshes in the mid-Atlantic →

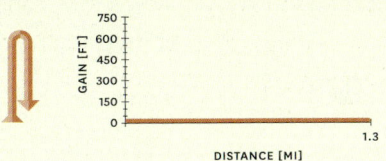

GAIN [FT]: 0, 150, 300, 450, 600, 750
DISTANCE [MI]: 1.3

LENGTH 1.3 miles out and back

ELEVATION GAIN 10 ft.

HIKE TIME + EXPLORE 1 hour

DIFFICULTY Easy—packed-earth path with mild elevation

SEASON Year-round; best in spring, when thousands of migrating shorebirds stop here on their way north.

GET THERE Take US-13 South from Middletown. Turn left onto Road 12 / Smyrna Leipsic Road. After 4.3 miles, turn left onto Road 84 / Big Woods Road. After 0.2 miles, continue onto Raymond Neck Road. After 1.7 miles, turn left onto Finnis Pool Road. After 1 mile, turn right onto Dutch Neck Road. Continue until you reach the small parking lot next to the trailhead.

Google Maps: bit.ly/timberbombayhook

RESTROOM At visitor center

FEE $4 per vehicle

TREAT YOURSELF Reward yourself with a specialty milkshake from MomMom's Ice Cream Shop, just 10 miles south of the refuge.

Bombay Hook National Wildlife Refuge
(302) 653-9345
Facebook @bombayhookwildliferefuge

Lenni-Lenape. Soon after starting, look for the foundation of a tower from World War II. If you walk off the path a few steps, you can actually walk into the foundation to explore. Back on the path, look up in the trees to see if you can spot any birds. The most common ones along this trail are red-bellied woodpeckers, flickers, and warblers. After half a mile, arrive at an opening where you will see a huge, beautiful sweetgum tree. This is a great place to take a break and power up. Next, you'll come across a field with views of Shearness Pool. Return to the path and head back to the trailhead the way you came. If time allows, continue driving around the refuge so you can keep admiring this beautiful wildlife sanctuary.

SCAVENGER HUNT

Great blue heron

Look for one of the tallest birds in Delmarva (which includes Delaware, the eastern shore of Maryland, and a small strip of land in Virginia). Only the bald eagle has a larger wingspan and weight! When flying, the great blue heron tucks in its neck, and its long legs trail behind. On land, it moves slowly until it is ready to quickly strike its prey. Play heron tag and move like a heron to catch your hikemate.

Ardea herodias only weighs 5 to 6 pounds

Tidal salt marsh

These coastal wetlands are flooded with saltwater brought in by the tides and drain as the tides recede. Tidal salt marshes are important because they help moderate the effects of climate change by isolating and storing carbon (emissions from cars and other pollution in the air) at a rate ten times faster than tropical forests! Take out your nature journal and draw your favorite part of the tidal salt marsh.

One acre of salt marsh can absorb up to 1.5 million gallons of floodwater

Bur marigold

Take a sniff as you hike! If you catch a scent of vanilla, you are probably walking past some bur marigolds. This annual (only blooms once and then dies) has a vanilla smell that attracts butterflies and bees; its blooms consist of seven to eight yellow petals from late autumn until first frost. Look closely—can you count how many tiny yellow disc florets make up the center?

Bidens laevis is a flowering plant in the daisy family

World War II headquarters building

The remains of this observation tower date from World War II. It stood 28 feet high and was home to the Army Air Force aerial rocket research program, which tested rockets by shooting them at targets in the swamp. In your journal, draw what the foundation and surrounding area looks like now; when you get home, draw what you think the building and surrounding area looked like during the war.

The Army Air Force took over much of the refuge during World War II

3

EXPLORE THE GREAT DUNE AT CAPE HENLOPEN

YOUR ADVENTURE

Adventurers, we are headed to the beach and the Great Dune, Delaware's highest sand dune, 80 feet above the ocean on the historical homeland of the Lenni-Lenape. The hike begins on the bike trail, so walk on the right side so bikers can pass on your left. You will soon see an iconic fire control tower from when the state park was a military base during World War II.

Take in the views from the Great Dune →

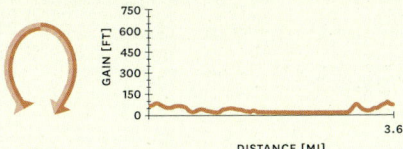

GAIN [FT]

750
600
450
300
150
0

3.6

DISTANCE [MI]

LENGTH 3.6-mile loop

ELEVATION GAIN 102 ft.

HIKE TIME + EXPLORE 2.5 hours

DIFFICULTY Moderate—combination of packed-earth and paved paths with mild elevation, except at the Great Dunes, where you will be walking up a short but sharp incline in the sand

SEASON Year-round; best in spring and autumn, as bugs can be fierce in summer.

GET THERE Traveling south from Milford, follow signs to US Route 9 East. Turn left onto Dartmouth Road and continue until the stop sign. Turn left onto US-9 East / Freeman Highway for 2.8 miles. Turn right onto Cape Henlopen Drive. The park entrance is approximately 1 mile past the Cape May-Lewes Ferry terminal. Once in the park, drive to the Herring Point parking lot right before the campsite and walk across the street to the trailhead.

Google Maps: bit.ly/timberwalkingdunes

RESTROOM At trailhead

FEE $5 per vehicle for DE residents, $10 nonresidents

TREAT YOURSELF Cool off after all of your hard work with a hand-dipped chocolate ice cream cone from 2 Dips, which is only 1.5 miles down the road heading west.

Cape Henlopen State Park
(302) 645-8983
Facebook @capehenlopenstatepark

After exploring, return to the path and go left. Over the next half mile, you will pass five WWII bunkers! Power up at a bench in between them, and stay right as you pass a paved trail that goes left. Next, watch for a small trail pole on the right side that points you to the dunes' walking trails. Walk through maritime forests, then peaceful salt marsh lands. You'll pass several right turns, but stay straight until you reach a wooden footbridge. Turn right, crossing it, then take another right at a bench. Cross another footbridge and then veer off the main path to the left, taking the small path to the dunes. Ask rangers if it is okay to climb, as it is a sensitive area. Finish the loop and return to the trailhead. To explore other parts of the park, including the fishing pier or beach, book a campsite at Cape Henlopen State Park Campground.

SCAVENGER HUNT

Prickly pears

Look but don't touch these cacti that sprawl on the ground—they got their name for a reason! Touching them can hurt and irritate the skin. In early summer, they produce beautiful yellow flowers. Find some rocks nearby and see if you can make a mosaic in the shape of a prickly pear. When finished, return all the rocks to where you found them.

Opuntia species are flat-stemmed, spiny cactuses

Sandy laccaria

Did you know that mushrooms can grow in sand? It's true! Sandy laccaria do. These mushrooms have a symbiotic relationship (where both members of a partnership benefit) with the roots of coastal pines along the path and can grow only under them. Do you have a symbiotic relationship with anyone? How many mushrooms can you find on this hike?

Laccaria trullisata has a scaly cap surface

WWII bunker

Secret bunkers were built within the sand dunes to house heavy artillery during World War II—they provided a perfect cover. This site closed in 1964, but the bunkers still stand. Today, some are used for storage by the Parks service, while others are empty. Would you be brave enough to explore their underground tunnels?

Access to the bunkers is limited to park officials

The Great Dune

The Great Dune is the largest sand hill between Cape Cod, Massachusetts, and Cape Hatteras, North Carolina. It formed over thousands of years by wind, waves, and currents bringing sand to the mouth of Delaware Bay. During World War II, the Army added more sand to hide a bunker. At the foot of the dune, see how fast you can run through the sand.

The Great Dune was once called the Great Sand Hill

WWII fire control tower

The US Army built eleven observation towers in Delaware between 1939 and 1942. Most are sealed shut, but this tower is restored and open to the public. Climb up to get panoramic views of Lewes, the Atlantic Ocean, and Delaware Bay. Imagine looking out from this tower as a soldier during World War II.

Fire Tower 7 is located at the start of the hike

4

ROAM AROUND TRAP POND

YOUR ADVENTURE

Adventurers, today we will explore the historical homeland of the Lenni-Lenape and one of Delaware's first state parks. Begin by hiking under the canopy of tall loblolly pines on the wide gravel Bob Trail. Please be mindful that you are sharing this path with horseback riders, so keep your eyes and ears open. Take the first left to an open grassy area with picnic tables

View of Trap Pond →

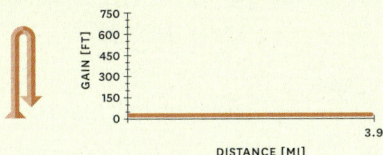

LENGTH 3.9 miles out and back

ELEVATION GAIN 43 ft.

HIKE TIME + EXPLORE 2 hours

DIFFICULTY Moderate—a combination of packed-earth and gravel paths with mild elevation

SEASON Year-round; lovely in spring when the bald cypress trees are full of color.

GET THERE From Georgetown, take West Market Street to Road 62 / East Trap Pond Road and follow for 11 miles to DE-24 West. Turn right and after 0.25 miles turn left onto Trap Pond Road. Drive 2 miles to the parking lot past the Bald Cypress Nature Center.

Google Maps: bit.ly/timbertrappond

RESTROOM At the nature center and at the parking lot by the historical church

FEE From 1 March to 30 November, $4 per vehicle for DE residents, $8 nonresidents

TREAT YOURSELF Stop by the bakery at the Dutch Country Market 5 miles west of the park to pick up some fresh peach pie, the official state dessert of Delaware.

Trap Pond State Park
(302) 875-5163 | Facebook @ TrapPondStatePark

and a pier over the pond. Head back to Bob Trail and pass a bench. Turn left when you arrive at the road, and walk carefully along it a short ways; the trail picks up again on your left. The trail becomes narrower as you zigzag through the trees, until you come to an opening that leads you to a historical old country church on the left side of the trail, the Bethesda Methodist Episcopal Church. Explore the church and graveyard, have a power-up stop, and use the restroom located by the adjacent parking lot before returning to the trail and starting your trip back to the trailhead. Look up for magnificent birds perched above and look out past the trees to pondside views of the bald cypress trees. Consider staying longer so you can have more time to explore this amazing state park. Take advantage of free bike rentals in summer by camping at the Trap Pond State Park campground.

SCAVENGER HUNT

Bald cypress trees

Have you ever seen a tree growing in the water? Today you will! Many bald cypress trees grow in the shallow standing water of Trap Pond, the northernmost park that features them. These trees drop needles in winter, giving them the name "bald." This unique sight will make a great addition to the drawings in your nature journal.

Taxodium distichum is a deciduous conifer

Pileated woodpecker

Listen for these large, mostly black birds often recognized by their prominent red crest like a mohawk on their heads. This largest woodpecker in North America whacks at dead trees and fallen logs looking for ants. If you can't spot any, see if you can find some of the rectangular holes they leave in the wood.

Dryocopus pileatus lives in deciduous forests

Tawny grisette

Look for this mushroom with its orange to brown cap and a tall, slender stem. Did you know that all fungi begin as tiny spores that spread by wind, water, and even animals? The only way they grow is if they happen to land on an appropriate food source. Draw this mushroom in your nature journal so you can compare it to mushrooms you find on other hikes. Be sure to look underneath at its gills—how many can you count?

Look for *Amanita fulva* in summer and autumn

Old country church

This community gathering place is over 150 years old. Although there were once many similar churches throughout this area, it is one of the few that remains unchanged today.

Bethesda Methodist Episcopal Church was built in 1879

Canada goldenrod

Keep your eyes peeled for this perennial (grows back every spring) wildflower native to eastern North America. It blooms in late summer to early fall with bright yellow to golden flowers. Bees often feed on the nectar of these plants, which makes them very important for the environment. Look around—do you see any bees flying near these beautiful wildflowers?

Solidago canadensis

ADVENTURES IN
MARYLAND

Welcome

Welcome to the Old Line State, adventurers! This history-rich state was the seventh to enter the Union, and was named after Queen Henrietta Maria, the wife of Charles I, who was king of Great Britain and signed a charter establishing Maryland as a colony in 1632. It's been called "America in Miniature" due to its wide variety of topography (the physical features of the land) ranging from sandy dunes in the east, to low marshlands near the Chesapeake Bay, to gently rolling hills in the Piedmont region and forested mountains in the Appalachian Plateau in the west. We'll start our journey on the eastern part of the state and work our way west. We'll begin by hiking to a lighthouse that sits atop a 100-foot bluff, then we'll explore one of the largest remaining freshwater tidal marshes within the upper Chesapeake Bay—the largest estuary in the country. Next, we'll be climbing to a rock formation known as the King and Queen Seat. Our journey will continue when we hike to Maryland's second-highest vertical drop waterfall, explore a hemlock gorge, chase waterfalls at Maryland's oldest state park, and hike under a magical tunnel of trees on our way to a small, secluded beach at the end of an island. We then hunt for fossilized shark teeth, experience the Underground Railroad, and climb Maryland's only monadnock (isolated hill), before hiking part of the Appalachian Trail on our way to the first monument dedicated to the memory of George Washington. Our final adventures in this state will have us hiking to the largest cascading waterfall in Maryland, exploring a 3,118-foot tunnel said to be the greatest engineering marvel along the Chesapeake and Ohio Canal, climbing to a 90-foot fire tower that sits on a mountain summit 3,000 feet above the ground, and then finally exploring Swallow Falls and Maryland's highest waterfall. Keep in mind Maryland's motto of "strong deeds, gentle words" and be strong but gentle on the trails in this great state.

Young explorers taking a break and admiring the magnificent Swallow Falls

5

LOOP YOUR WAY AROUND TURKEY POINT LIGHTHOUSE

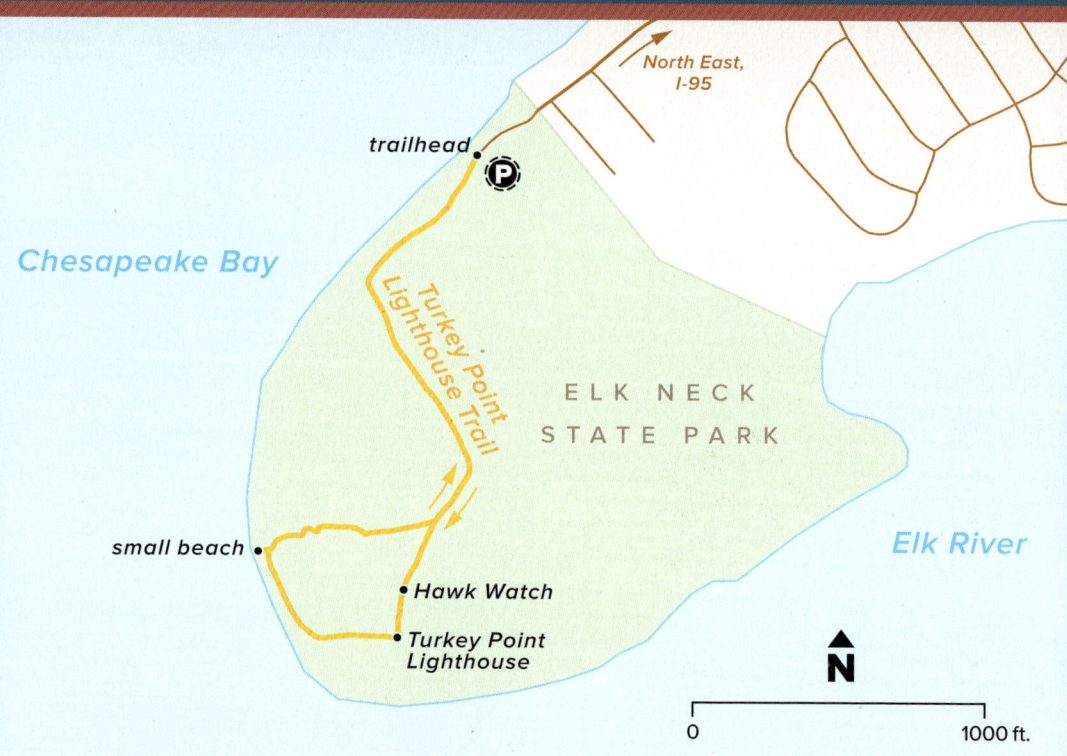

Chesapeake Bay

North East, I-95

trailhead

Turkey Point Lighthouse Trail

ELK NECK STATE PARK

small beach

Hawk Watch

Turkey Point Lighthouse

Elk River

N

0   1000 ft.

YOUR ADVENTURE

Adventurers, let's take a walk on the historical homelands of the Lenni-Lenape to a lighthouse high atop a 100-foot bluff with spectacular views of the Chesapeake Bay. Follow a gravel path through a small, wooded area where you can see a variety of wildlife—insects, butterflies, birds, and even elk. You'll soon reach a fork—go right to take a small loop to the

View of Turkey Point Lighthouse as you see it for the first time from the trail →

GAIN [FT]

750
600
450
300
150
0

DISTANCE [MI]

LENGTH 2.0-mile lollipop loop

ELEVATION GAIN 154 ft.

HIKE TIME + EXPLORE 1.5 hours

DIFFICULTY Easy—gravel path with mild elevation

SEASON Year-round; best in fall for hawk-watching.

GET THERE Take MD-272 / Main Street south from the town of North East for 11.5 miles as you pass through Elk Neck State Park, then through a small private community. The trailhead is at the very end of MD-272 in Elk Neck State Park.

Google Maps: bit.ly/timberturkeypointlighthouse

RESTROOM Seasonally at the lighthouse

FEE None ($5 to enter lighthouse when open on Saturdays and Sundays)

TREAT YOURSELF On your way back to I-95, stop at Chesapeake Bay Coffee Co. on Main Street for some delicious homemade donuts.

Elk Neck State Park
(410) 287-5333
Facebook @ElkNeckStatePark

water. Shortly after, carefully walk off the trail and over a few rocks to find a small beach. Power up and enjoy the amazing views of the Chesapeake Bay. Return to the path and walk up a slight incline until you leave the wooded area. When you emerge from the clearing and round the corner, you will see Turkey Point Lighthouse. Enjoy views from atop the cliffs. Did you know the bluffs you are standing on are visible for several miles out in the bay? Check out the vines and shrubs on both sides of the field, as well as the tall red cedar trees. Continue down the path to Hawk Watch, an open field where you can look for several species of migratory hawks, especially in fall. Continue until you reach the fork again; stay straight to head back to the parking lot. Consider extending your stay by camping at one of the tent sites or cabins available at Elk Neck State Park.

SCAVENGER HUNT

Sassafras

Look for this large tree with bright green, mitten-shaped leaves of 2 to 3 lobes. Fragrant yellow-green flowers bloom in April to June, and in late summer they produce small, dark blue oval-shaped fruits on bright red stalks. Gently shake hands with the mitten-like leaves as you walk by.

Sassafras albidum has a very recognizable leaf shape

Wild rye and wheat grass

Can you spot these perennial plants with spike-shaped seedheads and long, bristly awns that cause the stems to droop? Perennial plants regrow every spring; annual plants only grow for one season. Gently brush your hand along the stalks. Are they hard or soft?

Elymus species can be seen along the edges of the path

Common five-lined skink

Along the trail, try to find a common five-lined skink. The young reptiles are easy to spot with their five yellow or white stripes on their heads and bright blue tails. Try sketching this amazing creature in your nature journal, then fill in its beautiful colors when you get home.

Only the young *Plestiodon fasciatus* has a blue tail

Turkey Point Lighthouse

This lighthouse is 31.5 feet high and visible for 13 miles. A keeper's quarters used to be located next to the lighthouse. Fun fact: Turkey Point had more women lighthouse keepers than any other lighthouse on the Chesapeake Bay. Four out of the ten keepers here were women, and female keepers held the role for 89 of its 115 years. What do you think the life of a lighthouse keeper was like?

The Turkey Point lighthouse was built in 1833

Red-tailed hawk

Look up in the sky while walking through Hawk Watch, and you might see a hawk like the red-tailed soaring above. Eight types of migratory hawks can commonly be seen soaring overhead or perched high in trees, and their wing shapes are all different—see if you can tell the difference as they fly above. The best viewing times are between 9 a.m. and noon, as well as the morning after the passage of a cold front, or during the fall migratory season.

Buteo jamaicensis is the most common hawk in North America

6

ADVENTURE TO OTTER POINT CREEK

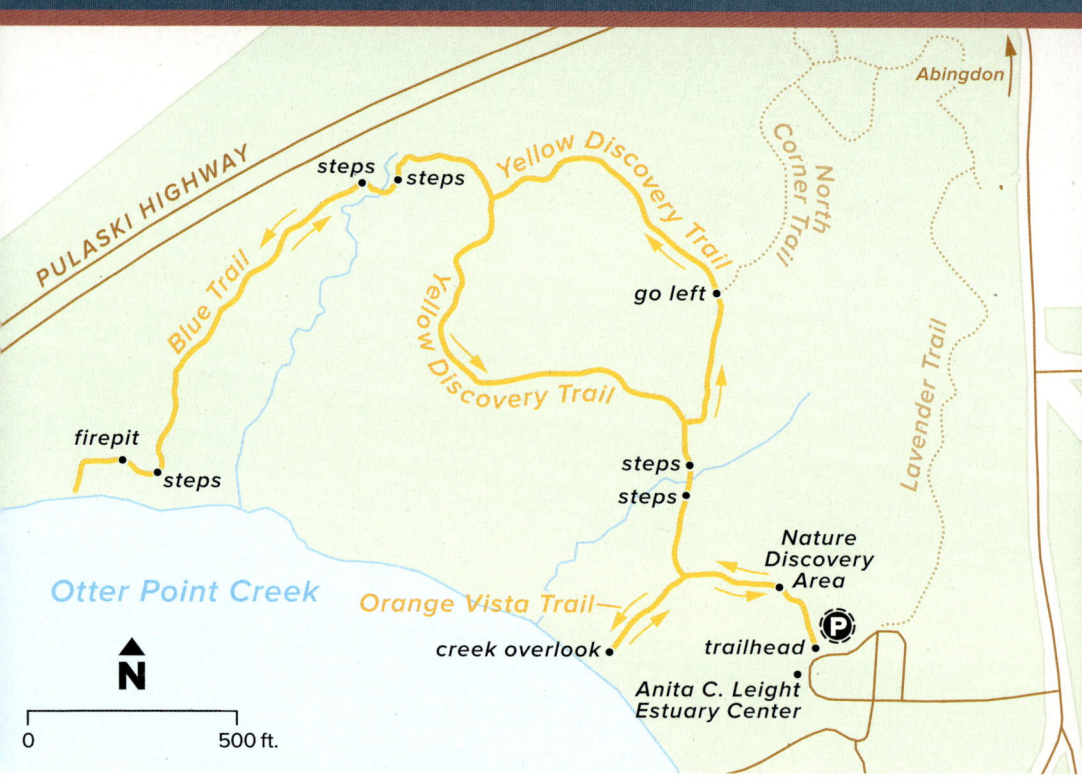

YOUR ADVENTURE

Adventurers, get ready to see some amazing flora as you walk along Otter Point Creek Natural Area, one of the largest remaining freshwater tidal marshes within the upper Chesapeake Bay. The Yellow Discovery Trail begins to the right of the nature center on the historical homelands of the Susquehannock. As soon as you turn the first bend, you'll reach the nature

The pier over Otter Point Creek →

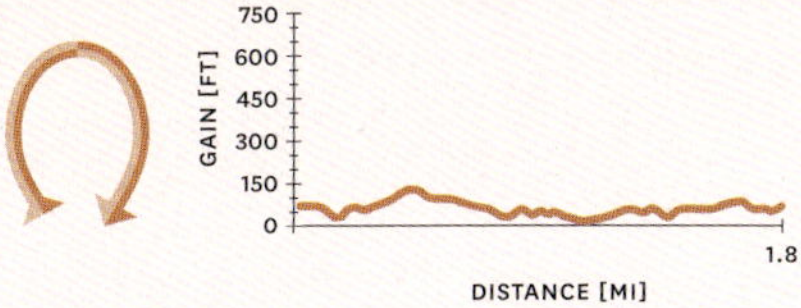

GAIN [FT]

750
600
450
300
150
0

1.8

DISTANCE [MI]

LENGTH 1.8-mile loop

ELEVATION GAIN 180 ft.

HIKE TIME + EXPLORE 1.5 hours

DIFFICULTY Moderate—packed-earth paths and a series of natural steps with mild elevation

SEASON Year-round. Spring features blooms and birds returning from migration.

GET THERE From Abingdon, take Abingdon Road southeast to cross US-40 West and continue on Otter Point Road for 0.4 miles. Turn right into the driveway at the Anita C. Leight Estuary Center entrance sign.

Google Maps: bit.ly/timberottercreek

RESTROOM At the nature center

FEE None

TREAT YOURSELF Don't miss the freshly made ice cream at Broom's Bloom Dairy, just 5 miles north on Rt. 543.

Anita C. Leight Estuary Center
(410) 612-1688
Facebook @ACLEC

discovery area, a play space made of mostly natural materials. At the next fork in the path, turn left on the Orange Vista Trail, then walk a short distance to get to an overlook of 9-mile-long Otter Point Creek, a shallow tributary of Bush River, which leads into the Chesapeake Bay. Hike back to the Yellow Discovery Trail and turn left; you will start to see signs highlighting the flora along the path. Cross the creek and come to a fork. Go right to the pier to start a small loop, go left at the next turn then go straight on the Blue Trail. Wind your way through the woods, going up and down more steps, until you emerge into an open field with picnic tables and a firepit. Consider lunching here. Continue to a long wooden pier featuring views of Otter Point Creek. Explore, then return to the Blue Trail and wind your way back to the Yellow Discovery Trail. Turn right, then stay straight past the Orange Vista Trail and Green Overlook Trail until you reach the start of the hike. If you have time, stop at the visitor center to explore their hands-on exhibits about the Chesapeake Bay ecology and local flora and fauna.

SCAVENGER HUNT

Black-eyed Susan

Look for this common wildflower, easily recognized because by an almost black center and bright yellow petals. They can reach almost 4 feet in height, and they bloom between June and September. Black-eyed Susans attract butterflies and bees, the main pollinators of this plant. How many petals do you count on one flower?

Rudbeckia hirta is Maryland's state flower

Sweetbay magnolia

What's that smell? This small tree has creamy white flowers of 9 to 12 petals. They bloom open in the morning and close in the evening during late spring to midsummer. Then, after the flowers fade, they produce a cluster of dark red fruit. Put your nose close to the tree to see if you can smell its beautiful light lemon scent.

Magnolia virginiana leaves smell spicy when crushed

Beautyberry

Look for this shrub's lavender flowers in summer and its bright purple berries that grow in clusters around the plant's stems in late summer and early fall. These berries are a crucial food source for many birds that call this park home. How many berries can you count on one stalk?

Callicarpa americana (*Callicarpa* means "beautiful fruit." Do you agree?)

North American river otter

Look for this playful semi-aquatic mammal splashing about in the aptly named Otter Point Creek. It has adaptations (features that evolved to help them thrive in a certain environment) on its body that make it perfect for the river—short legs and webbed feet, a long body, and a long strong tail. What adaptations do you have that make you suited for land?

Otter Point Creek is an important part of the Chesapeake Bay's ecosystem

7

SPEND THE DAY AS ROYALTY AT THE KING AND QUEEN SEAT

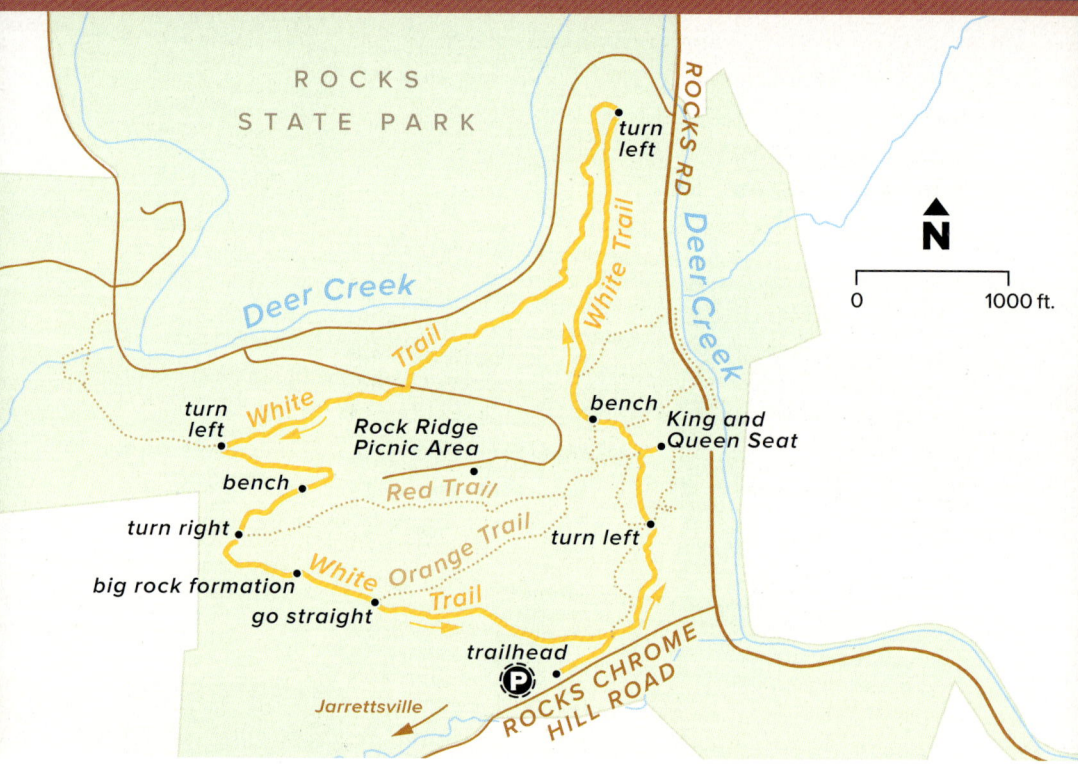

YOUR ADVENTURE

Adventurers, are you ready to do some social climbing to reach royalty status? Today you will explore Maryland's first state park, in the historical homelands of the Susquehannock. A narrow path leads up a moderate incline on rocky terrain. Follow the white blazes on the trees and at the fork, turn right to take this loop counterclockwise. After about ten minutes,

The King and Queen Seat are made of quartzite and were formed millions of years ago →

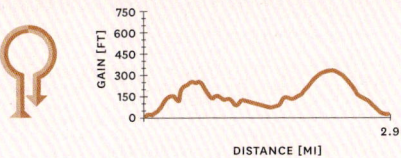

LENGTH 2.9-mile lollipop loop

ELEVATION GAIN 469 ft.

HIKE TIME + EXPLORE 2 hours

DIFFICULTY Moderate—packed-earth path with rock scrambles, plus large rocks at summit with moderate incline

SEASON Year-round; best during fall foliage.

GET THERE Head north on Baldwin Mill Road from Jarrettsville. Turn right onto Jarrettsville Road. After 2 miles, turn left onto Old Federal Hill Road. After 0.6 miles, turn right onto Chrome Hill Road. After 1.6 miles, turn left onto Rocks Chrome Hill Road. The parking lot will be on your left and is located next to the ranger's office. The trailhead is at the end of the parking lot.

Google Maps: bit.ly/timberkingandqueenseats

RESTROOM At trailhead

FEE None

TREAT YOURSELF After this challenging adventure, you deserve some homemade ice cream from Jarrettsville Creamery, located just 5 miles southwest from the trailhead.

Rocks State Park
(410) 557-7994
Facebook @Rocks-State-Park

you will see the rock formations known as the King and Queen Seat on your right. Skilled hikers may climb out on the rock formations, but please use extreme caution, as they hover almost 200 feet above the Deer Creek Gorge below. If you choose to admire them from afar, which we recommend, you can still enjoy amazing views of Harford County's rolling hills and farmlands. This is a beautiful place for a power-up or to climb on rocks closer to the trail. Once you are ready to continue, return to the White Trail, passing the Red Trail, where you will walk on a rocky incline. Power up at the next bench. Pass a rock scramble and come to a junction with the Blue Trail. Stay left to continue on the White Trail. Rest at another bench and pass the Red Trail again (if you still have energy, you can hike a half mile into the Rock Ridge Picnic Area on the Red Trail). Your reward is a downhill back to the trailhead. Pass a big rock formation, go straight at another junction with the Yellow Trail, hit the junction where you started, and go right, back to the parking lot.

SCAVENGER HUNT

King and Queen Seat

This natural rock outcrop towers 190 feet above Deer Creek with breathtaking views. It is made of quartz-pebble metaconglomerate and was formed millions of years ago. The surrounding rocks eventually eroded away, leaving this tall tower. The seats were a ceremonial gathering place for the Susquehannock people. Sit on a closer rock formation and pretend to be the king or queen of the forest!

This area was once called "The Rocks of Deer Creek"

Hay-scented fern

Take a sniff as you pass this feathery plant. When you brush by, it releases a fragrance similar to freshly mown hay. It doesn't have flowers but reproduces with spores at the bottom of each of its pinnules, or leaves. Can you find the frond, stalk, blade, and pinna of the fern? How is it different from other plants?

The feathery fronds of *Dennstaedtia punctilobula* turn golden brown in autumn

Black walnut

Can you spot this deciduous tree, which can reach up to 75 feet tall? How tall is the one you see today? It takes 12–15 years for these to begin bearing nuts. When they do, the fruit consists of three layers—a green fleshy husk; a hard, thick, black inner shell; and an oily kernel. If you find one on the ground, observe its size, coloring, and texture and record it in your nature journal.

Juglans nigra nuts ripen in early to mid-autumn

Chicken of the woods mushroom

It is easy to spot this mushroom because of its vibrant yellow and orange colors and its large size. Look closely: can you see its pores (small holes)? This mushroom is edible and considered a delicacy in some parts of the world. People who have eaten it say it tastes like chicken, which is how it got its name. Have you ever eaten something that tasted like chicken but wasn't?

Laetiporus species make fruit from May to September

8

RELAX BELOW KILGORE FALLS

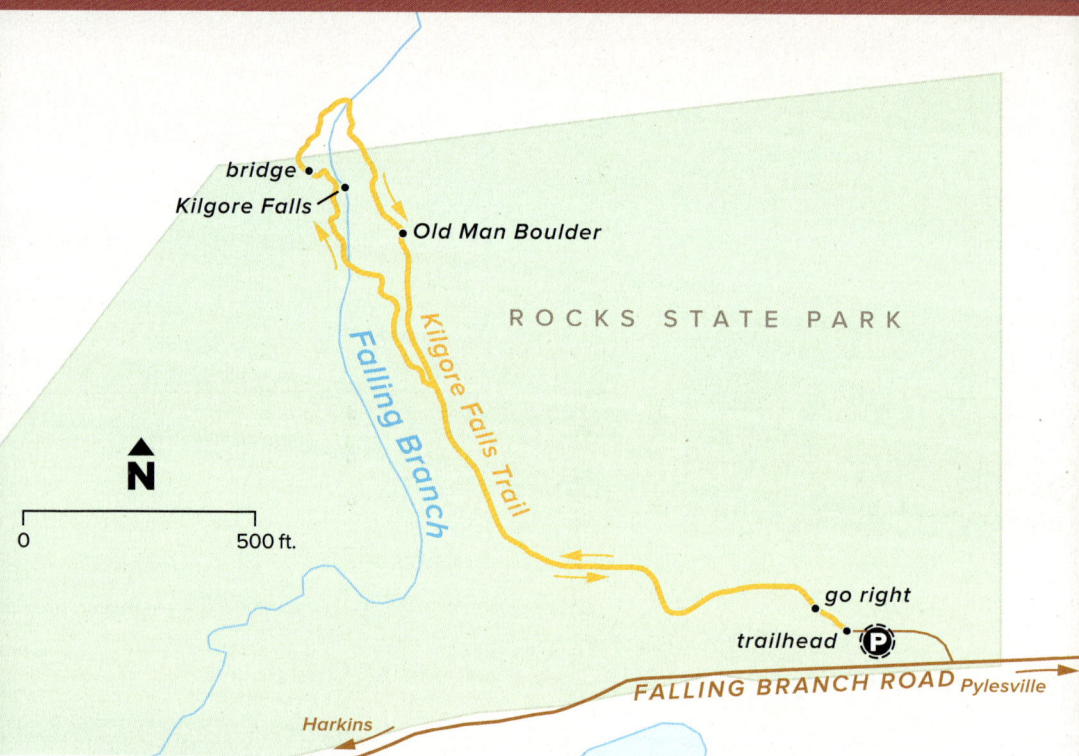

- bridge
- Kilgore Falls
- Old Man Boulder

ROCKS STATE PARK

Falling Branch

Kilgore Falls Trail

N

0 — 500 ft.

go right

trailhead

FALLING BRANCH ROAD *Pylesville*

Harkins

YOUR ADVENTURE

Adventurers, today we will explore the Falling Branch area of Rocks State Park in the historical homelands of the Susquehannock. Enjoy the path down toward the falls, where you will cross a small wooden bridge and walk through woods. If you are quiet, you can almost immediately hear the rushing of the falls. When you reach a fork in the path, veer left, then carefully

A wooden bridge on the way to Kilgore Falls →

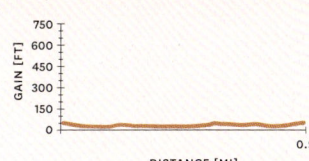

GAIN [FT]

750
600
450
300
150
0

0.9

DISTANCE [MI]

LENGTH 0.9-mile lollipop loop

ELEVATION GAIN 85 ft.

HIKE TIME + EXPLORE 2 hours

DIFFICULTY Easy—level, packed-earth path mixed with rocky areas and roots with mild elevation

SEASON Year-round, but especially fun in early autumn when it is less crowded but you can still swim in the watering holes.

GET THERE From Pylesville, take St. Marys Road west to where it joins Clermont Mill Road and turn right onto Falling Branch Road. In 0.4 miles, the parking lot will be on your right.

Google Maps: bit.ly/timberkilgorefalls

RESTROOM At trailhead

FEE None. Reservations are required (YourPassNow.com/ParkPass/md/kilgore) from 1 May to Labor Day. Passes become available each Monday prior to your visit.

TREAT YOURSELF Cool off with some ice cream from Bonkey's Ice Cream and Snoballs, just off Main Street in Whiteford. Their ice cream is made fresh daily and within three days of milking cows from a local farm!

Rocks State Park
(410) 557-7994
Facebook @Rocks-State-Park

use stepping stones to cross the water. Soon you'll arrive at Kilgore Falls. The water is cold but makes a perfect swimming hole. Wear your bathing suit and water shoes so you can wade and explore the granite cliffs and rock-covered river bottom. Be careful on the slippery rocks, and remember that the depth drops to over 10 feet near the falls, so you may not want to go too far from the shoreline. If you don't want to get as wet, you can play further downstream or have a power-up on one of the large rocks and watch the beautiful falls. When you're ready, follow the path along the left side of the falls over a small wooden bridge. Climb a steep stone staircase to view the falls from above before crossing a creek and looping around to return to the trailhead. Be sure to stay straight at the fork where you went left last time.

SCAVENGER HUNT

Viscid violet cort

It is hard to miss this bell-shaped mushroom that grows in clusters under trees from August through October. Why? The new mushroom will have a bright purple cap that is hard to miss; the color will fade to light lilac or even white or yellow as it matures. How many mushrooms can you count in each cluster?

The cap and stalk of *Cortinarius iodes* is coated in a sticky slime

Kilgore Falls

The water flowing down Kilgore Falls and over these large boulders travels through all three Maryland state parks before flowing into the Susquehanna River. How much water do you think flows over the waterfall each minute?

At 17 feet, this is Maryland's second-highest vertical drop

Schist pebbles

While wading through the water, you will see that the bottom is covered in thousands of schist pebbles. These are pieces of bedrock that have broken off larger schist rock formations and are now breaking down into smaller pieces by the water as part of the rock cycle. Collect as many different pebbles as you can and make a mosaic. When finished, return all the pebbles to where you found them.

Enjoy wading through the beautiful colored pebbles under the water by the falls

Potted touch-me-nots

Look for these summer-blooming wildflowers with orange flowers and red or dark-orange spots. The leaves have a coating that repels water, making it bead up and look like jewels. This is why it's also called spotted jewelweed. They're called touch-me-nots because if you touch their seeds, they burst open! Draw one in your nature journal to compare it to other wildflowers you find on hikes.

Impatiens capensis was used as a medicinal herb by several Indigenous tribes

Profile boulder

There are many huge boulders on this adventure. After you have climbed the stone steps and are above the falls, search for a large boulder that looks like a profile of a man's face. This rock formation is about 550 million years old!

Schist boulder that looks like the profile of a man's face

9

ADVENTURE AROUND THE HEMLOCK GORGE

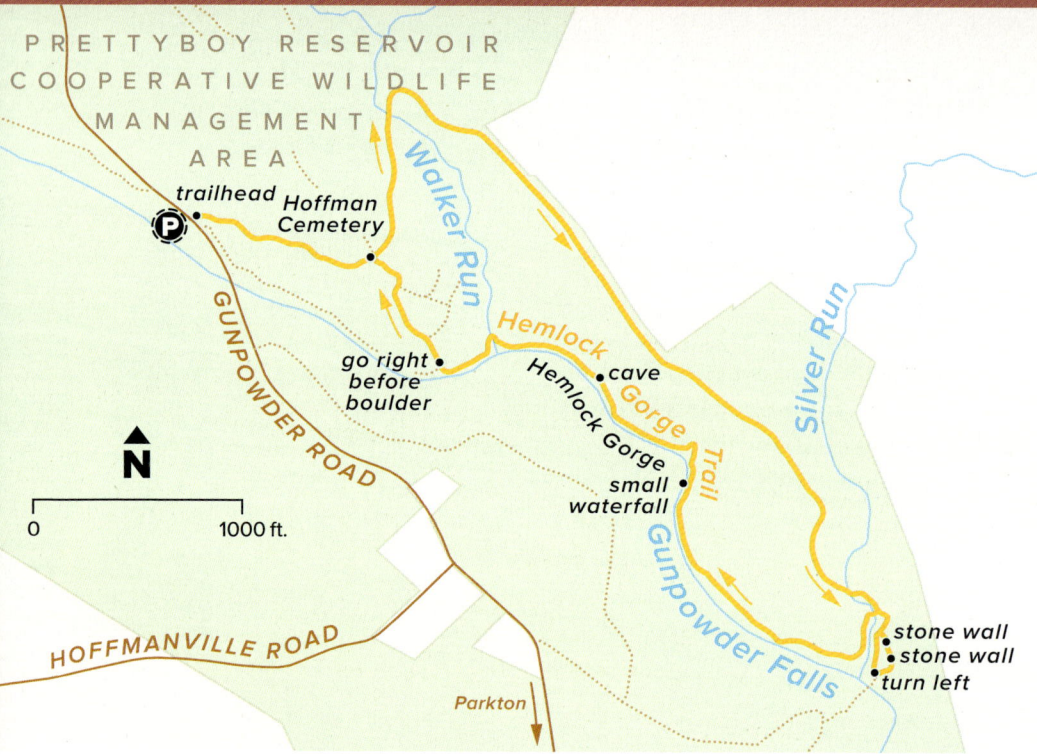

PRETTYBOY RESERVOIR COOPERATIVE WILDLIFE MANAGEMENT AREA

trailhead
Hoffman Cemetery

Walker Run

Hemlock Gorge

Silver Run

GUNPOWDER ROAD

go right before boulder

Hemlock Gorge Trail

cave

small waterfall

Gunpowder Falls

N

0   1000 ft.

stone wall
stone wall
turn left

HOFFMANVILLE ROAD

Parkton

YOUR ADVENTURE

Adventurers, get ready for beautiful sights and a bit of history in the Hemlock Gorge area, in the historical homelands of the Susquehannock. Start on a narrow path that quickly leads to the Hoffman Gunpowder Burying Ground. Take a few minutes to walk through the historical graveyard. Stay straight past the cemetery to continue down a hill and over the first stream,

A view of Hemlock Gorge from above →

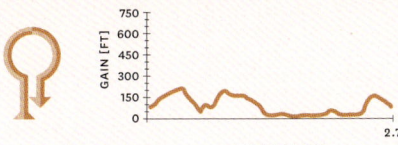

GAIN [FT]

750
600
450
300
150
0

2.7

DISTANCE [MI]

LENGTH 2.7-mile lollipop loop

ELEVATION GAIN 453 ft.

HIKE TIME + EXPLORE 2 hours

DIFFICULTY Moderate—a combination of packed-earth paths and rocky terrain with moderate elevation

SEASON Year-round, but best during spring when the water is flowing through the river and the flora is blooming.

GET THERE Follow I-83 north from Towson to Exit 31, Middletown Road. Continue on Middletown Road for about 5 miles. Turn left on Beckleysville Road, then slight right onto Cotter Road, which turns into Clipper Mill Road. Turn right onto Gunpowder Road. There is a clearing in the vegetation on the left side of the road where several cars can park. While the trailhead is not marked, it is located across the street from the parking area.

Google Maps: bit.ly/timberhemlockgorge

RESTROOM None

FEE None

TREAT YOURSELF Enjoy a crab dip–topped jumbo pretzel from Freeland Crab and Seafood, just 10 minutes east on Middletown Road.

Prettyboy Reservoir Cooperative Wildlife Management Area
(410) 260-8367
Facebook @MarylandDNR

crossing Walker Run. For the next mile and a half, wind your way around and up and down rolling hills. The path can be rocky at times, and you will have to navigate over roots and rock scrambles and walk along some exposed edges—be sure to hold younger hands here. After several more water crossings, you'll arrive at a small waterfall. There are many large rocks that provide a good spot to admire this hidden beauty. Farther down the path, you'll arrive at an area known as Hemlock Gorge. Hemlocks are evergreen trees with sweeping branches that provide dense cover. A gorge is a narrow valley with steep, rocky walls. Pause to admire the abundant hemlocks—special because they can only be found in old forests like this one. Immediately beyond, you'll come to a small cave made by the rock formations above the gorge. When you are done exploring here, follow the trail along the hillside to the last stream crossing. Stay straight to close the loop, and hike the final quarter mile back to the trailhead.

SCAVENGER HUNT

Eastern white pine

This is the only pine to grow needles in bundles, called fascicles, of five. Can you count them? These were called "mast pines" because they were perfect for ship-building. Why do you think people might have wanted to build a ship out of these trees?

Pinus strobus can grow for over 200 years

Historical graveyard

Buried here is William Hoffman, who was born in 1740 in Germany and moved to Maryland in 1775. He was Maryland's first paper manufacturer. Walk through the graveyard and look for the oldest gravestone you can find.

The Hoffman Gunpowder Cemetery was a burial ground from 1778 to 1890

Cave

Did you know that caves like this one form by the dissolution of limestone? When rainwater picks up carbon dioxide from the air and it seeps into the soil, it slowly dissolves the limestone along the joints of the rock. In some places it dissolves enough to form caves. What kind of animals do you think might call this cave home?

Find this small cave in the Hemlock Gorge

White moss

Look for these non-flowering plants. They have stems and leaves, but instead of roots, they have rhizoids, small hairlike structures that absorb water and nutrients underground. Go by the river, place your fingers in the water, and pretend your fingers are moss that can absorb the water just by touching it.

Leucobryum albidum is sometimes called cushion moss

Gunpowder Falls

Sit down on the large rocks here and enjoy the sight and sound of the cascading water in the midst of the forest. Drop leaves in the falls and watch them quickly float downstream to 79-square-mile Prettyboy Reservoir, which provides drinking water to 1.8 million people in the Baltimore area!

Admire the beauty of this tucked-away waterfall

10

CHASE WATERFALLS AT PATAPSCO VALLEY

PATAPSCO VALLEY STATE PARK

trailhead

• Swinging Bridge

Cascade Falls

• swimming hole
go right

small falls

go right

Garrett's Pass Trail

Cascade Creek

Upper Cascade Falls Trail

Cascade Falls Trail

Ridge Trail

RIVER ROAD

Patapsco River

I-95, Ellicott City

wooden bridge

go right   wooden bridge

N

0   1000 ft.

YOUR ADVENTURE

Adventurers, wear your water shoes and get ready for some fun—you get to see three waterfalls! You will be exploring the historical homelands of the Susquehannock and Piscataway in Maryland's oldest state park. Begin on the Cascade Falls Trail, then take a left and another left. In less than a quarter of a mile, you'll arrive at the first area where the Patapsco River

Cascades Falls is 9 feet tall →

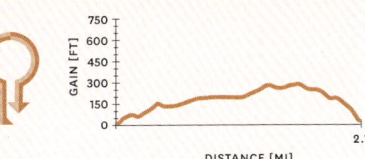

GAIN [FT]
750
600
450
300
150
0
2.1
DISTANCE [MI]

LENGTH 2.1-mile lollipop loop

ELEVATION GAIN 305 ft.

HIKE TIME + EXPLORE 1.5 hours

DIFFICULTY Moderate—a combination of packed-earth paths and rocky terrain with moderate elevation

SEASON Year-round, but best during spring so you can enjoy the many swimming holes before it becomes crowded. Updates are on Maryland State Parks' Twitter.

GET THERE Take I-95 South from Baltimore. Exit 47A-B for Interstate 195 East. After 0.6 miles, take Exit 3 for US-1 / Washington Blvd. toward Elkridge. In quick succession turn right on Washington Blvd., right onto South Street, and left onto Park Entrance Road. Pay for entry at the Avalon area entrance, then drive to a stop sign, turn left, and follow to the Orange Grove area. The trailhead is opposite the Swinging Bridge.

Google Maps: bit.ly/timberpatapscovalley

RESTROOM At trailhead

FEE April through October on weekends and holidays, $3 per person for MD residents, $5 nonresidents; all other times $2 per vehicle for MD residents, $4 nonresidents.

TREAT YOURSELF Reward yourself with fresh donuts from Bakery Express 5 miles east in Halethorpe.

Patapsco Valley State Park
(410) 461-5005 | Facebook @MDStateParks

cascades over the rocks. Soon afterward are the next falls—Cascade Falls. They are approximately ten feet high, with a pool at the base, perfect for wading. When done exploring, cross the water and climb a set of steps. Stay right on the Cascade Falls trail; pass the Ridge Trail on your left. Continue on the slightly hilly trail that ranges from smooth surfaces to rock scrambles. The last falls is a great power-up stop. Afterward, stay straight; you'll see Garrett's Pass Trail on your right. Cross a stream over one wooden bridge and then another, walk through the water, and then go right and up to stay on the Cascade Falls Trail. Pass by Garrett's Pass Trail again and stay straight. You'll hit another junction—stay right here. At the next junction, stay straight, ignoring the other part of Garrett's Pass Trail. Start heading downhill and reach your original fork. Stay straight. Back at the trailhead, carefully cross the parking lot and the road to the large swinging bridge over the Patapsco River. Walk across the bridge and read about the history of the mill that was once located there. Then, if you haven't had your fill of this beautiful park, consider extending your stay by camping at the Hilton or Hollofield Campgrounds.

SCAVENGER HUNT

Common garter snake

Watch for these harmless reptiles. They have three stripes from the back of their head all the way down to their tails. They are considered small snakes, as they are usually only about 24 inches long. If you cannot spot one of them, you might be able to find some of their favorite foods: slugs, worms, or mice.

Thamnophis sirtalis is one of the most common snakes in North America

White wood asters

Look for this plant with heart-shaped leaves. It grows at ground level and prefers partial shade. Do you prefer shade or sun? Try sketching one of these beautiful flowers in your nature journal, paying close attention to the shape of its 6–10 petals.

Eurybia divaricata's white flowers bloom late summer through mid-autumn

Daddy long legs

Did you know that, although they are part of the Arachnid family, daddy long legs are not spiders? Also called harvestmen, they often play dead to trick potential predators. They are omnivorous and mostly eat small insects, mites, spiders, snails, and vegetable matter. Fun fact: daddy long legs have been found in fossils over 400 million years old! Are you able to lie completely still to trick a predator? Freeze and see how long you can go without moving.

Opiliones can be found on every continent except Antarctica

Swinging bridge

The Swinging Bridge is a suspension footbridge made of a wooden deck supported by large cables. It enables pedestrians to cross the Patapsco River. Take your time crossing this impressive bridge while soaking in the river and forest scenery. If you are feeling brave, try running across the bridge—you might feel it move slightly under your feet!

The Swinging Bridge has been refurbished since it was built in 1856

11

WALK UNDER A MAGICAL TREE TUNNEL AT WYE ISLAND

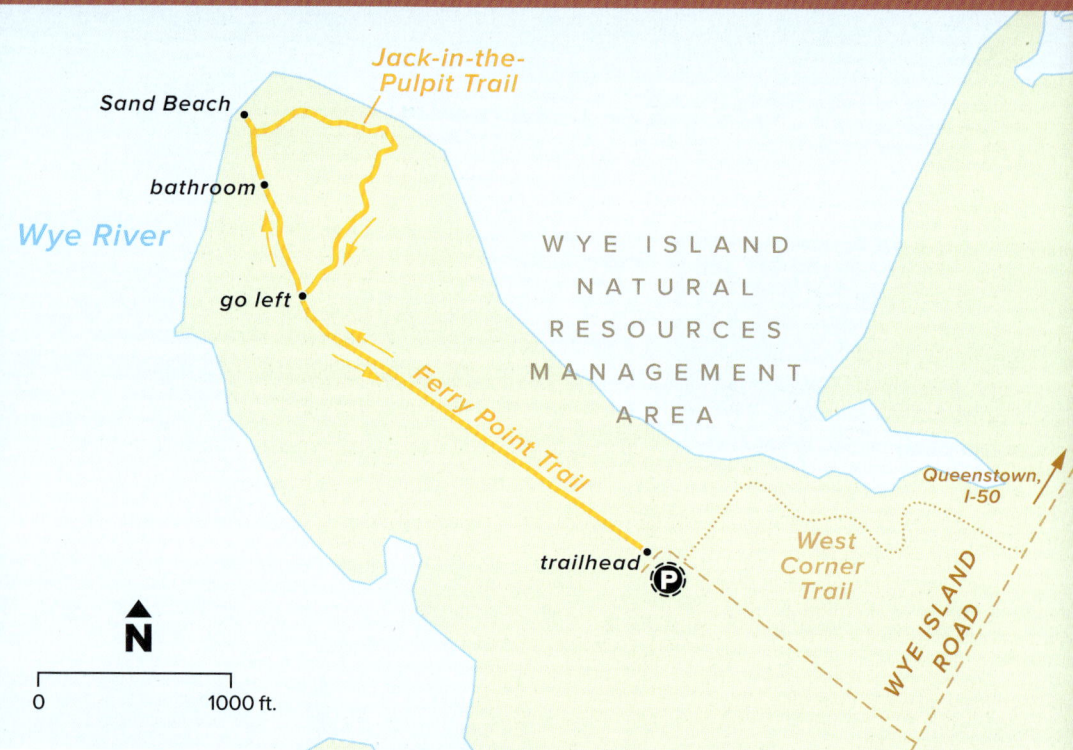

Sand Beach

Jack-in-the-Pulpit Trail

bathroom

Wye River

go left

Ferry Point Trail

WYE ISLAND NATURAL RESOURCES MANAGEMENT AREA

Queenstown, I-50

trailhead

West Corner Trail

WYE ISLAND ROAD

N

0   1000 ft.

YOUR ADVENTURE

Adventurers, welcome to Wye Island, where you can hike under a magical tunnel of trees on your way to a small, secluded beach. You will begin your hike on a wide dirt trail under a canopy of Osage orange trees in the historical homelands of the Susquehannock and Ozinie. These trees have a very distinctively shaped fruit—look for fallen softball-size Osage

The entrance to the trail is a canopy of Osage orange trees →

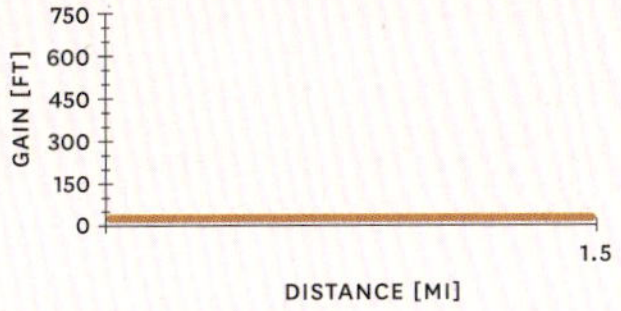

GAIN [FT]

750
600
450
300
150
0

1.5

DISTANCE [MI]

LENGTH 1.5-mile lollipop loop

ELEVATION GAIN 26 ft.

HIKE TIME + EXPLORE 1 hour

DIFFICULTY Easy—a combination of packed-earth paths and rocky terrain with mild elevation

SEASON Year-round. Best time to see the Osage orange trees in bloom is May through July.

GET THERE Travel north on Route 50 West / Ocean Gateway from Easton to the Maryland Route 213 traffic light. Turn left onto Carmichael Road and travel 5 miles until you cross Wye Island Bridge. Follow signs to the trailhead parking lot.

Google Maps: bit.ly/timberwyeisland

RESTROOM At trailhead

FEE None

TREAT YOURSELF Take a 30-minute drive west to Kent Island Crab Cakes in Stevensville and treat yourself to Maryland's famous snack.

Wye Island Natural Resources Management Area
(410) 827-7577
Facebook
@WyeIslandNaturalResourcesManagementArea

oranges scattered along the trail. As you walk along the red-blazed path, these unique trees form a canopy above you. You'll first reach a fork. Let's go clockwise here, so stay left. Soon you will reach a sandy shore and Drum Point. There is a wooden picnic table perfect for a power-up stop. Take some time here to enjoy the beautiful views of the Wye River and tidal grasses. Although swimming is prohibited, walk along the shoreline to see if you can find any horseshoe crabs or other critters. As you return to the trail, instead of staying on the path you hiked in on, turn left to take a small detour and hike through a dense forest. You will quickly loop back around to the main path, where you will continue back to the trailhead.

SCAVENGER HUNT

Osage orange trees

These small deciduous trees have branches that grow up into a round shape. Between May and July, they produce a fruit that is round and bumpy and about the size of a grape-fruit. Surprisingly, it is green in color, not orange as its name might make you think. Pick up a fallen fruit to get a sense of its size and weight; inside the fruit is a milky sap that can cause rashes in humans, so please do not break the fruit open or touch an open fruit.

Maclura pomifera wood has been used by Indigenous peoples to make bows

Horseshoe crabs

Did you know that these arachnids (part of the spider family, not the crab family) are considered living fossils, since they have been around for more than 400 million years? That means they existed before dinosaurs! Despite that, the horseshoe crab has barely evolved from the way their ancient relatives looked, because their body structure is extremely effective for survival. They have a hard exoskeleton and ten legs used for walking on the sea floor. Do your best crabwalk on your hands and feet when you reach the beach.

Limulus polyphemus can live for more than 20 years

Twisted branches

In addition to the magical overhanging Osage orange trees, you will also see many trees that have intertwined branches. This is due to a natural phenomenon known as inosculation, when branches, trunks, or roots of two trees grow together. With a hiking mate, intertwine your arms and see how long you can walk like that.

It is unusual for trees of different species to grow together

Common reed

When you reach the point, you will see many swaying reeds by the water. When spread out in small clusters, they can provide cover for birds and small mammals. However, they usually grow in large, impenetrable clumps that provide little value for wildlife. What do you think might be hiding in these?

Genus *Phragmites* has a thick stalk that can reach 13 feet in height

12

HUNT FOR SHARK TEETH AT CALVERT CLIFFS

Chesapeake Bay

CALVERT CLIFFS STATE PARK

Orange Trail

beach

restrooms

765

service road

Red Trail

Alexandria

small waterfalls

go right

bench

bridge

boardwalk

bridge

trailhead

Yellow Trail

Blue Trail

S. SOLOMONS ISLAND ROAD

Lexington Park

2

N

0   2000 ft.

YOUR ADVENTURE

Adventurers, put your explorer hats on and grab your shovels and sand sifters. Today we are hunting for fossils and shark teeth in the historical homelands of the Susquehannock, Patuxent, and Piscataway! The hike begins on the wood-chip Red Trail, past a one-acre fishing pond on your left. Take a right after the pond, over a wooden bridge onto a sandy path through

These cliffs were formed over 10 million years ago →

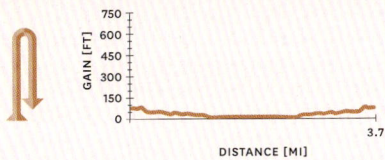

GAIN [FT]
750
600
450
300
150
0
3.7
DISTANCE [MI]

LENGTH 3.7 miles out and back

ELEVATION GAIN 98 ft.

HIKE TIME + EXPLORE 3 hours

DIFFICULTY Moderate—sand paths and wood bridges with mild elevation

SEASON Year-round, but especially fun in warmer seasons as you are hiking to a secluded beach.

GET THERE Head southeast on MD-2 South / MD-4 South / Solomons Island Road. Turn left onto Calvert Cliff State Park Drive, and the park entrance will be on the right.

Google Maps: bit.ly/timbercalvertcliffstrailhead

RESTROOM At trailhead and at beach

FEE $5 per vehicle for MD residents, $7 nonresidents

TREAT YOURSELF Indulge in some key lime pie at the Lotus Kitchen, 6 miles south off Solomons Island Road.

Calvert Cliffs State Park
(443) 975-4360
Facebook @Calvert-Cliffs-State-Park

the woods. Stay straight at the next junction and turn right after you pass the service road. Pass a small waterfall and walk along wetlands constructed by beavers. Stay straight past the Yellow Trail to continue on the Red Trail. Pass another wooden bridge, then power up on the benches just before you cross the Blue Trail. Stay straight again on the Red Trail and cross a wooden bridge, still staying straight. You'll pass three more benches and hear and see different birds and frogs in the marsh on the right. After a little over a mile, you will reach the cliffs and beach. Look for the large sign showing what kinds of fossils and shark teeth are found in this area (there have been over 600 species of fossils!). Enjoy sifting through the sand to see what shells, rocks, and other prehistoric finds you can uncover. Splash your feet in the cool water and then have a picnic lunch at one of the many tables. Return to the path and trailhead by retracing your steps, staying straight on the Red Trail the whole way back.

SCAVENGER HUNT

Fossilized shark tooth

While huge megalodon teeth are among the most sought-after at Calvert Cliffs, it's more common to find smaller shark teeth. How did they get here? During the Miocene Epoch, about 17 million years ago, the area that is now Calvert Cliffs was covered by a warm, shallow sea where sharks lived. After approximately 10,000 years trapped in the cliffs, the minerals in the sediment replace the natural structure of the tooth. What is left behind is essentially a rock in the shape of a tooth, which we call a fossil. Now it is your turn to sift through the sand and see if you can find a fossilized shark tooth, invertebrate, or crab claws! Normally you should leave anything you find when hiking, but here the state park allows collecting.

Fossilized crab claw and fossilized shark tooth

Beaver

While you might not always spot a beaver, you can often hear them and see their handiwork along the path. Beavers are large semi-aquatic mammals that cut down trees by biting them down. This creates ecosystems used by a wide variety of other species, including birds who nest here. Do you see any logs that have been chewed by beavers?

Castor canadensis has front teeth that grow continuously throughout its lifetime

Northern watersnake

Can you spot this common non-venomous aquatic snake? It can stay underwater for 1.5 hours without coming up for air! How long can you hold your breath?

Nerodia sipedon grows to be 2–4 feet long

Common puffball

These mushrooms were given their names because of the "puffs" of brown dust-like spores that release when the mature fruit body is disturbed. When young, puffballs are white, but as they mature they become yellow-brown. Draw this mushroom in your nature journal and compare it to other mushrooms you have seen.

Lycoperdon perlatum (*Lycoperdon* translates to "wolf fart" in Latin)

13

FOLLOW THE UNDERGROUND RAILROAD EXPERIENCE TRAIL

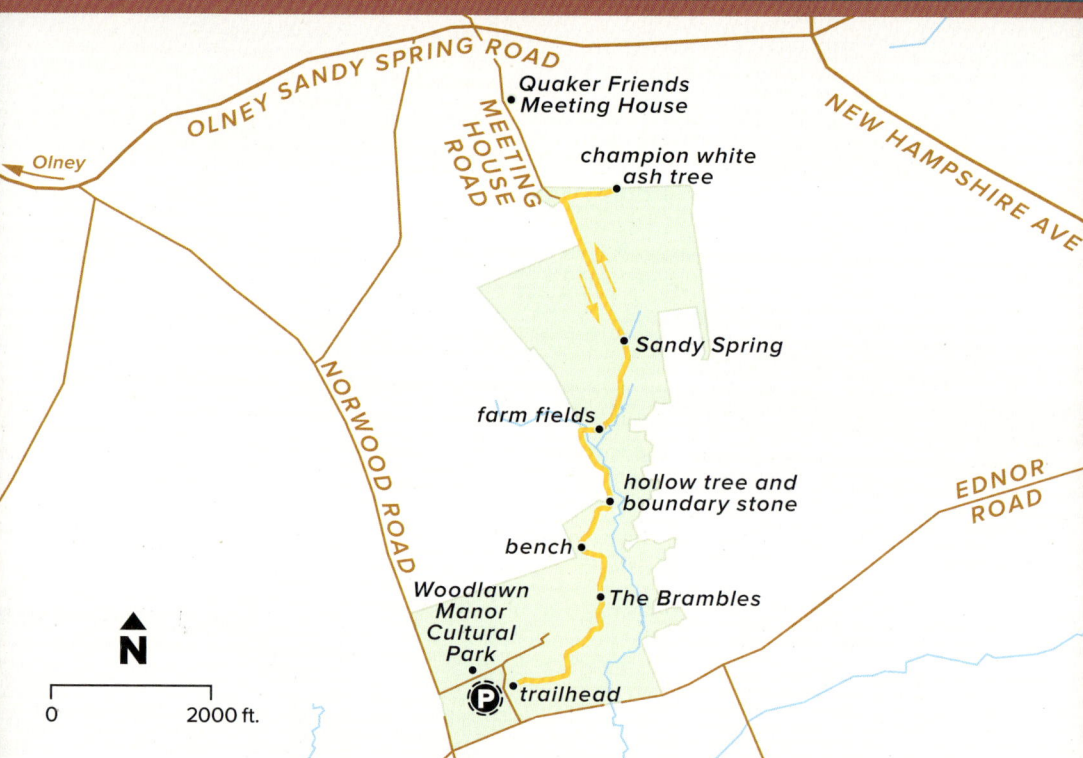

OLNEY SANDY SPRING ROAD

MEETING HOUSE ROAD

NEW HAMPSHIRE AVE

Olney

Quaker Friends
Meeting House

champion white
ash tree

Sandy Spring

NORWOOD ROAD

farm fields

hollow tree and
boundary stone

EDNOR
ROAD

bench

Woodlawn
Manor
Cultural
Park

The Brambles

trailhead

N

0   2000 ft.

YOUR ADVENTURE

Adventurers, today we will travel on the historical homelands of the Anacostan and Piscataway. Imagine it is 1850 and slavery is legal, so aiding enslaved people who seek freedom is a federal offense. The term "Underground Railroad" refers to a nineteenth-century secret network of people who helped enslaved persons travel to freedom in northern states and Canada.

An outbuilding at Woodlawn Manor →

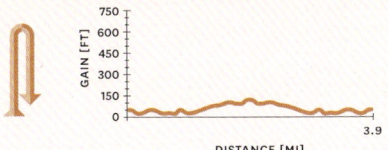

GAIN [FT]

750
600
450
300
150
0

3.9

DISTANCE [MI]

LENGTH 3.9 miles out and back

ELEVATION GAIN 207 ft.

HIKE TIME + EXPLORE 1.5 hours

DIFFICULTY Moderate—a combination of wide natural-surface and gravel paths with mild elevation. Please note that the trail is not suitable for some strollers and is not ADA accessible.

SEASON Year-round, but best during winter when you can see what the landscape looked like when there were fewer areas to hide.

GET THERE Take 29 South from Columbia to MD-198 and follow 1 mile to MD-650. Turn right and after 1 mile, turn left onto Ednor Road, following it to the parking lot inside Woodlawn Manor Cultural Park.

Google Maps:
bit.ly/timberundergroundrailroad

RESTROOM At visitor center

FEE None

TREAT YOURSELF Don't leave the area before grabbing a specialized European dessert 3 miles south at Flowers Bakery Café.

Woodlawn Manor Cultural Park
(301) 929-5989
Facebook @WoodlawnManorPark

Before the Civil War, the Underground Railroad was active in this area. Freedom seekers knew the freed African Americans and Quakers of Sandy Spring would help them. The network was never literally underground or an actual railroad, and there was no single route used. Today you will take a journey similar to those taken by many runaways seeking freedom. Begin by walking on a short stone path past the Woodlawn Museum. Turn left onto a grass field and look for a large information sign about the trail. Take a trail map to guide you through the parts of the Underground Railroad experience, all marked along the path. Walk along a wooden fence by a horse pasture. Turn right onto a trail and follow it past woods, brambles, a hollow tree and boundary stone, and farm fields—all marked by signs. Cross the stream on a bridge and emerge into a meadow. Pass Sandy Spring on the right. After stopping to get a closer look and have a power-up, continue and turn right at the fork to see the three-hundred-year-old champion white ash tree. Retrace your steps back to the trailhead. On the way, you'll pass the Woodlawn Museum. If it's open, consider stopping to view the exhibits here for a small fee.

SCAVENGER HUNT

Woodlawn barn

This three-story barn is constructed of rubble stone and timber. It is an example of a building that could have been used to hide freedom seekers. Sketch this barn, including the cornerstone high on the side of the building engraved with "1832WP" in your journal. Then sketch a barn you might want to build today.

Woodlawn Manor's stone barn was constructed in 1832

Common milkweed

Look for this perennial (comes back every year) that gets its name from the milky sap in its leaves and stems. Flowers are small with pink to purple petals that bloom from June through August. Can you see any monarch caterpillars on it? They can only eat milkweed.

Over 450 insects feed on *Asclepias syriaca*

Sandy Spring

The local community took its name from Sandy Spring, which provided fresh water that filtered naturally through sandy soil. All the farms nearby had a path leading to this spring, so it became a natural meeting place and trail marker for freedom seekers on the Underground Railroad. The date "1775" on the concrete archway refers to the year local Quakers held the first Sandy Spring Friends Meeting. What do you think this area looked like 180 years ago?

The concrete archway over the spring was built in 1914

Hollow tree and boundary stone

Large hollow trees like this one were often used by freedom seekers as hiding places. The boundary stone marked the dividing line between two manors. Boundary stones were often used as markers for people trying to follow the trail north. Stand inside the hollow tree and imagine what it was like to hide and sleep in this small space.

Hollow trees enabled freedom seekers to light fires for warmth and cooking while hiding

SCALE SUGARLOAF MOUNTAIN

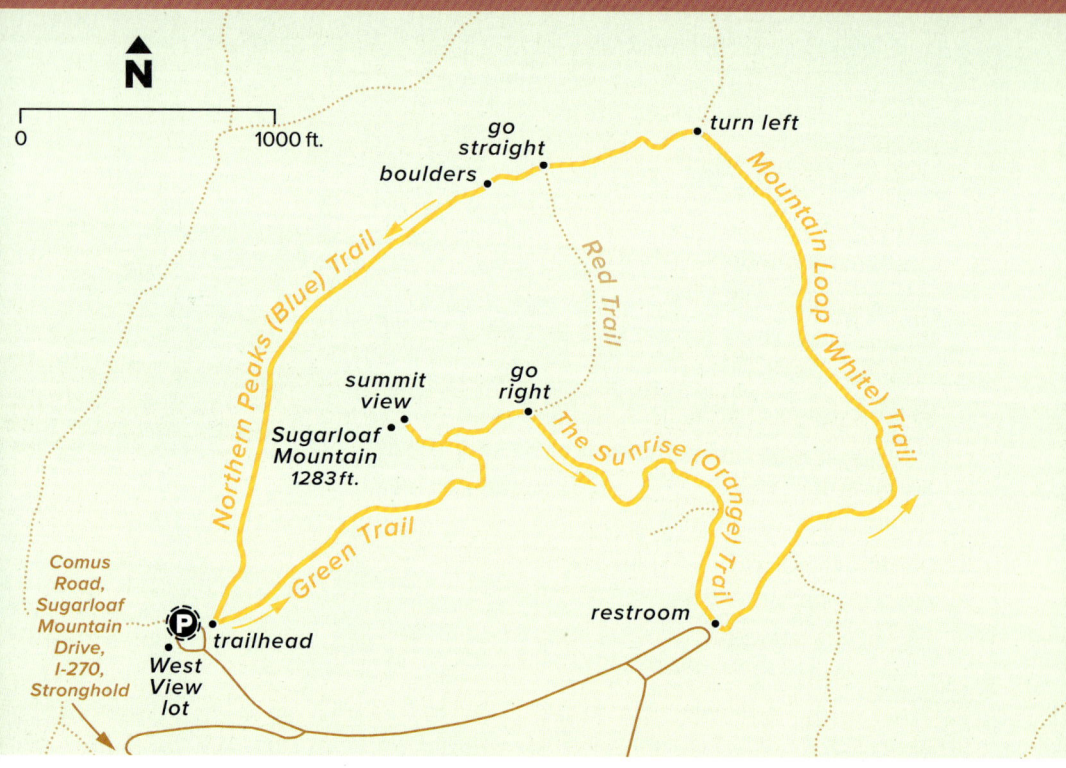

N

0   1000 ft.

go straight

turn left

boulders

Mountain Loop (White) Trail

Northern Peaks (Blue) Trail

Red Trail

summit view

go right

Sugarloaf Mountain 1283 ft.

The Sunrise (Orange) Trail

Green Trail

Comus Road, Sugarloaf Mountain Drive, I-270, Stronghold

P

trailhead

West View lot

restroom

YOUR ADVENTURE

Adventurers, are you ready for a challenge? Today we will explore the historical homelands of the Manahoac and Piscataway—and climb to the top of a mountain! Early pioneers gave Sugarloaf Mountain its name because its shape reminded them of the loaves sugar commonly came in back then. Start your journey in the West View lot; the first part of your adventure will

The incredible view from the summit of Sugarloaf Mountain →

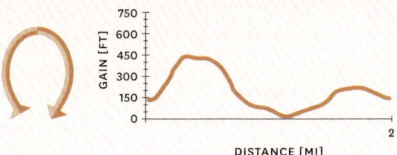

GAIN [FT]
750
600
450
300
150
0

2

DISTANCE [MI]

LENGTH 2.0-mile loop

ELEVATION GAIN 489 ft.

HIKE TIME + EXPLORE 2 hours

DIFFICULTY Challenging—rocky path and stone steps at the beginning, then slight inclines and declines throughout with high elevation gain

SEASON Year-round; best during fall foliage.

GET THERE Take I-270 South from Frederick to the Hyattstown exit. Follow Route 109, then turn right onto Comus Road. This will bring you right to the Sugarloaf Mountain entrance. Take the road up the mountain and park in the West View parking lot.

Google Maps: bit.ly/timbersugarloaf

RESTROOM At the East View and West View parking lots

FEE None; donations accepted

TREAT YOURSELF Go 9 miles north and grab some ice cream nachos (yes, you heard us right) from Sweet Babe's Creamery in Urbana.

Sugarloaf Mountain
(301) 874-2024
Facebook @Sugarloaf-Mountain

be the hardest. Go right, or counterclockwise, on the blazed Green Trail; climb a steep incline and beautiful natural stone steps. Consider stopping to admire the boulders along the way and take power-up stops as needed. At the summit, you will have earned an amazing view of the Maryland countryside! Sugarloaf Mountain is unique—it is the only monadnock, or solitary small mountain surrounded by level plains, in all of Maryland. At an elevation of 1,282 feet, Sugarloaf Mountain stands more than 800 feet above the farmland below. You will also observe a massive plate of quartzite at the summit. Turn left on the blazed Red Trail and then right at the fork to the blazed Orange Trail. Arrive at the East View lot, which has a portable bathroom. Consider having a power-up stop at the picnic tables next to another overlook with incredible mountain-top views. Continue to loop around the mountain, staying straight on the blazed White trail and turning left, back onto the Blue Trail, which loops you back to the trailhead. After you leave the park, be sure to look back at the mountain you just climbed to see how high it looks!

SCAVENGER HUNT

Stone Steps

At the beginning of the hike, you will climb steep stone steps cut into the rock. While they may be challenging to climb, imagine how hard it would be if they were not here! Count the steps as you go—how many are there?

Rustic stone steps help your ascent

False Caesar's mushroom

Look down occasionally to see if you can spot mushrooms growing along your path. False Caesar's mushrooms are often found under pine trees in wooded areas from spring through autumn. They can be easy to spot due to their bright red caps that are covered with warts ranging in color from pale yellow to white.

Amanita parcivolvata can grow alone or in groups

Boulders

The rugged cliffs on the summit are primarily quartzite, a hard metamorphic rock formed when sandstone is squeezed and heated underneath other mountains. Pure quartzite is usually white, but you might see shades of red and pink. It is hard, so it erodes slowly, which is why it sticks around in cool shapes like these! Clank two pieces together—what do you notice?

These boulders are composed primarily of quartzite

Mossy maze polypore

Look for this wood-decomposing fungus that grows on logs and dead hardwood trees. Notice how it grows in semicircular shapes projecting from the wood? It can be observed year round in dense, overlapping clusters. What does its shape remind you of?

Cerrena unicolor is a very common bracket fungus

15

"THRU-HIKE" WASHINGTON MONUMENT STATE PARK

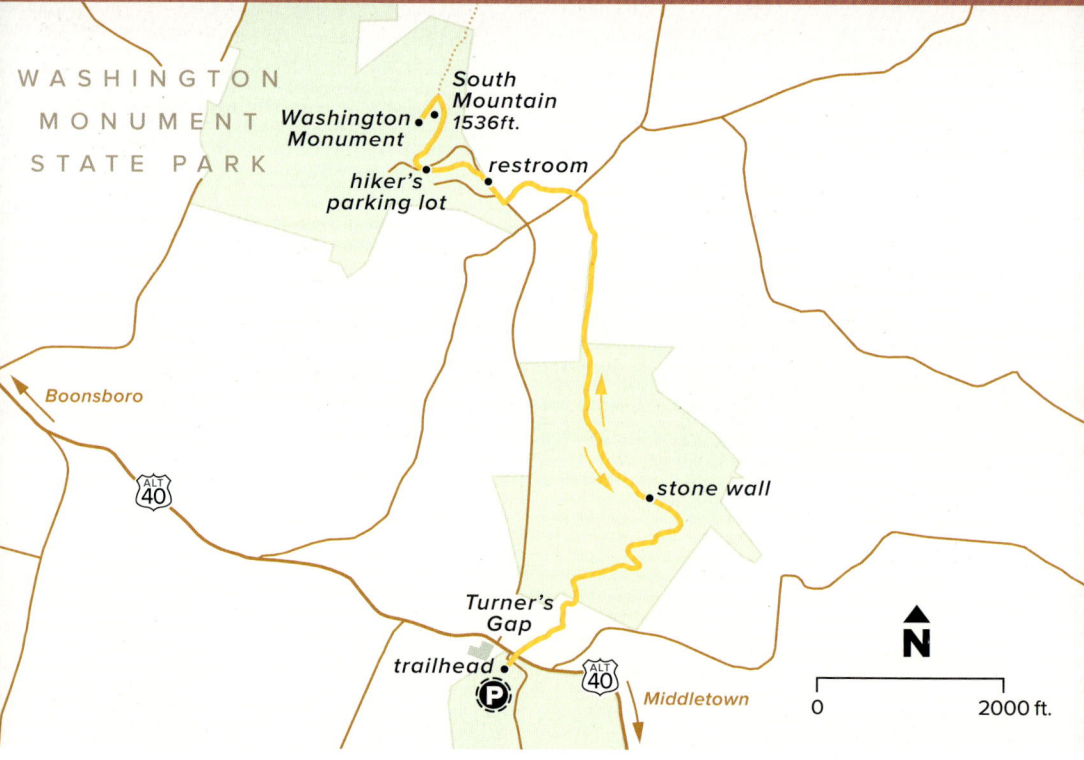

YOUR ADVENTURE

Adventurers, step back in time! We will work our way through the historical homelands of the Massawomeck to the Washington Monument. But first we get to hike part of the Appalachian Trail. Did you know the Appalachian Trail can be hiked from Georgia to Maine for 2,194 miles, and some people do it in summer as a "thru-hike"? Does that sound fun? While we will hike

The Washington Monument is a 40-foot-tall stone tower, the first ever to honor the nation's first president →

GAIN [FT]

750
600
450
300
150
0
                                              4.3

DISTANCE [MI]

LENGTH 4.3 mile out and back

ELEVATION GAIN 925 ft.

HIKE TIME + EXPLORE 2.5 hours

DIFFICULTY Challenging—packed-earth path with high elevation gain

SEASON Year-round; best during fall foliage.

GET THERE Take I-70 East from Hagerstown to Exit 32A and merge onto US-40 East. In 2.5 miles, turn right on MD-66 S for 4.3 miles, then turn left onto North Main Street / Old National Pike. At the traffic circle, continue straight. Turn right into Turner's Gap and Old South Mountain Inn parking lot. Please note: you will need to cross a street to get to the trailhead, so please be careful with little explorers.

Google Maps: bit.ly/timberwashingtonmonumentstatepark

RESTROOM 1.8 miles along the trail

FEE None

TREAT YOURSELF Cool off with some homemade ice cream from South Mountain Creamery a few minutes south on Bolivar Road.

Washington Monument State Park
(301) 791-4767
Facebook @MDStatePark

only a small part, it will lead to amazing views. Carefully cross the busy street from the parking lot at Turner's Gap by Old South Mountain Inn. The first part of the adventure is on a zigzaggy incline on a packed-earth trail with rocky spots. Wind through the woods, going up and down inclines on a path that narrows. Pass a stone wall, and before you hit the two-mile mark, you'll come across an Appalachian Trail and state park parking lot; there is a restroom and water here. Next, the trail inclines sharply and turns to packed earth with rocks and wooden logs for steps. Walk through the hikers' parking lot, then take a sharp right onto a gravel path with a steep incline. Several placards teach about George Washington, as you wind up this steep but paved final part of the trail to arrive at the top of South Mountain and see the Washington Monument, which was modeled to look like a Revolutionary War cannon. Take the narrow steps to the top for incredible panoramic views of three states before retracing your steps to the trailhead. Want to stay longer? Consider camping 7 miles down the road at Little Bennett Campground.

SCAVENGER HUNT

White-tailed deer

Look for the white underside of this deer's tail. They display and wag their tails when they sense danger. They are common along this part of the Appalachian Trail. The quieter you are, the more likely you will be able to spot one of these beautiful animals.

Odocoileus virginianus is the smallest member of the North American deer family

Monument steps

Located on the top of South Mountain, the Washington Monument is a 40-foot stone tower built by the citizens of Boonsboro in 1827 to honor the first president of the United States. The steps are narrow, but the views you get from the top are worth the effort. Count how many steps there are to the top!

How many steps to get to the top of the monument?

Barberries

Can you spot this perennial plant with yellow flowers and red berries? The berries are oblong, scarlet red to purple, and contain one to three small black seeds. How many berries are on one branch? How many berries do you think grow on each tree?

Genus *Berberis* often grows in open woods or pastures

Appalachian Trail

Look for hikers passing with big (really big) packs. Millions hike parts of the AT every year, but only a few hundred complete the whole thing. From here to either end, at Mount Katahdin in Maine or on the southern end in Georgia, is over 1,000 miles away! Could you hike that far? Be a "trail angel" and pack an extra snack for a hungry thru-hiker. Ask them their trail name and make up one for yourself. It can be an inside joke or just something you like. Peanut Butter? Dinosaur?

This white blaze marks the epic trail

16

MOSEY ALONG TO CUNNINGHAM FALLS

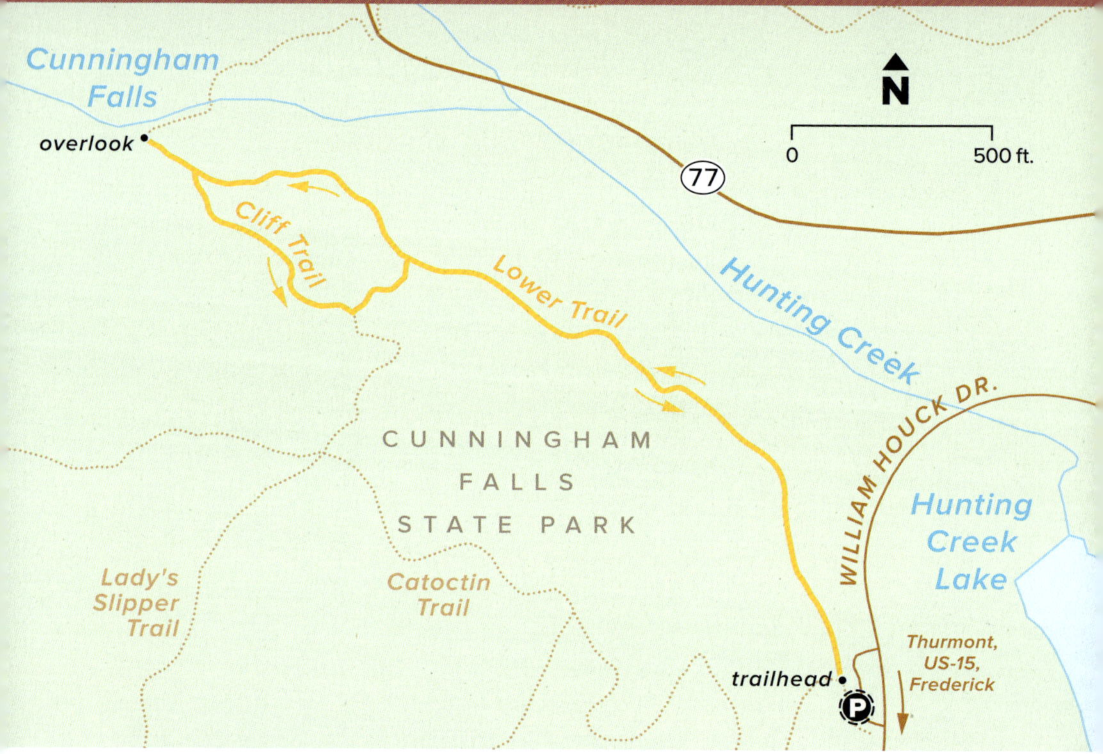

Cunningham
Falls

overlook •

Cliff Trail

Lower Trail

Hunting Creek

77

N

0   500 ft.

CUNNINGHAM

FALLS

STATE PARK

WILLIAM HOUCK DR.

Hunting
Creek
Lake

Lady's
Slipper
Trail

Catoctin
Trail

trailhead •

P

Thurmont,
US-15,
Frederick

YOUR ADVENTURE

Adventurers, today we will explore the historical homelands of the Piscataway and the Susquehannock in the beautiful Catoctin Mountains, part
of the Blue Ridge and Appalachian Mountain ranges—formed 250 million
years ago! Journey about half a mile up the gradual incline on the smooth,
red-blazed Lower Trail, staying straight past a left turn (we'll take that on our

Cunningham Falls is the largest cascading waterfall in Maryland →

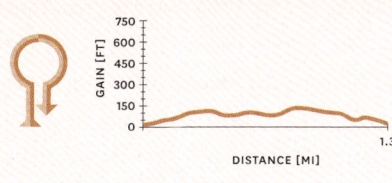

GAIN [FT]

750
600
450
300
150
0

1.3

DISTANCE [MI]

LENGTH 1.3-mile lollipop loop

ELEVATION GAIN 157 ft.

HIKE TIME + EXPLORE 1 hour

DIFFICULTY Moderate—packed-earth path with moderate elevation

SEASON Year-round, but best during spring for blooms and a rushing waterfall.

GET THERE Take US-15 North from Frederick to MD-77 West, then turn left on Catoctin Hollow Road. In 1 mile, turn right on William Houck Drive. The parking lot is 0.5 miles on the left, and the trailhead is on the west side of the lot.

Google Maps: bit.ly/timbercunninghamfalls

RESTROOM None near trail; try Catoctin Hollow Road near the boat ramp by the state park office

FEE $3 per person for MD residents, $5 nonresidents

TREAT YOURSELF Just north on US-15 you can pick your favorite candy from the barrels at Gateway Candyland.

Cunningham Falls State Park
(301) 271-7574
Facebook @Cunningham-Falls-State-Park

way back) until you reach a small wooden boardwalk where you can view the flowing falls. Take your time admiring them, maybe powering up on a small snack before continuing. While it might be tempting to climb the rocks for a closer look, for both your safety and the preservation of this natural area, leaving the trail and climbing the rocks is discouraged. After the rocks, go right; you'll soon hike by large granite boulders and up stone steps. Loop back around to the original path, following it back to the trailhead. Need more time to explore? Extend your stay by camping at the William Houck Campground.

SCAVENGER HUNT

Hickory tussock moth caterpillar

When these insects are young, they are communal eaters, meaning they eat with other caterpillars. Are you a communal eater? Amazingly, older hickory tussock moth caterpillars don't eat *anything*—they don't have functional mouth parts! Their black-and-white fuzzy bodies look tempting to pet, but their hairs might irritate your skin. Best to look but not touch. Instead, do your best wiggly caterpillar impression for a hike mate.

Lophocampa caryae is a type of tiger moth

Common morel

This prized edible mushroom is so sought after that parks like Cunningham Falls have to set limits. Mushroom hunters may only collect up to a half gallon per day. Note: some mushrooms are poisonous, so always use caution and never consume a mushroom that a professional doesn't recognize. If you pick one, check with a ranger before tasting it. How do you like to eat your mushrooms? On pizza or pasta, or by themselves?

Morchella esculenta is called a sponge mushroom because of its honeycomb-like caps

Wild hydrangeas

Look for these multi-stemmed shrubs with clusters of greenish-white flowers that open in June and last until early August. Feel their large, rounded leaves that have "teeth" along their edges. The actual flowers are tiny and grow in the middle of four bracts, which look like petals, but are actually special leaves. How many flowers total can you count in one cluster? They're a favorite of pollinators—can you spot any bees pollinating them today?

Hydrangea arborescens

Eastern American toad

Can you spot this large amphibian that eats a variety of insects—as well as snails, earthworms, and beetles—by shooting out its sticky tongue to catch prey? Did you know toads can eat up to 100 bugs a day? While walking to and from the falls, see if you can find bugs that a toad might like to snack on. Try to eat your snack like a toad, sticking your tongue out to "catch" it!

Anaxyrus americanus does not drink water but absorbs moisture directly through its skin

Golden trumpet mushroom

These tiny mushrooms make a big impression with their bright orange fruits. Look for them growing in clusters May through November. When young, the caps are bell-shaped, but as they mature, the outer part expands, turning the center concave, like a bellybutton. Take out your nature journal and draw this mushroom in your collection of fungi sketches.

Xeromphalina campanella grows on dead logs

17

EXPLORE THE PAW PAW TUNNEL

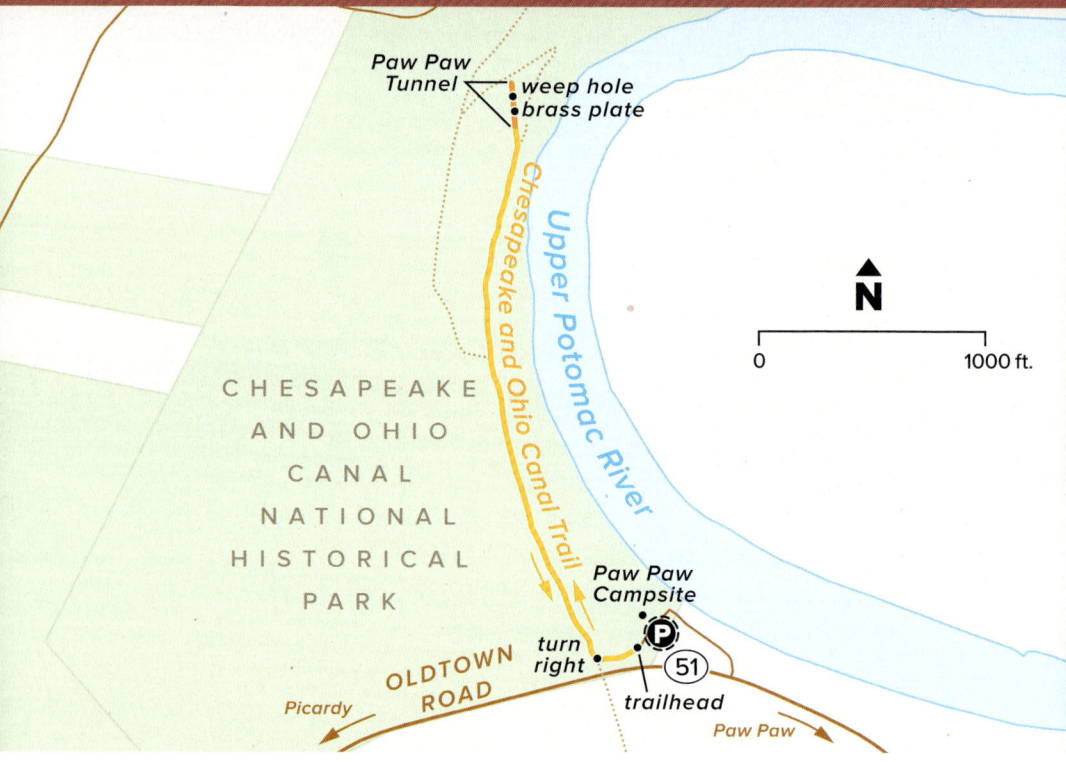

Paw Paw
Tunnel
weep hole
brass plate

Chesapeake and Ohio Canal Trail

Upper Potomac River

N

0   1000 ft.

C H E S A P E A K E
A N D   O H I O
C A N A L
N A T I O N A L
H I S T O R I C A L
P A R K

Paw Paw
Campsite

P

turn
right

51

OLDTOWN
ROAD

Picardy

trailhead

Paw Paw

YOUR ADVENTURE

Adventurers, grab your flashlights and get ready to explore a canal tunnel that is over 170 years old and full of history! The Paw Paw Tunnel is located on the historical homelands of the Piscataway and Susquehannock. It is said to be the greatest engineering marvel of the 184.5-mile-long Chesapeake and Ohio Canal. It was dug so boats could take a shortcut through

The entrance to the Paw Paw Tunnel →

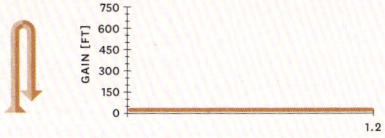

LENGTH 1.2 miles out and back

ELEVATION GAIN 33 ft.

HIKE TIME + EXPLORE 1 hour

DIFFICULTY Easy—a wide, packed-earth path to the tunnel (be careful of the few uneven spots and large puddles), then a narrow path in almost complete darkness with mild elevation gain. Must bring a flashlight or headlamp!

SEASON Year-round, but best during winter when bats hibernate in the tunnel. Note that sections of the towpath and trails may intermittently be closed for repair; check the National Park Service's official current park conditions webpage before departing.

GET THERE From Cumberland, take MD-51 (Oldtown Road) South to just before the Paw Paw Bridge. The parking lot will be on your left.

Google Maps: bit.ly/timberpawpawtunnel

RESTROOM At trailhead

FEE None

TREAT YOURSELF Cool off after your adventure with a purple cow patty sundae from Purple Cow Soft Serve in Paw Paw.

Chesapeake and Ohio Canal National Historical Park
(301) 739-4200
Facebook @chesapeakeandohiocanal

the mountain, eliminating 6 miles along a windy stretch of the Potomac River. However, what began in 1838 with an estimated budget of $33,000 and a timeline of two years ended up taking fourteen years and costing over $600,000—it nearly bankrupted the C&O Canal Company. Engineering can be complicated work! Head out on a wide, packed-earth path, past beautiful pawpaw trees. Soon you will see milepost 155.2 on your right, which marks the west entrance to the Paw Paw Tunnel. Turn right, take out your flashlight, and explore 3,118 feet of history. You can find everything from weep holes (a place for water to escape), rope burns (smooth grooves worn into the wooden railing by towlines), rub rails (wooden planks fastened to the brick liner to protect the tunnel), brass plates, and even mushrooms and insects. You'll probably hear water trickling through the bricks overhead, and at some spots you might even feel water dripping on you. Once you reach the end of the tunnel, turn around and retrace your steps back to the trailhead. If you are up for more of a challenge—and if the rest of the trail is open—consider continuing on the Paw Paw Tunnel Hill Trail for a longer loop, adding about two additional miles to your adventure, or spending the night at the nearby Paw Paw Campground.

SCAVENGER HUNT

Survey markers

Shine your light on the walls of the tunnel to find brass plates called survey markers, some of which are originals from the 1800s. As you look for the plates, imagine what it was like to work in these dark, dangerous conditions while building the tunnel.

Brass plates mark every 100 feet

Original bricks

Six million bricks were used to construct the 3,118-foot-long tunnel. It was a slow process, with only 12 feet of bricks going in each week. Before inserting the bricks, laborers had to remove 200,000 cubic yards of material through vertical shafts as they slowly worked their way forward, using pick-and-shovel labor in between black-powder blasts.

The bricks have remained intact since the tunnel's opening in 1850

Northern long-eared bats

While exploring, don't just look down—make sure you look up too! You might find some of these flying mammals sleeping above. These federally threatened northern long-eared bats use the canal as a refuge in winter because it provides constant temperatures, high humidity, and relatively still air. Would you want to spend winter in here?

Myotis septentrionalis emerges at dusk to feed

Stone steps

The entrance to the tunnel is a semicircular arch made of coarse limestone and sandstone. Sandstone steps lead up on both sides. The main components of this sandstone are quartz, feldspar, and rock fragments. Stand in front of the stairs and look up to the top step—how many steps do you think there are? Count with your eyes—do not climb, as they are old and possibly unstable.

Stone steps along the west entrance to the tunnel

18

ASCEND TO HIGH ROCK IN SAVAGE RIVER STATE FOREST

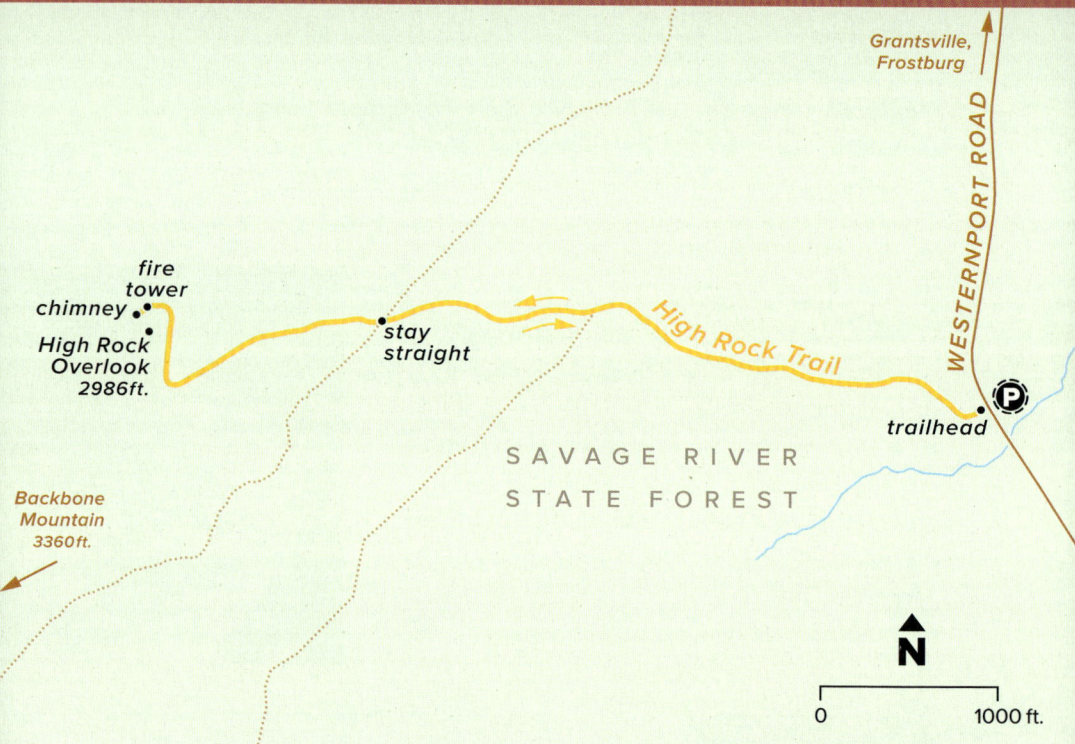

fire tower

chimney

High Rock Overlook 2986ft.

stay straight

High Rock Trail

trailhead

Grantsville, Frostburg

WESTERNPORT ROAD

Backbone Mountain 3360ft.

SAVAGE RIVER STATE FOREST

N

0   1000 ft.

YOUR ADVENTURE

Adventurers, today you are going to climb to the top of Big Savage Mountain in Maryland's largest state forest, on the historical homelands of the Massawomeck and Shawnee. Begin your adventure on a wide, packed-earth path that used to be an access road. You'll begin to notice a moderate incline as you walk between tall trees. The grade steepens quickly, so be sure to stop

A view from the 2986-foot summit at dusk →

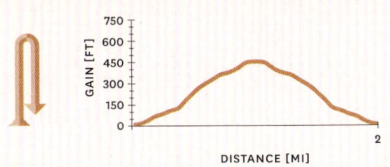

LENGTH 2 miles out and back

ELEVATION GAIN 456 ft.

HIKE TIME + EXPLORE 1 hour

DIFFICULTY Moderate—grassy, even path; rock scrambles at the summit; high elevation

SEASON Year-round; best during fall foliage.

GET THERE Follow McAndrews Hill Road east through New Germany State Park to Westernport Road and turn south. Follow for 7.9 miles, over the Savage River to the top of Backbone Mountain. Look for a yellow gate on the right at a small left-hand curve in the road, 1.5 miles after the intersection with Pine Swamp Road. Parking is available at a small pullout on the left. Trailhead is at the yellow gate on the other side of the road.

Google Maps: bit.ly/timberhighrocktrailhead

RESTROOM None

FEE None

TREAT YOURSELF Drive north through Savage River State Forest and treat yourself to a cinnamon roll from the Cornucopia Café in Grantsville.

Savage River State Forest
(301) 895-5759
Facebook @MarylandDNR

and power up as needed. After about a mile, the trail turns sharply to the right; there will be a steep incline before you wind back to the left. When you round that last corner, you will see an impressive sight—an abandoned fire tower rising 90 feet above you. Though it seems tempting to climb up the tower to get a better view, it's not allowed—instead, take a narrow trail west, to ruins of an old ranger station and then to High Rock Overlook. You can stand on the large boulders here to admire the 180-degree views over the Savage River Gorge below and the neighboring Meadow Mountain. Please be careful with little explorers, as there are no barriers, and the rocks can be slippery if wet. Consider bringing lunch and having a picnic at this altitude of 2,986 feet, or stay and watch the sky light up in beautiful colors at sunset. If you are feeling especially adventurous, consider spending the night at one of the fifty-two primitive roadside campsites nearby.

SCAVENGER HUNT

Boulders

The boulders at the summit of Big Savage Mountain are made of Pottsville Formation sandstone and are around 300 million years old! Sandstone is a sedimentary rock made of compacted sand that forms in two stages. First, layers of sand build up as it collects on the ground or a sea floor. Next, the sand particles are compacted by pressure from the layers above them and they cement together. Touch the boulders—how do they feel? Are they soft or hard? Smooth or rough?

Boulders at the peak of Big Savage Mountain, 2986'

Historical fire tower

This tower, built in 1934, is a stunning sight as you near the summit of the mountain. Fire observers would staff this tower and inform the forest warden of a fire's location, size, and intensity by observing the volume, density, and color of the smoke. This helped the warden determine how many firefighters would be needed to fight the fire. How many steps do you think lead to the top?

This fire tower stands approximately 90 feet high

Raccoon

Keep an eye out for these mammals with masks and bushy, ringed tails. Raccoons are omnivores who will eat almost anything—including fish, nuts, insects, and sometimes mice or squirrels. In your nature journal, draw yourself wearing a raccoon mask near the tower.

Procyon lotor is usually nocturnal but you might still see one

Old chimney

The ruins of a chimney and foundation of an old ranger's cabin from the 1930s are located near the base of the tower. Imagine what it would have been like to work in the tower 100 years ago and sleep in this cabin at nearly 3,000 feet of altitude—what modern conveniences would you have missed?

Remains of a chimney from a ranger's cabin

19

FIND FOUR AT SWALLOW FALLS

MAPLE GLADE ROAD

Muddy Creek Falls

overlook

Youghiogheny River

SWALLOW FALLS STATE PARK

trailhead

bridge

rock overhangs

Canyon Trail

old-growth forest

N

0   1000 ft.

turn left

Lower Swallow Falls

Upper Swallow Falls

Tolliver Falls

Herrington Manor, Oakland

SWALLOW FALLS ROAD

YOUR ADVENTURE

Adventurers, today you will explore four waterfalls and some 300-year-old hemlocks in the historical homelands of the Monongahela culture and the Osage, Shawnee, and Massawomeck nations. In the summers of 1918 and 1921, Henry Ford, Thomas Edison, and Harvey Firestone (of car, electricity, and tire fame, respectively) gathered and camped here—they called

Muddy Creek Falls is the highest waterfall in Maryland →

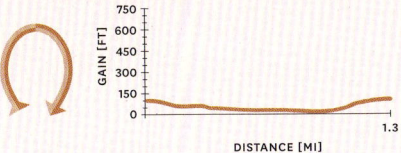

GAIN [FT]

750
600
450
300
150
0

1.3

DISTANCE [MI]

LENGTH 1.3-mile loop

ELEVATION GAIN 108 ft.

HIKE TIME + EXPLORE 1 hour

DIFFICULTY Moderate—a combination of wide, packed-earth paths and some rocky terrain with mild elevation

SEASON Year-round; best during fall foliage.

GET THERE From Oakland, take Herrington Manor Road north to bear right onto Swallow Falls Road. In 1.3 miles, turn left on Maple Glade Road, then turn right into the state park.

Google Maps: bit.ly/timberswallowfalls

RESTROOM At trailhead

FEE $3 per vehicle for MD residents, $5 nonresidents

TREAT YOURSELF Stop and get an ice cream cone at the Swallow Falls Country Store, located just outside the park entrance.

Swallow Falls State Park
(301) 387-6938
Facebook @MDStateParks

themselves "The Vagabonds." Be aware that you are in black bear country; if you see one, make noise and back away slowly. Begin under the large trail sign by the parking lot. Turn left to go clockwise around the Canyon Trail loop. Follow a boardwalk, then reach the first overlook for Muddy Creek Falls. After admiring the view, bear slightly left back to the trail and head down to the base of the falls. Here, you can walk onto the rocks or just sit and admire the beauty. Continuing on, walk along the sandstone cliffs and steps. The trail will wind around a bend. Get a good view of the Youghiogheny River before climbing stairs, hiking over a wooden bridge, and passing under two high rock overhangs. Stay straight past a right-branching trail and arrive at Lower Swallow Falls. Go left over another wooden staircase to arrive at Upper Swallow Falls. On the path, wind to the base of Upper Swallow Falls, a popular swimming hole in warm weather. After taking a dip or enjoying a power-up, leave the river to reach the final waterfall, the low but beautiful Tolliver Falls, which spills out into a pool. Bear right into the oldest stand of hemlocks and white pine trees in Maryland. Complete the loop, then turn left back to the trailhead. To experience this park like Edison, Ford, and Firestone, stay at one of the many campsites in the state park.

SCAVENGER HUNT

Youghiogheny River

The 132-mile-long Youghiogheny River flows through Swallow Falls State Park, creating four waterfalls. *Youghiogheny* is a Lenape word meaning "a stream flowing in a contrary direction." The river was given this name because it runs north its entire course. Do *you* do something that's opposite the way most people do things?

The "Yough" is the only river in western Maryland that does not flow south into the Potomac River

Muddy Creek Falls and Tolliver Falls

The water coursing over these waterfalls drops through rocks that are about 300 million years old. Look closely and see if you can tell the different kinds apart. Sketch the falls in your nature journal, labeling them by name to remember which is which later.

Muddy Creek Falls (top) is 53' high, while Tolliver Falls (bottom) is only 6'

Brittlegills

Look for this fungus with red caps and a cream-colored center. The cap sometimes fades to pink due to sunlight or rain. Gently touch the gills underneath—do you see how they got their name, brittlegills? Where in the forest do they seem to like to grow?

Genus *Russula* gets its name from its red caps

Blackburnian warbler

It's not easy to spot these small colorful songbirds, since they build their nests high in hemlocks, but on a quiet day, you can hear their distinctive song—a series of high "swi" notes that ascend in pitch. Listen for them, then take a turn mimicking their beautiful song.

Setophaga fusca spends winter in southern Central America and South America

ADVENTURES IN
DC

Adventurers, it is time to explore the nation's capital—the District of Columbia. Washington, DC, was established in the Constitution of the United States on July 16, 1790, to serve as the hub of government. President George Washington chose its exact location along the Potomac and Anacostia Rivers. Both Maryland and Virginia agreed to give land to the new "district" so that it would be distinct from the rest of the states. It's only 61.4 square miles and is located on a fall line, the border of two substantially different geographical landscapes—the hard rock of the Piedmont Plateau and the soft sediments of the Atlantic Coastal Plain. The landscape has changed a lot. Marshland and swamp became the National Mall. Tiber Creek used to flow down what's now Constitution Avenue. We'll hike through historical gardens in the middle of the city and explore an island and national memorial in the Potomac River and its tidal marshlands. As you drive between hikes, reflect on the District's motto: "justice for all." How can you demonstrate justice for all through your outdoor adventures?

20

ROAM AROUND DUMBARTON OAKS

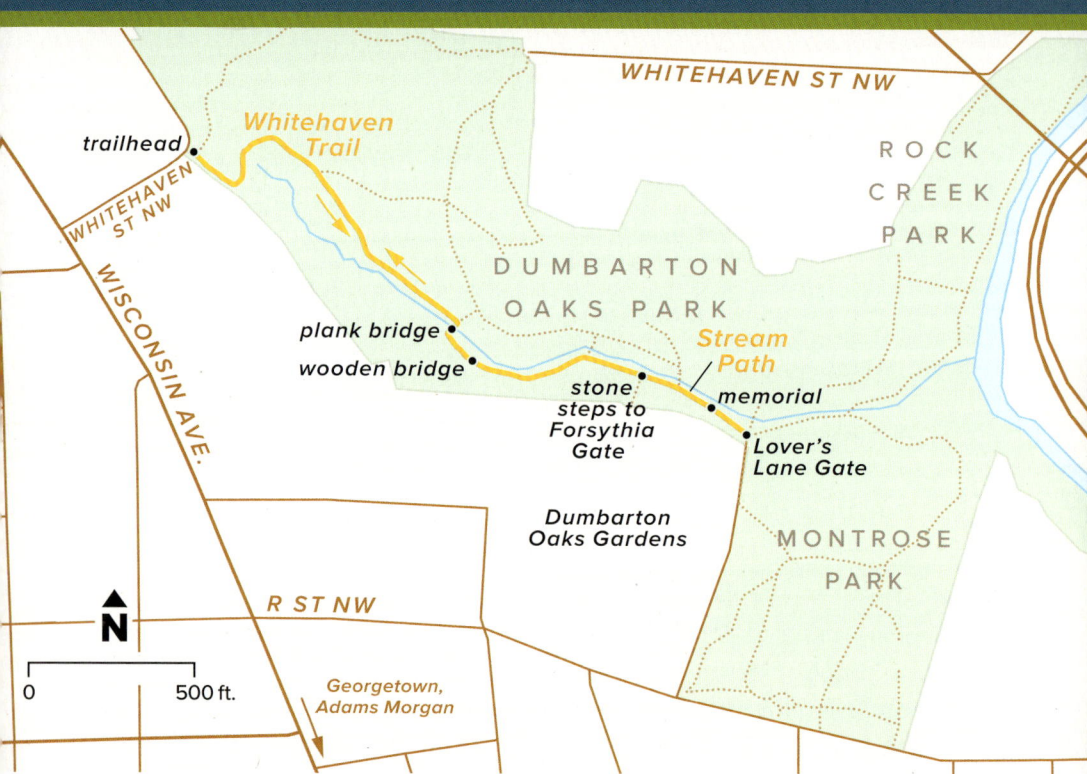

YOUR ADVENTURE

Adventurers, are you ready to walk through history? These are the historical lands of the Anacostan and Piscataway. This acreage was later donated by Ambassador Robert Woods Bliss and his wife, Mildred Barnes Bliss, in 1940 to Harvard University. This garden was designed by Beatrix Farrand, one of the first professional female landscape architects in US

Stone clapper bridge over the water →

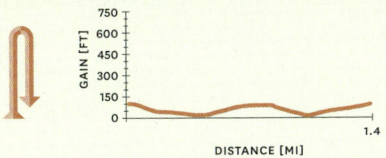

GAIN [FT]

750
600
450
300
150
0

1.4

DISTANCE [MI]

LENGTH 1 mile out and back

ELEVATION GAIN 157 ft.

HIKE TIME + EXPLORE 45 minutes

DIFFICULTY Easy—combination of packed-earth and paved paths with mild elevation

SEASON Year-round, but best during spring when trees are full and flowers are blooming.

GET THERE Take Wisconsin Ave. NW south to turn left (east) on Whitehaven Street NW. Look for street parking near the trailhead where the road curves—there is no parking at the park.

Google Maps: bit.ly/timberdumbartonoakspark

RESTROOM Down R Street at Montrose Park

FEE None

TREAT YOURSELF Enjoy to a delicious pastry from Pâtisserie Poupon, half a mile away from the park on Wisconsin Avenue.

Dumbarton Oaks Park
(202) 895-6000
Facebook @doaksDC

history. Begin your journey by stepping off the city street onto a narrow packed-earth path. Soon you will pass by a wood plank bridge over a small man-made waterfall. Walk over another small wood bridge and past several more man-made cascades and small ponds along the path. Look for beautiful old limestone steps that lead up to a magnificent arch with an iron gate on the right side of the path. After admiring the gardens you can see through the gate, return to the path to find a stone arbor on the other side of the water. A little farther and you'll arrive at the wooden gates of Lovers' Lane. If you have time, you can continue on to explore Montrose Park. When you're ready, turn around and retrace your steps.

SCAVENGER HUNT

Forsythia Gate

It's worth taking the small detour up the limestone veneer steps to the Forsythia Gate, which is named for the yellow-blooming shrubs that flank the stairs. This stone arch and iron gate separate Dumbarton Oaks Park and Dumbarton Oaks Gardens. Count the steps as you walk up to peek through the bars.

Stone steps leading to the Dumbarton Oaks Gardens

Gray arbor memorial

Across the water from the trail, you'll see a memorial to William James Gray, the first groundskeeper of the Dumbarton Oaks Gardens. It's made of coarse rubble stone set in mortar and was originally covered by a rustic timber arbor that is now gone. Sketch this structure in your nature journal now, and later sketch what you think it looked like when it was built 85 years ago.

This memorial was built in 1937

Waterfall

Beatrix Farrand's 1921 design for this area included a carefully phased transition from formal gardens near the mansion to informal gardens farther away. The woodland landscape includes numerous artificial waterfalls and ponds. Consider sitting by one of these waterfalls and enjoying the quiet time in nature—all within the city limits!

One of the waterfalls designed by Beatrix Farrand

Burdocks

Look for these purple-reddish flower heads from June to October. In fall, the flower heads change into prickly burrs composed of thirty to forty seeds hidden inside spherical pods that resemble a thistle. This is a great wildflower to draw in your natural journal—compare it to flowers found in the more formal gardens.

Genus *Arctium*

Lovers' Lane gate

The Lover's Lane entrance to Dumbarton Oaks Park from Rock Creek Park consists of a two-part wooden gate that hangs between stone piers. Along the side of this entrance is a 7-foot-high stone retaining wall. Is someone *you* love near you on this path? Give them a hug.

This gate was constructed in the early 1930s

21

CIRCLE THEODORE ROOSEVELT ISLAND

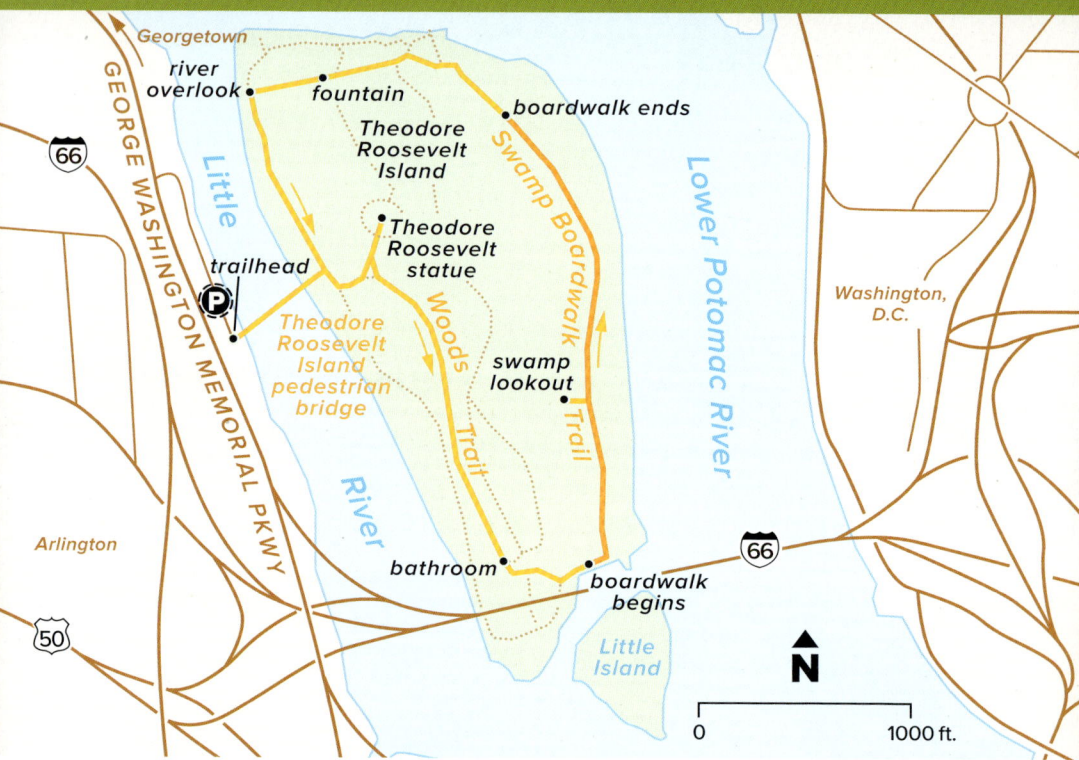

YOUR ADVENTURE

Adventurers, today we will walk around an entire island! This area provided fishing, foraging, and hunting grounds for the Nacotchtank (Anacostan) until the early 1700s. In the 1930s, the island was rewilded from the neglected, overgrown farmland it had become, as tribute to President Theodore Roosevelt, a great outdoorsman and conservationist. To start,

Cross the Theodore Roosevelt Island pedestrian bridge to begin your journey →

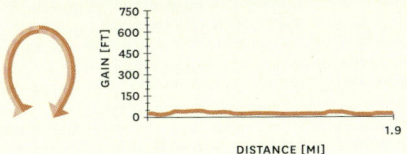

GAIN [FT]
750
600
450
300
150
0
1.9
DISTANCE [MI]

LENGTH 1.9-mile loop

ELEVATION GAIN 56 ft.

HIKE TIME + EXPLORE 1 hour

DIFFICULTY Easy—a combination of wide, packed-earth paths and wooden boardwalks

SEASON Year-round, but best during early spring for blossoms.

GET THERE Take the George Washington Memorial Parkway north past Ronald Reagan Washington National Airport. In about 4 miles turn right toward Theodore Roosevelt Island. Park at the south end of the lot near the pedestrian bridge.

Google Maps: bit.ly/theodorerooseveltisland

RESTROOM On the trail

FEE None

TREAT YOURSELF Stop at Captain Cookie & the Milkman for a made-to-order ice cream sandwich with freshly baked cookies, across the river near the White House and National Mall.

Theodore Roosevelt Island
(703) 289-2500
Facebook @TheodoreRooseveltIsland

cross the Potomac River on the Theodore Roosevelt Island pedestrian bridge. Turn right on the Swamp Trail and then left to reach Roosevelt Memorial Plaza. Here, find a huge statue of Theodore Roosevelt. After exploring, return to the path and begin to loop around the island on the trail closest to the water. Pass bathrooms on the left before you round the path and get up-close views of the Theodore Roosevelt Bridge. Look for ducks! Loop to the left on the Swamp Boardwalk Trail over the tidal marsh to several overlooks on your left. Return to a packed-earth path—you may have views of the Kennedy Center and Watergate Hotel, depending on how full the trees are. Before turning left to loop back around to the trailhead, walk a few steps off the trail for a clear view of the Washington Harbor Complex. Follow the Swamp Trail—you'll be close to the water, so keep little ones away from the edge of the path. You'll pass two trails on your left, the Upland and Woods Trails, but keep going straight. If you have time at the end, return to the Roosevelt Memorial Plaza for a picnic lunch or a much-earned power-up.

SCAVENGER HUNT

Statue of Theodore Roosevelt

This island was gifted to the US government in 1932 to honor conservationist and former president Theodore Roosevelt. He was the first president to make conserving America's natural resources a top priority. During his time in office, almost 230 million acres of land were placed under the protection of the federal government. If you could say one thing to President Roosevelt, what would it be?

Theodore Roosevelt was America's twenty-sixth president

American robin

This songbird can be easily spotted and identified by its reddish-orange chest and cheery song. It sings almost 2,000 times a day! It is not just the American robin that calls this island home—there are almost 200 species of birds that visit throughout the year. Download a checklist from the park website before your visit and see how many birds you can spot.

Turdus migratorius is comfortable in both cities and forests

Tidal marsh

This island showcases three different ecological zones: upland forest, swamp, and tidal marsh. Can you tell the difference between the three? The marsh is an almost treeless area of open water. At low tide, the stream flows under the boardwalk. At high tide, the bridge can be nearly flooded.

The boardwalk over the tidal marsh

Mallards

Can you spot a male mallard? They have dark, iridescent green heads and bright yellow bills. Females are brown. Mallards are "dabbling ducks" because they feed in the water by tipping forward to graze on underwater plants. They often stay in groups, not just with other mallards,

but also with dabbling ducks of other species. Pretend they are leading a game of Simon Says and mimic each new behavior you see.

Anas platyrhynchos can live in almost any wetland habitat

ADVENTURES IN
VIRGINIA

Adventurers, we are heading west and entering the Old Dominion State (so called because it was the "oldest dominion" in America of the kings and queens of England). Virginia was the first English colony, and it's the state that has produced the most US presidents—eight! The Cherokee, Powhatan, and Nottoway, among many others, all lived on the land that is now Virginia, and many words that we use in English today originated from their languages, including hickory, chipmunk, skunk, raccoon, and moccasin. As you travel, you'll notice five distinct regions: Along the coastline there are lowlands, salt marshes, and swamps that make up the Atlantic Coastal Plain. Moving west, there is the Piedmont region, which contains rolling foothills and river valleys. If you enjoy climbing mountains, you will enjoy the Blue Ridge region, made up of the steep parts of the Appalachian Mountains. Heading farther west, you will arrive at the Appalachian Ridge and Valley region, full of many natural bridges and caverns to be explored. Then comes the Appalachian Plateau, a forested area of winding rivers and flat-topped rocks. Our forested adventures (62 percent of the state is covered in forest!) will begin in the northern part of the state. We'll take in views of the Great Falls, then hike through a historical and scenic nature preserve. Next it's on to Shenandoah National Park to climb the second-highest peak, Stony Man, explore five waterfalls, and summit Dark Hollow. Continuing our journey south, we'll tiptoe through the 4,264-foot-long Blue Ridge Tunnel, hit Humpback Rocks, hike along the waterfall with the highest vertical drop east of the Mississippi River, Crabtree Falls, and wind around Blackwater Creek. We'll wade into Bear Creek, Beaver Lakes, and Taskinas Creek before walking around the mysterious bald cypress trees at First Landing State Park. At Chincoteague National Wildlife Refuge, we'll spy wild ponies, then explore the forested Occoneechee State Park, go spelunking in a cave named Devil's Den, and hike to the hidden Stiles Falls. Then it's off to see the 30-foot cascading Roaring Run waterfall, the 66-foot Cascades Falls, an abandoned N&W Railway tunnel, wild ponies at Grayson Highlands, and Pinnacle Natural Area Preserve and the very wide Big Falls. As you travel, keep in mind that the state slogan is "Virginia is for lovers"—let yourself fall in love with each beautiful region in this gorgeous state.

Young adventurers take in the views while hiking at Grayson Highlands State Park

22

FOLLOW THE CANAL TO GREAT FALLS

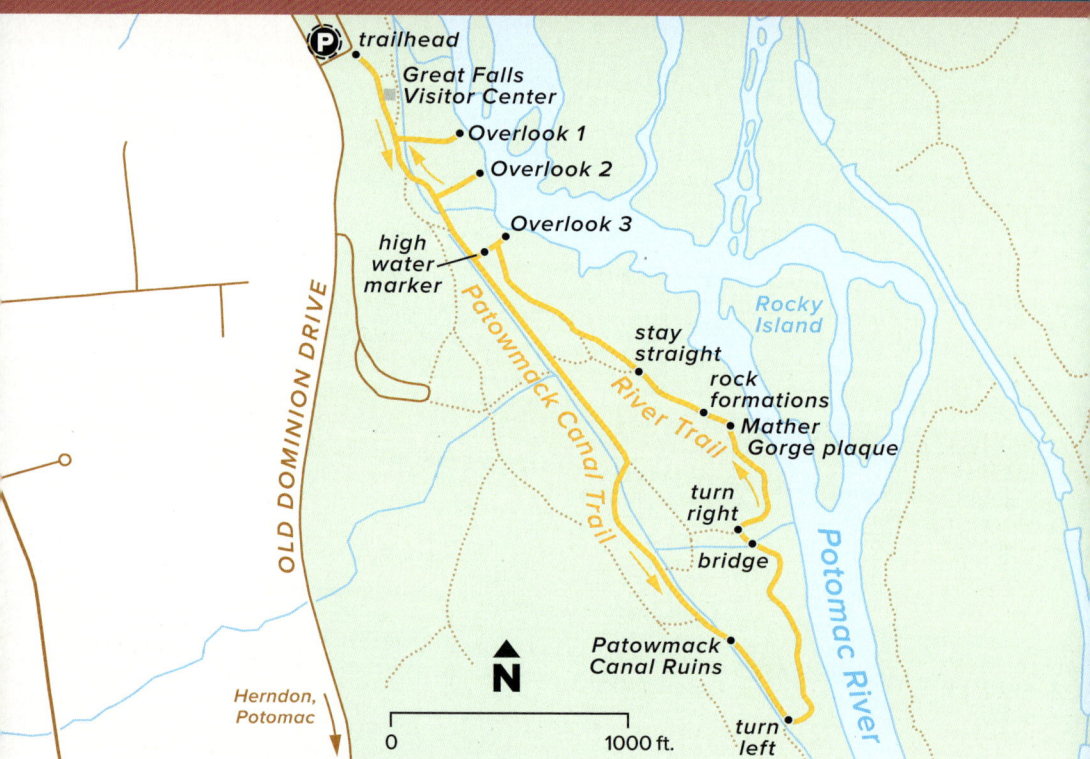

trailhead

Great Falls Visitor Center

Overlook 1

Overlook 2

Overlook 3

high water marker

OLD DOMINION DRIVE

Patowmack Canal Trail

River Trail

Rocky Island

stay straight

rock formations

Mather Gorge plaque

turn right

bridge

Potomac River

Patowmack Canal Ruins

turn left

N

Herndon, Potomac

0   1000 ft.

YOUR ADVENTURE

Adventurers, let's get ready to view some magnificent waterfalls while taking a stroll through history on the historical homelands of the Piscataway and Manahoac. You'll begin immediately on the Patowmack Canal Trail. Two overlooks on your left provide fantastic views of the beautiful cascading Great Falls below—the result of the Potomac River dropping 76 feet in

View of the magnificent waterfall from Overlook 2 →

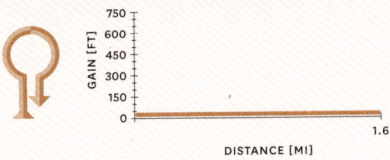

LENGTH 1.6-mile lollipop loop

ELEVATION GAIN 30 ft.

HIKE TIME + EXPLORE 1.5 hours

DIFFICULTY Easy—mostly dirt and grass paths; some stairs; a couple rock scrambles

SEASON Year-round; best in spring for blooms and rushing waterfalls.

GET THERE Take VA-7 East from Ashburn. Turn left onto VA-193 East / Georgetown Pike. In 5 miles, turn left onto Old Dominion Drive. Follow just over a mile to the visitor center parking lot.

Google Maps: bit.ly/timbergreatfallspark

RESTROOM At visitor center

FEE $20 per vehicle

TREAT YOURSELF Head south about 6 miles on Old Dominion Drive for some delicious scones and gourmet cakes at Sweet Stuff Deli.

Great Falls State Park
(703) 757-3101
Facebook @Great-Falls-Park

less than a mile, while also having to squeeze through Mather Gorge. This makes Great Falls the steepest rapids on any river in the eastern United States! Near Overlook 3 on your left, you will see a high-water marker that shows just how high it has flooded in the past century. Turn left onto the River Trail, then stay straight at the fork in the path. Climb over some fun rock scrambles while you work your way to Mather Gorge. It's named after Stephen Mather, the first director of the National Park Service; a plaque was placed along the gorge in his honor. At the next fork, turn left to go over a long wood bridge and up the steps on the other side. Turn right onto the Patowmack Canal Trail. You're walking through the remains of the Patowmack Canal, built starting in the late 1700s! Take another left turn to close the loop and return to the path you hiked in on. Finish by walking back past the Overlooks—you might want to stop one more time to have a snack and get one final glimpse of the falls in all their glory.

SCAVENGER HUNT

Potomac River high-water marker

Near Overlook 3, watch for a high-water marker that shows where the Potomac reached in the 1900s. Look up—some markers will be way over your head! Try to figure out what would be covered if the water were at one of the markers today. Would you be able to see any of the rocks in the river, or even the overlook you are standing on?

The highest water levels recorded were in 1936

Eastern red cedar in rock

We often think trees need a lot of soil to grow, but if you look carefully here, you'll see that many plants and trees are also able to grow in cracks along the cliff. Plants can take root in small amounts of soil and debris that collect in the pockets of the rocks. Name one thing *you* can do that might seem impossible to others!

Juniperus virginiana can grow in rocks if its roots find hidden water sources

Virginia pine

The sparse, eroded cliff soil in the gorge offers a fine home for the Virginia pine, which can live up to 150 years. It is small compared to other pines, growing 15 to 40 feet tall. Pines grow clusters of needles (called fascicles) instead of leaves. The cones of this species are thin and woody and grow to be 1.5 to 2.5 inches long. Look up at a Virginia pine—how many pine cones can you count on one tree?

Pinus virginiana is an evergreen tree

Patowmack Canal ruins

The Patowmack Company was organized in 1784 by George Washington, with the goal of constructing a series of five canals to make the Potomac River navigable from Ohio to the Chesapeake Bay. This canal was completed in 1802. Today, you can see remnants of its locks, as well as portions of the canal itself. What cargo do you think this canal transported over 200 years ago?

These waterways were an engineering feat when construction started in 1785

23

FIND THE ROCK QUARRY AT GOVERNMENT ISLAND

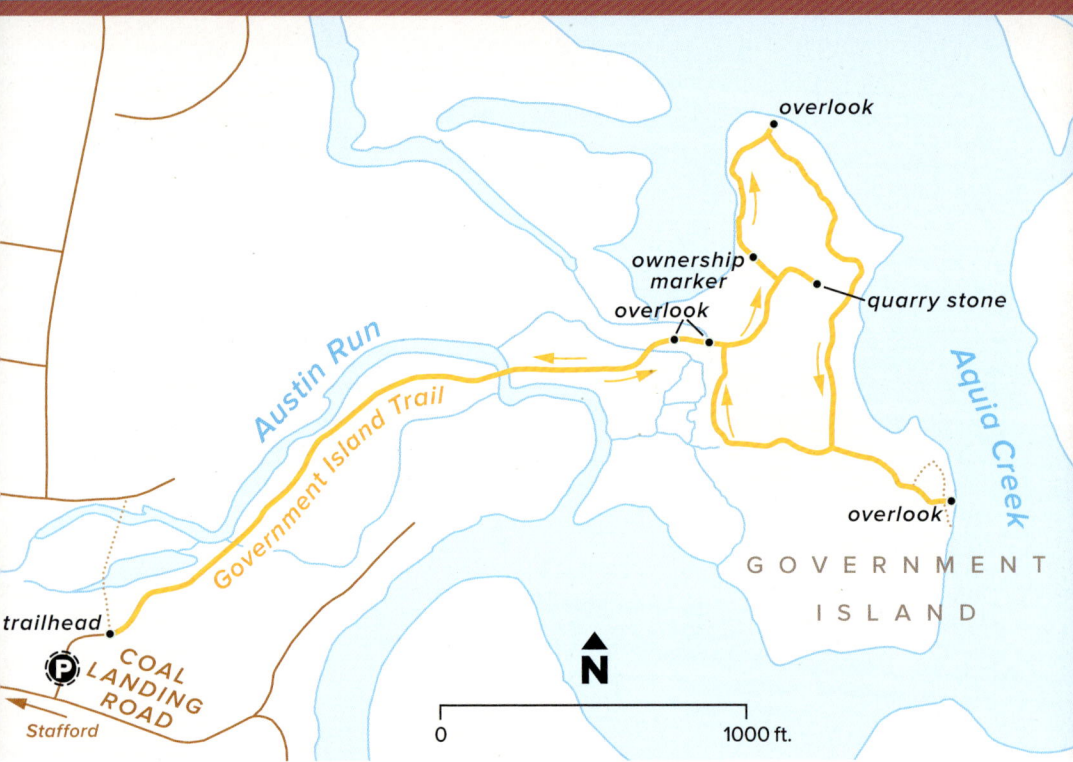

YOUR ADVENTURE

Adventurers, get ready to hike through a historical scenic nature preserve and archeological site on the historical lands of the Patawomeck and Doeg. Captain John Smith visited this area in 1608 to negotiate trade with the Patawomeck. Your journey begins on the wide, paved Government Island Trail. It features wooded areas and is parallel to Austin Run. From the

View of Aquia Creek from Government Island →

GAIN [FT]

750
600
450
300
150
0

1.75

DISTANCE [MI]

LENGTH 1.75-mile lollipop loop

ELEVATION GAIN 56 ft.

HIKE TIME + EXPLORE 1 hour

DIFFICULTY Easy—a combination of dirt, paved, and boardwalk trails with no elevation

SEASON Open March through October; best in spring for birds and blooms.

GET THERE Take US-1 North in Stafford to turn right onto Coal Landing Road. In just under a mile, the Government Island Parking Lot will be on your left. The trailhead is at the far end of the lot.

Google Maps: bit.ly/timbergovernmentisland

RESTROOM At trailhead

FEE None

TREAT YOURSELF Grab a burger at the Mason-Dixon Café just off US-1 in Stafford.

Government Island Park
(540) 658-4871
Facebook @StaffordHistory

boardwalk, look down to observe aquatic plants, birds, and other wild-life—placards along the way tell about the ecosystem. The first overlook has benches for a power-up. At the end of the boardwalk, turn left and cross over the wetlands. The hiking trail becomes a dirt path as you enter the largely shaded forest. Soon you'll come to the historical quarry on the right. A bit farther down the path you'll see an ownership marker from 1791. As you continue to loop around the island, follow the path to the left to an over-look of Aquia Creek. Retrace your steps back to the path. Turn left to find a sign showing artifacts from the Patawomeck that have been recovered here. Stay left and continue circling the island. Turn left at the fork to hike to another water overlook. Return to the path to find the boardwalk again, then retrace your steps to the parking lot.

SCAVENGER HUNT

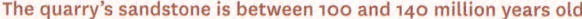

Aquia sandstone

This quarry was purchased by George Washington in 1791. Its sandstone was used in the construction of the US Capitol Building and the White House! It was also referred to as "freestone" because of its ability to be carved without split-ting. Look closely—can you see pebble-size quartz and clay pellets cemented together?

The quarry's sandstone is between 100 and 140 million years old

Spatterdock

Look for this perennial aquatic plant—its leaves might be underwater or floating just on top. The flowers are deep yellow and bloom at or just above the surface from June through September. It stabilizes pond banks and provides cover for many aquatic animals. Look closely for a few minutes—do you see any creatures?

Nuphar advena, also called yellow pond lily

Ospreys

While on the overlooks, see if you can spot one of these very large hawks that love the water. They search for prey by circling over relatively shallow water and hovering briefly before diving feet-first to grab a fish with their talons. They carry their catch back to the nest to eat it. Put your snack on the ground, pretend your hands are talons, and snatch your "prey" for lunch!

Pandion haliaetus is brown above and white below

Ownership marker

In 1791, the federal government acquired all but 1 acre of this entire island. The last acre belonged to Robert Steuart, a stonemason from Baltimore, Maryland. He marked his property with four stone boundary markers, the largest of which still remains and is clearly marked with his initials: R. S. How do *you* mark things that are yours?

Ownership marker from the 18th century

Tidewater

Government Island sits near where Austin Run meets 28-mile-long Aquia Creek. This later flows into the 405-mile-long Potomac River. While Government Island is commonly referred to as an island, it is actually a peninsula joined to the main-land by tidal wetlands. As adjacent tidal creeks and marshes rise, they cover the land with water.

View of the tidewater region along Government Island

24

SUMMIT THE STONY MAN

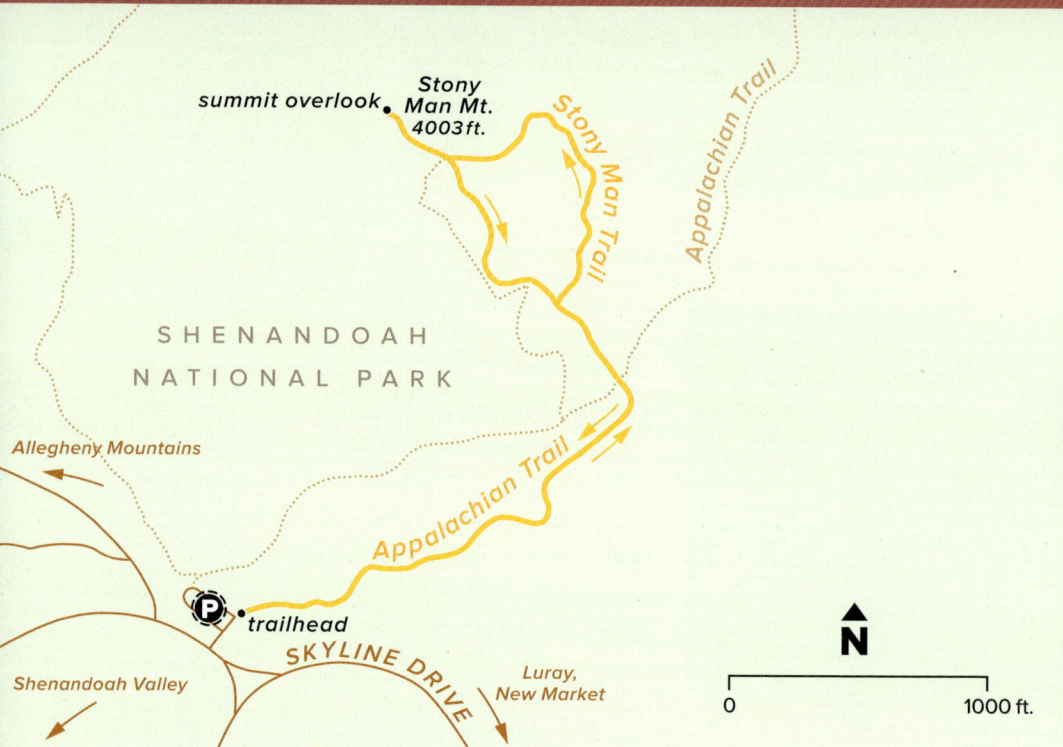

Stony Man Mt. 4003 ft.

summit overlook

Stony Man Trail

Appalachian Trail

SHENANDOAH
NATIONAL PARK

Allegheny Mountains

Appalachian Trail

trailhead

SKYLINE DRIVE

Shenandoah Valley

Luray,
New Market

N

0   1000 ft.

YOUR ADVENTURE

Adventurers, today you will see some of the best views in the area and climb to the second-highest peak in Shenandoah National Park at 4,010 feet! You'll be on the historical homelands of the Shawnee, Manahoac, and Monacan. In the late 1800s, long before we used the word "hike" in English, vacationers to Skyland Resort would say they'd "tramp" on these same

Seen from a distance, the rocks on the summit resemble a man's face →

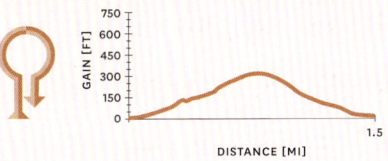

DISTANCE [MI]

LENGTH 1.5-mile lollipop loop

ELEVATION GAIN 318 ft.

HIKE TIME + EXPLORE 1.5 hours

DIFFICULTY Moderate—a combination of packed-earth paths and rocky terrain with moderate elevation

SEASON Year-round, but best during fall foliage. Note that while Shenandoah National Park is open year round, Skyline Drive may be closed in winter due to weather. Always check for closures before you head out.

GET THERE In Shenandoah National Park. At milepost 41.7 along Skyline Drive, the Stony Man lot has ample parking. The trail begins at the upper right end of the parking area.

Google Maps: bit.ly/timberstonyman

RESTROOM Just down the road at the Skyland visitor center

FEE $30 per vehicle

TREAT YOURSELF Enjoy a signature blackberry ice cream pie from Skyland Hotel, just up the road on Upper Loop.

Shenandoah National Park
(540) 999-3500
Facebook @shenandoahnps

trails. Begin on the famous Appalachian Trail (often called the AT), watching for blue blazes that mark the Stony Man Trail. You will soon arrive at a Y junction; veer right (you will explore the other path on the return trip). Turn right again to arrive at the summit. This collection of large rocks can be scrambled on, but please be careful, as they can be very slippery when wet. Find a safe spot to sit and enjoy the magnificent views of the Shenandoah Valley and the Allegheny Mountains to the west. On the way back, turn right at the junction and loop around the mountain on the blue-blazed trail to the junction with the AT. Retrace your steps to the parking lot. Want more of this beautiful national park? Consider camping at one of SNP's four main campgrounds.

SCAVENGER HUNT

Wild turkeys

Don't be surprised if you see these gobbling birds walking by on the trail! They are a common sight here. Their diet consists mostly of fruit, grass, seeds, and acorns. Acorns are high in protein, fat, and carbohydrates—these help wild turkeys survive winter. Look on the ground for a V-shape scratched in the leaf litter. That's how you know where a wild turkey has been searching for acorns.

Meleagris gallopavo can run up to 25 mph

Greenstone boulders

The many boulders and rock formations near the summit today are made of greenstone that is about 570 million years old. It started out as basalt lava rock that "cooked" deep underground to become metamorphic rock. Amazingly, the oldest rocks in Shenandoah National Park are even older—approximately 1.1 *billion* years old. The Earth is about 4.5 billion years old, so these rocks have been around for almost a quarter of the time that Earth has been around! In your nature journal, draw what you think these mountains looked like billions of years ago.

Basalt lava transforms under extreme heat into greenstone

Common bonnets

These gilled mushrooms have gray or brown bell-shaped caps and thin, fragile stems. Common bonnets grow in small clusters among the mosses on forest floors or on logs, stumps, or the dead wood of deciduous trees. In your nature journal, draw some fairies flitting around these bonnets.

Mycena galericulata is very common in the mid-Atlantic region

Scarlet tanager

During spring and summer, listen for the raspy song of the male scarlet tanager. If you stand still, you can often see a flash of bright red high in the tree branches above as the birds change perches or look for food. Males trade their red feathers for yellowish-green feathers in fall, making them the same color as the females. When males and females have distinct differences, it's called "dimorphism."

Piranga olivacea migrates to South America in fall

25

DESCEND INTO DARK HOLLOW FALLS

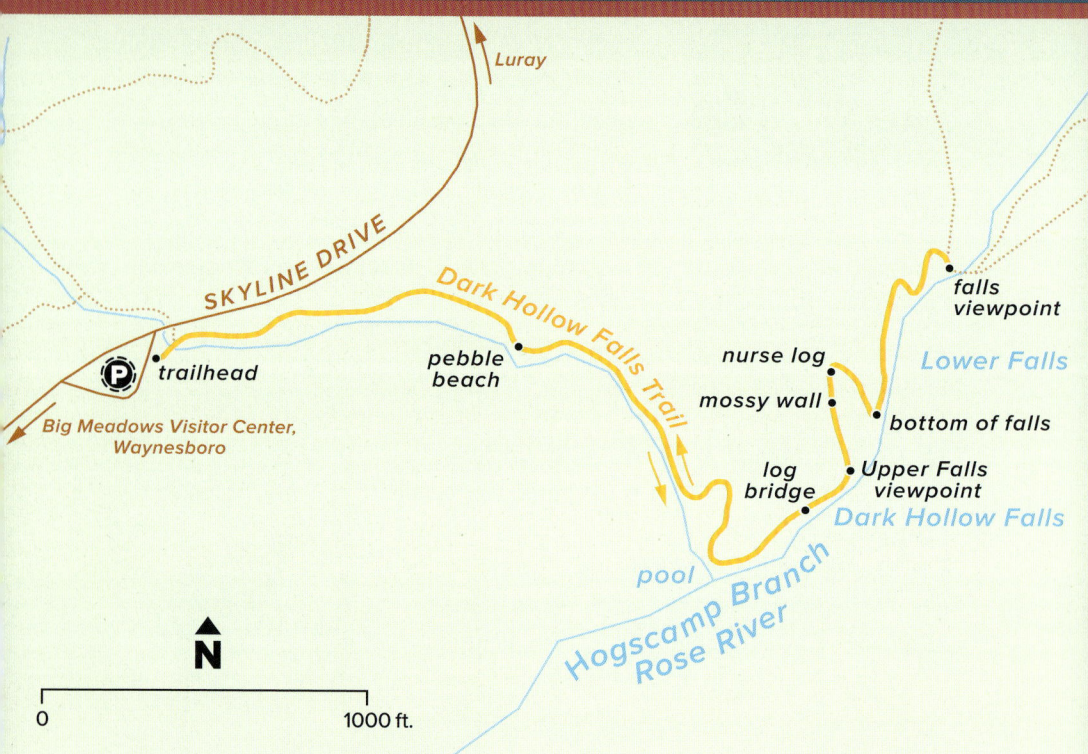

Luray

SKYLINE DRIVE

Dark Hollow Falls Trail

P trailhead

pebble beach

nurse log

mossy wall

falls viewpoint

Lower Falls

bottom of falls

log bridge

Upper Falls viewpoint

Dark Hollow Falls

Big Meadows Visitor Center, Waynesboro

pool

Hogscamp Branch

Rose River

N

0   1000 ft.

YOUR ADVENTURE

Adventurers, let's gear up to see not one . . . not two . . . but *five* waterfalls! You're on the historical homelands of the Shawnee, Manahoac, and Monacan. You'll first head downhill with a creek babbling next to you all the way on the Dark Hollow Falls Trail. Watch for play spots to dip your toes along the 8.8-mile-long Rose River, which meets up with the 34-mile-long

These falls cascade dramatically over several levels of rock →

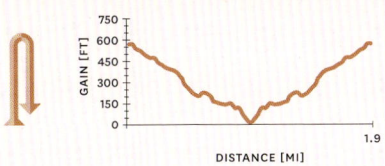

GAIN [FT]

750
600
450
300
150
0

1.9

DISTANCE [MI]

LENGTH 1.9 miles out and back

ELEVATION GAIN 584 ft.

HIKE TIME + EXPLORE 2 hours

DIFFICULTY Challenging—short, but the way back up is steep

SEASON Year-round. Note that while Shenandoah National Park is open year round, Skyline Drive may be closed in winter due to weather. Always check for closures before you head out.

GET THERE In Shenandoah National Park. The trailhead is just off Skyline Drive across the road from Harry F. Byrd Sr. Visitor Center, 28 miles south of the North entrance on 211 and 20 miles north of the Swift Run Gap entrance.

Google Maps: bit.ly/timberdarkhollow

RESTROOM Across the street at the visitor center

FEE $30 per vehicle

TREAT YOURSELF The New Market Taproom at Big Meadows Lodge has personal pizzas and ice cream, a great way to relax after climbing out of Dark Hollow.

Shenandoah National Park
(540) 999-3500
Facebook @ShenandoahNPS

Robinson River. The first falls is delicate and tiny and features a big pool with a huge flat rock you can sun yourself on like a lizard. Pass a log bridge, then arrive at the Upper Falls viewpoint. Continue down to see the entire falls from the lower viewpoint—feel the splash on your face! After a power-up stop, keep trekking down. You'll pass three more falls until you reach a bridge and road at the bottom that allows you to look all the way up the creek! Turn back the way you came. Consider camping at Big Meadows across the street.

SCAVENGER HUNT

Hay-scented fern

Feel the soft, hairy texture of these fronds. Ferns have a frond, then a blade, and then each leaf is called a pinna. Look closely—these pinna split again, into pinnules, and then one more time. Smell a frond—do you think it smells like hay, as it's named for?

Look for *Dennstaedtia punctilobula* spores under the pinnae in summer

Mountain laurel

June is mountain laurel's month in the park! Take a piece of paper from your nature journal and try folding an origami laurel bloom. You can often tell you're in a laurel thicket even when these shrubs aren't blooming, because of their shiny, pointed leaves.

Kalmia latifolia

Wineberry

This isn't a raspberry or blackberry, but it's from the same plant family. Wineberries are covered in a bristly calyx (special leaves that protect the petals and the flower). Put a snack from your lunch in your palm and shape your hand like a calyx to protect it.

Rubus phoenicolasius

Wild hydrangea

This shrub has big ovate leaves with small teeth around the edges. A stalk of white flower clusters sprouts from it in late spring and summer. They love water and can't grow without a lot of it—how much water do *you* need to drink every day?

The seed pods of *Hydrangea arborescens* look like water jugs

Moss

Look for these green noodles festooning the sides of rocks—there are 208 different species of moss in this park! This species has small leaves coming out of a short stem, but it is different from many other plants because it doesn't have "veins" to carry water inside. See if you can count how many leaves one stem has.

Green mosses like this are in a class called Bryopsida

26

TACKLE THE TOP OF BLACKROCK SUMMIT

YOUR ADVENTURE

Adventurers, are you ready to summit Blackrock? You'll be trekking on the historical homelands of the Shawnee, Manahoac, and Monacan as you complete a loop around this geologic feature. To get started, take the quick left on the white-blazed Appalachian Trail. You'll gradually ascend, passing through tons of mountain laurel, and coming to a junction with a concrete

Can you believe these rocks at the summit used to be on the seabed of an ancient body of water? →

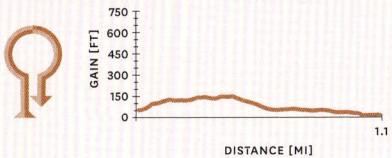

GAIN [FT]

750
600
450
300
150
0

1.1

DISTANCE [MI]

LENGTH 1.1-mile lollipop loop

ELEVATION GAIN 162 ft.

HIKE TIME + EXPLORE 1 hour

DIFFICULTY Moderate—short; some rocks and roots on the approach; optional rock scramble at summit

SEASON Year-round. Note that while Shenandoah National Park is open year round, Skyline Drive may be closed in winter due to weather. Always check for closures before you head out.

GET THERE In Shenandoah National Park. The trailhead is on the west side of Skyline Drive, 19 miles south of Swift Run Gap entrance station and 20 miles north of Rockfish Gap entrance station.

Google Maps: bit.ly/timberblackrock

RESTROOM At trailhead

FEE $30 per vehicle

TREAT YOURSELF Loft Mountain Wayside, just up Skyline at Mile 79.5, has grab-n-go sandwiches and snacks.

Shenandoah National Park
(540) 999-3500
Facebook @ShenandoahNPS

AT post. Stay straight to continue on the AT. Soon you'll hit the bundle of rocks that make up Blackrock summit! The final concrete AT marker is an access point for a fairly easy scramble up the rocks, but this is at your own discretion—best for older or experienced kiddos. If you opt out of climbing it, you've still reached some amazing 360-degree views! Continue around the rock, then descend on a wider trail, the Blackrock Hut Fire Road. You'll pass the AT junction from the start of the hike—continue right on this wider trail to complete the loop. Consider making a full weekend adventure of it by camping at Loft Mountain Campground just a few minutes north.

SCAVENGER HUNT

Sassafras

Put your hand up to the leaves of this tree—sassafras is unique because its leaves can be different shapes. Look for oval leaves, mitten-shaped leaves, or three-lobed leaves, all on the same plant! If you find a leaf on the ground, crush it up and see if you can smell its spicy root beer aroma.

Sassafras albidum

Appalachian Trail marker

These trail markers guide thru-hikers—people who hike the full length of the AT—from Georgia to Maine. What would it be like to camp every night? To see so many different states? To have to pick up food every few days and haul everything you need on your back? Would you like to do it one day? Why or why not?

The full AT runs 2,194 miles and takes 5 to 7 months to hike

Gall

Galls are growths that occur on the leaves, twigs, roots, or flowers of many plants. If you find one still attached, look closely without touching—is there anything inside? Many are created by wasps—they insert their eggs in plants, which swell to create a protective home around the larvae. They don't hurt the plant.

The paper-thin shell of an empty gall sometimes falls from its tree

Lichen

This isn't a plant—but what *is* it? It is actually algae and fungus working together. There are over 800 types of lichen on the East Coast! Keep your eyes peeled for different types as you hike. This kind is "crustose," like a crust.

Lichen is a slow-growing organism

Blackrock talus

A pile of rocks broken up into small chunks on or near a summit is called talus. The talus here is made of quartzite. Water, ice, and roots break down large rocks into smaller pieces. Pick up two rocks and compare how different their edges are. Can you guess what force might have caused each to erode?

Scramble gently over these rocks, if you dare

27

FIND YOUR WAY THROUGH BLUE RIDGE TUNNEL

Waynesboro

west entrance

250

SKYLINE DRIVE

N

0   1000 ft.

Charlottesville

64

AFTON DEPOT LANE

trailhead • P

Blue Ridge Tunnel Trail

64

east entrance

YOUR ADVENTURE

Adventurers, are you ready to explore a pitch-black 4,273-foot-long tunnel on the historical homelands of the Monacan, Shawnee, and Manahoac? Begin on a wide gravel path, passing interpretative signage on the history of the tunnel. Mileage markers every 0.25 miles help you follow your progress. An active railroad track runs along the trail; this is a new route that takes

Entrance to the Blue Ridge Tunnel →

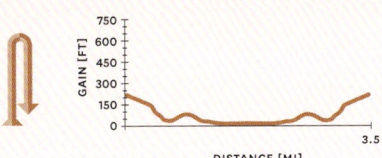

GAIN [FT]

750
600
450
300
150
0

3.5

DISTANCE [MI]

LENGTH 3.5 miles out and back

ELEVATION GAIN 367 ft.

HIKE TIME + EXPLORE 2 hours

DIFFICULTY Moderate—a gravel path with some elevation; trail is completely dark, so be sure to bring a flashlight or headlamp

SEASON Year-round. Best in fall for foliage and fog escaping the tunnel, and winter is nice for icicles on wet walls near the tunnel portals.

GET THERE From I-64 exit onto US-250 East. Travel 1.5 miles and turn right on VA-6 / Afton Mountain Road. In 0.5 miles, turn right on Afton Depot Lane and follow to the parking lot at the end.

Google Maps: bit.ly/timberblueridgetunnel

RESTROOM At trailhead

FEE None

TREAT YOURSELF Blue Mountain Brewery, just a few minutes south on Critzer Shop Road, has a great kids menu and beautiful view. Keep driving south after, along the famed Nelson 151 trail, for even more fun eateries and B&Bs.

Blue Ridge Tunnel
(434) 263-7130
Facebook @ClaudiusCrozetBlueRidgeTunnel

trains to the Blue Ridge Tunnel replacement built in 1944. In a little over a half a mile, arrive at the Blue Ridge Tunnel, also called the Claudius Crozet Tunnel, after its engineer. It was constructed between 1850 and 1858 and is 16 feet wide and 20 feet high and a little over 0.8 miles long. Most of its sides and ceiling are exposed bricks. Before you enter, take out your flashlight to safely navigate the almost-mile-long trek through the completely dark tunnel. Take your time to find all the animals that call this tunnel home— salamanders, crayfish, frogs, toads, turtles, and bats! You'll exit the tunnel at the west end; notice the stone-lined arch crafted by Irish stonemasons. It stands in contrast to the east entrance, which looks more rustic. After exiting the tunnel, power up before retracing your steps to the trailhead.

SCAVENGER HUNT

Box turtle

On your way to and from the tunnel, look for these reptiles. They hibernate during cold weather by burrowing deep under soil and leaves as early as October then re-emerge in April or May. Be sure to step quietly and gently around one. If it gets frightened, it will pull its head and legs into its shell until it feels safe.

Genus *Terrapene* has a dome-shaped carapace, or shell

Eastern crayfish

Can you spot this shellfish in one of the small streams inside the tunnel? Crayfish are most active at night, when they feed on snails, worms, insect larvae, and tadpoles. When they molt their shell, they usually eat their old skeleton to retain

the nutrients in it! They walk forward, but swim backward. Next time you go swimming, have a crayfish race by seeing who can swim backward the fastest.

Cambarus bartonii resemble small lobsters

Vesper bat

When awake, these bats rely on echolocation to navigate and find prey. This is a very useful skill, since they cannot see and live in dark, empty, damp areas. If you turn off your flashlight and yell inside the tunnel, are you able to guess how far away your hiking mate is?

Evening bats are in the family *Vespertilionidae*

Pickerel frog

This frog is relatively large and can be identified by the two rows of dark, squarish spots running down its back between its dorsolateral folds. They love this tunnel for its slow-moving water sources and areas with low, dense vegetation and cooler temperatures. Shine your flashlight on the sides of the tunnel to see if you can spot one!

The male *Lithobates palustris* attracts females with a snore-like call

Brook salamander

These amphibians look like a cross between lizards and frogs. Their bodies are long and slender, and their skin is moist. They have long tails and teeth on both top and bottom. Salamanders can sense vibrations but are unable to hear. The ones here have adapted to living in the tunnel's total darkness. What would you need to live in total darkness?

Salamanders of genus *Eurycea* are nocturnal

28

ROCK OUT AT HUMPBACK ROCKS

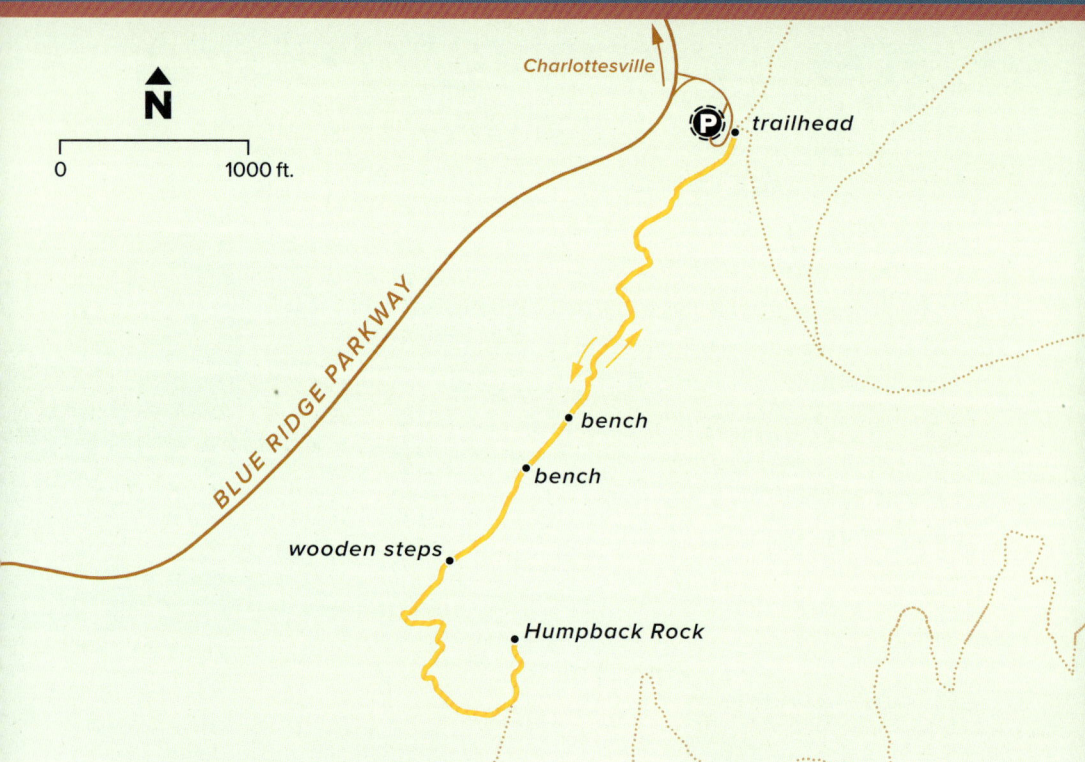

N

0   1000 ft.

Charlottesville

trailhead

BLUE RIDGE PARKWAY

bench

bench

wooden steps

Humpback Rock

YOUR ADVENTURE

Adventurers, are you ready for a challenge? Today you are going to climb a massive greenstone outcrop near the peak of Humpback Mountain in the Blue Ridge Mountains, on the historical homelands of the Monacan, Shawnee, and Manahoac. This rocky summit is unique for an area where most mountain peaks are heavily vegetated. Begin on the wide packed earth

To the north you can see Shenandoah National Park, to the east farmland, and to the southwest the woods and ridges of George Washington National Forest →

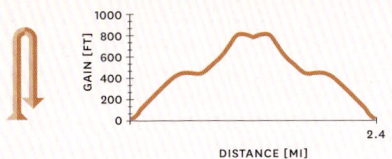

GAIN [FT]

1000
800
600
400
200
0

2.4

DISTANCE [MI]

LENGTH 2.4 miles out and back

ELEVATION GAIN 817 ft.

HIKE TIME + EXPLORE 1.5 hours

DIFFICULTY Challenging—packed-earth path, but a lot of elevation gain

SEASON Year-round; best in fall for foliage.

GET THERE Take the Blue Ridge Parkway south from I-64 for 6 miles and turn left into Humpback Rocks Recreation Area parking lot. Trailhead is at the far end.

Google Maps: bit.ly/timberhumpbackrocks

RESTROOM None

FEE None

TREAT YOURSELF Grab some pulled-pork barbecue sandwiches and mac and cheese at Paulie's Pig Out in Afton.

Blue Ridge Parkway National Park Service
(828) 348-3400
Facebook @BlueRidgeNPS

of the blue-blazed trail that immediately starts ascending. There are many benches along the path for power-up stops as needed. As you climb the mountain, the path will become rocky and covered in roots, and you will occasionally also have to scramble over rocks. When you reach a long set of wood steps, you'll know you've almost made it! At the top, turn left and pass a huge pile of rocks to arrive at Humpback Rocks proper. You've gained 800 feet of elevation in just a little over a mile of hiking! The summit rewards all of your hard work with a 360-degree view of the surrounding terrain from 3,080 feet. This very landmark guided wagon trains through this area in the 1840s. Enjoy the amazing scenery and catch your breath before retracing your steps back down to the trailhead.

SCAVENGER HUNT

Black bear

There are black bears living in the Blue Ridge Mountains, but they are quite shy. As long as you make noise along the path, you are unlikely to encounter one. If you do meet a bear on the trail, it is recommended that you maintain eye contact while backing away slowly. Never run away or try to approach one—black bears weigh 150 to 300 pounds and are able to run up to 30 miles per hour.

Ursus americanus scat reveals what the bear ate

Jack-in-the-Pulpit

During spring, look for a large, striped, hooded green-and-purple flower that blooms on a stalk the same height as the leaves. In fall, the flower produces a cluster of red berries. Put your arms over your head in the same way the flower arches—why do you think it's formed that way?

The berries, foliage, and roots of *Arisaema triphyllum* are poisonous to humans

Northern short-tailed shrew

These shrews are about the size of a meadow mouse, and their ears are almost completely hidden by their fur. They are active year round, both during the day and night. They build their nests under rocks and logs and create complex runways leading to and from these safe spots.

Blarina brevicauda are small and hard to spot

Whitewash lichen

Many of the greenstone rock formations on the summit are decorated with what appears to be a white or silver paint. This is a crustose lichen, which gets the food it needs to survive directly from the air—so it has no need for roots and can grow almost anywhere. Fun fact: 6 to 8 percent of Earth's land surface is covered by lichen! If *you* could live anywhere, where would it be?

Phlyctis argena provides a food source for some animals

Blackhaw

Keep your eye out for this shrub's stiff, spreading branches that form an irregular crown near the top. It blooms from April to May with numerous small white flower clusters. Then from September to October it makes bluish-black berries on long red stalks. Look closely—how many petals do each of the flowers have?

Viburnum prunifolium fruit is a favorite snack of white-tailed deer

29

NAVIGATE YOUR WAY ALONG CRABTREE FALLS

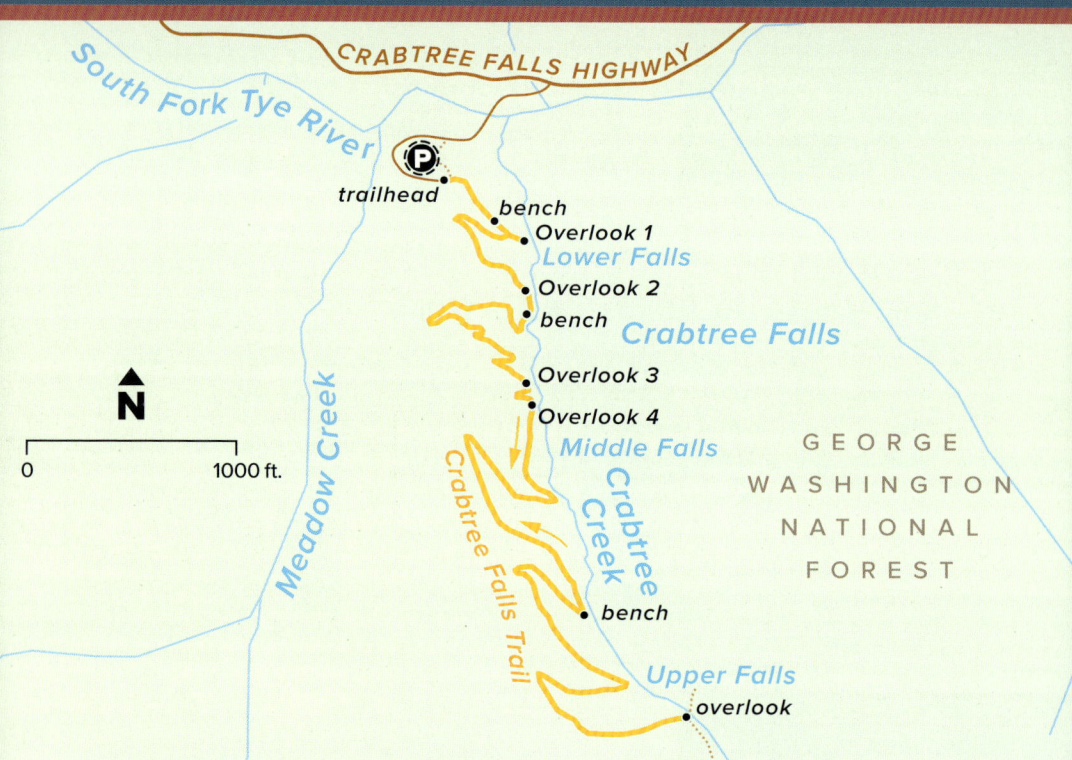

YOUR ADVENTURE

Adventurers, today we will climb over 1,000 feet of elevation to see the waterfall with the highest vertical drop east of the Mississippi River. We'll travel through the historical homelands of the Monacan, Shawnee, and Occaneechi. The falls is named after William Crabtree, who settled in this area in 1777. The first overlook is just a few hundred feet from the parking

View of Crabtree Falls from the trail →

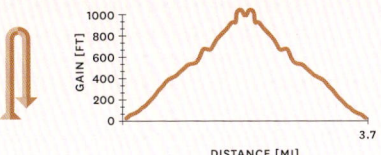

GAIN [FT]

1000
800
600
400
200
0

3.7

DISTANCE [MI]

LENGTH 3.7 miles out and back

ELEVATION GAIN 1,086 ft.

HIKE TIME + EXPLORE 2.5 hours

DIFFICULTY Challenging—a longer trek on a packed-earth path with high elevation gain

SEASON Year-round; best during fall foliage.

GET THERE From milepost 27 on the Blue Ridge Parkway, take VA-56 east for 6.6 miles and follow the signs to Crabtree Falls to the parking lot.

Google Maps: bit.ly/timbercrabtreefallsva

RESTROOM At trailhead

FEE $3 per vehicle

TREAT YOURSELF Grab some pre-hike snacks at Montebello Country Store, a couple miles east on VA-56.

Blue Ridge Parkway, George Washington National Forest
(434) 263-7015, (540) 291-2188
Facebook @BlueRidgeNPS

lot, along a paved trail. Take it if you like, then come back to the paved path and take a right to follow the Crabtree Falls Trail, a packed-earth but slightly rocky trail. Continue along the trail, passing another overlook over the lower section of the falls. Wind your way along the trail's inclines and switchbacks until you reach a third overlook for the top of the lower falls. Next, arrive at the base of the middle falls, a single drop of about 90 feet. Wind up the mountain until you reach the base of the upper falls and a fourth overlook. This is a strenuous hike, so power up on benches at the overlooks and vistas over the Tye River Valley. At the top, cross a bridge and enjoy amazing views from the summit and surrounding area, called Crabtree Meadows. When ready, retrace your steps back down. Want more? Camp at the Crabtree Falls Campground afterward.

SCAVENGER HUNT

Pear-shaped puffball

Can you spot these mushrooms? They grow in large clusters on decaying wood from July to November. While the outside is yellow to brown, the inside is pure white, like a marshmallow. How many mushrooms can you count on one log?

Apioperdon pyriforme (*pyriforme* is Greek for pear-shaped)

Wood fern

Did you know ferns are among the oldest plants on Earth, first developing hundreds of millions of years ago? Wood ferns like to live in forests, fields, and wet areas and thrive in moist, rich, well-drained soil. They can even grow on rock surfaces in moist, shady woods. Look underneath a frond to find their spores, which help them reproduce.

Genus *Dryopteris* on top of a boulder and steps

Mantleslug

This is a species of mollusk. It got its name because the mantle (the outer wall of the body) is unusually large and covers the entire dorsal (top) surface. They consume fungus and can often be found beneath loose bark on downed trees after it rains. Gently peek under some logs or branches to see if you can spot one!

Philomycus has smooth, shiny skin

Crabtree Falls

This falls is commonly referred to as the tallest waterfall in the East, but that is not really accurate, since it is actually a *series* of smaller waterfalls. There are three sections—can you spot them all? The lowest section is the tallest and has many drops; the middle section is a single drop through a crevice; and the upper features the largest single drop, over a massive 60-foot cliff.

Five major cascades and some smaller ones fall a total distance of 1,200 feet

Cemetery

Betsy and Achilles Fitzgerald raised ten children at Crabtree Falls. They lived in a one-room log cabin several hundred yards east of where these tombstones are located. The trail you are hiking takes you through the same areas where the Fitzgerald family once lived and worked. What chores would you need to do each day if you lived in a small cabin in the woods?

Pioneer graves—can you read the inscriptions?

MEANDER ALONG BLACKWATER CREEK

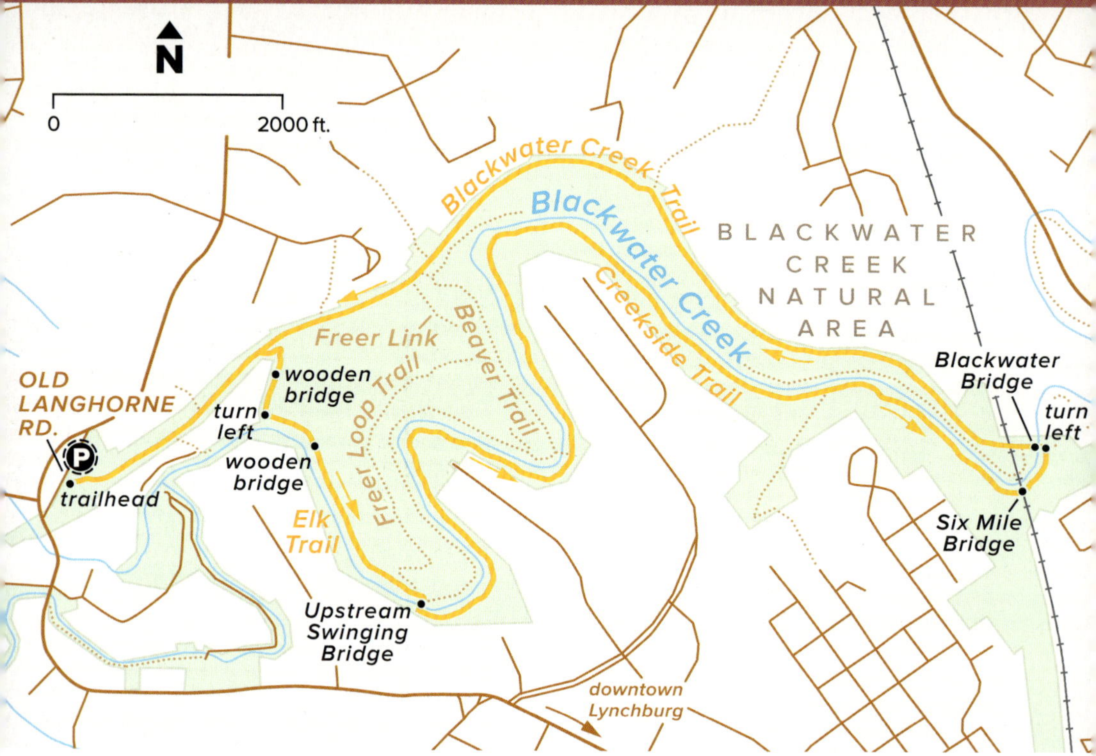

N

0   2000 ft.

Blackwater Creek Trail

Blackwater Creek

Creekside Trail

Beaver Trail

Freer Link

Freer Loop Trail

BLACKWATER CREEK NATURAL AREA

OLD LANGHORNE RD.

• wooden bridge

turn left

wooden bridge

Elk Trail

• trailhead

Upstream Swinging Bridge

Blackwater Bridge

turn left

Six Mile Bridge

downtown Lynchburg

YOUR ADVENTURE

Adventurers, today we will meander along the winding Blackwater Creek, through a forest, over a suspension bridge, and under an old railroad bridge on the historical homelands of the Monacan and Occaneechi. Begin by walking past the Awareness Garden (a special garden for those whose lives have been affected by cancer) on the flat, paved Blackwater Creek Trail, and

The railroad bridge above the trail →

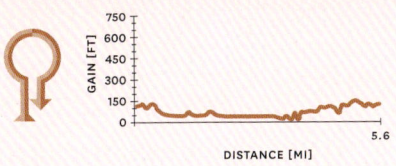

GAIN [FT]

750
600
450
300
150
0

5.6

DISTANCE [MI]

LENGTH 5.6-mile lollipop loop

ELEVATION GAIN 279 ft.

HIKE TIME + EXPLORE 2.5 hours

DIFFICULTY Moderate—a longer hike on packed-earth and paved paths with mild elevation

SEASON Year-round; best in fall for foliage.

GET THERE Take Langhorne Road in Lynchburg to where it intersects with Old Langhorne Road. The Awareness Garden parking lot is on the east side of the road, and the trailhead is at the far end.

Google Maps: bit.ly/timberblackwatercreek

RESTROOM At trailhead

FEE None

TREAT YOURSELF Cookie skillets await you at Rookie's, just a few minutes north on Norfolk Avenue.

Blackwater Creek Natural Area
(434) 455-5858
Facebook @lynchburgparks

soon turn right onto the packed-earth Elk Trail. Go over a small wooden bridge, turn left for the Creekside Trail, and go over the Upstream Swinging Bridge. Hike past a bend in the woods along the side of the creek, crossing a few rock scrambles; you will see the Downstream Bridge on the left. Continue winding through the woods, passing under a railroad bridge overhead before arriving at Six Mile Bridge and then Blackwater Bridge. Turn left to cross over the bridge. After exploring and having a power-up stop, follow Blackwater Creek Trail all the way back to the trailhead.

SCAVENGER HUNT

Upstream Swinging Bridge

This long, swinging suspension bridge sits high over Blackwater Creek. Don't be nervous—we know this bridge is tough because it was the only bridge in the park to survive a 2018 flood! In fact, three other bridges that were destroyed during the flood are being rebuilt and modeled after the design of this bridge.

Do you dare walk across this swinging suspension bridge?

Inky cap

Look for these mushrooms—they start off a whitish-cream color and darken as they age. Over time, their caps go from being bell-shaped to flat. Then their flesh begins to ooze into a black goo that, amazingly, can be used as ink for writing! Would you ever write with ink from a mushroom?

Coprinus atramentarius grows on wood

Sycamore tree

Look up on this trail and you might be able to spot a sycamore tree—the largest species of deciduous tree in the eastern United States. The bark has a camouflage pattern consisting of a grayish-brown outer bark that peels off in patches to expose the light-gray-to-white wood underneath. Rip a piece of paper out of your nature journal, hold it over the bark, and use your pen or pencil to make a rubbing.

Identify *Platanus occidentalis* by its seed balls that fall to the ground in spring

Six Mile Bridge

You will get to walk under the Norfolk Southern Six Mile Bridge No. 58, also known as the Six Mile Bridge. This is a historical Pratt truss railroad bridge that was originally constructed around 1853. This massive structure is 1,860 feet long and 150 feet high and was part of the Norfolk Southern Railroad. Would you want to ride a train across this high bridge?

Trestle bridge above part of the trail

Black rat

Look closely in the woods and you might be able to spot this mammal with relatively large ears and a tail that is nearly always longer than its body. Since the black rat is an agile climber, it often lives in high places, such as trees in forested areas. It mostly feeds on fruit, grain, cereals, and other vegetation.

Rattus rattus has an average lifespan of one year

31

MAKE YOUR WAY AROUND BEAR CREEK LAKE

YOUR ADVENTURE

Adventurers, today we will hike around a man-made lake in Cumberland State Forest on the historical homelands of the Occaneechi and Monacan. You will walk along the water and through the forest for much of the hike, giving you the opportunity to see many species of birds and wildlife. Consider bringing your bathing suit and taking a dip at the designated beach

View of Bear Creek Lake from the trail →

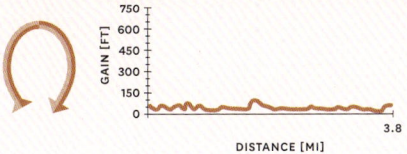

GAIN [FT]

750
600
450
300
150
0

3.8

DISTANCE [MI]

LENGTH 3.8-mile loop

ELEVATION GAIN 174 ft.

HIKE TIME + EXPLORE 2 hours

DIFFICULTY Moderate—packed-earth path and mild elevation, but a longer hike

SEASON Year-round; best in summer for swimming at the beach.

GET THERE From US-60 in Cumberland, take Forest View Road north 3.3 miles and turn right on Oak Hill Road. After 0.9 miles, turn right on Bear Creek Lake Road. Park at the beach parking lot.

Google Maps: bit.ly/timberbearcreeklaketrail

RESTROOM At the beach

FEE $7 per vehicle

TREAT YOURSELF Enjoy a dragon fruit lemonade and a scone from the Cumberland Coffee Co., just off US-60 on Stony Point Road.

Bear Creek Lake State Park
(804) 492-4410
Facebook @vaspbearcreeklake

area by the trailhead, or cast a fishing line—the lake is filled with many types of fish. There are also two playgrounds along the path. Start on the Channel Cat Loop by the beach area, heading south. Trek on wood stairs, go over a small wood bridge, and turn right on the Lakeside Connector Trail. Hike until you reach the Kestrel Trail. Turn right to stay on the Lakeside Connector Trail and cross a long wood bridge over several streams. Turn right as you continue to loop around the lake. At the intersection with a dirt road, turn right on the road, then quickly turn right to stay on the Lakeside Trail. Scramble over some rocks before turning right at the Lost Barr Loop and walk across two small wooden bridges. Next, leave the trail, turn right, and walk in the grass along Oak Hill Road—be sure to keep little explorers close by. Take the next right on Bear Creek Lake Road, head into the parking lot, and take the Channel Cat Loop again. Walk over three more small wood bridges, turn right, and you will arrive back at the trailhead. Reward your feet at the end by soaking them in the lake! Happy here? Consider camping at one of the state park's campsites.

SCAVENGER HUNT

Beaver

Have you heard the phrase "busy as a beaver"? Beavers are very busy at night—one beaver alone can chew through an 8-foot-thick tree trunk in just 5 minutes! You might not spot a live beaver on your hike, but look for evidence of them—such as tree trunks like this.

Tree trunks chewed by *Castor canadensis*

Fly agaric mushroom

This is of the most recognizable fungi in the world, due to its distinctive red cap and white stalk. They are usually found growing beneath pines, spruces, or birch trees between late summer and early winter. They are toxic for humans to eat, but some animals, like red squirrels and slugs, can eat them.

Amanita muscaria is a gilled mushroom

Hairy woodpecker

Try to spot this small but powerful bird foraging along trunks and the main branches of large trees. The hairy woodpecker has a long, almost thorn-like bill that it uses to tear off bark and drill holes in search of insects. Its search creates a wavy pattern—can you see traces of this bird's presence on any nearby trees?

Dryobates villosus makes smaller holes than larger species of woodpeckers

Christmas fern

Can you find a frond of one of these ferns? The frond has a stalk (like a stem), and its little fingerlike leaves are called pinnae. They grow opposite each other along the stem. Since they can be found all year long, including in winter, they are often used for decorating holiday wreaths, hence the name "Christmas fern." Have you ever decorated your home for the holidays with this fern?

Polystichum acrostichoides

32

LOOP BEAVER LAKE IN POCAHONTAS STATE PARK

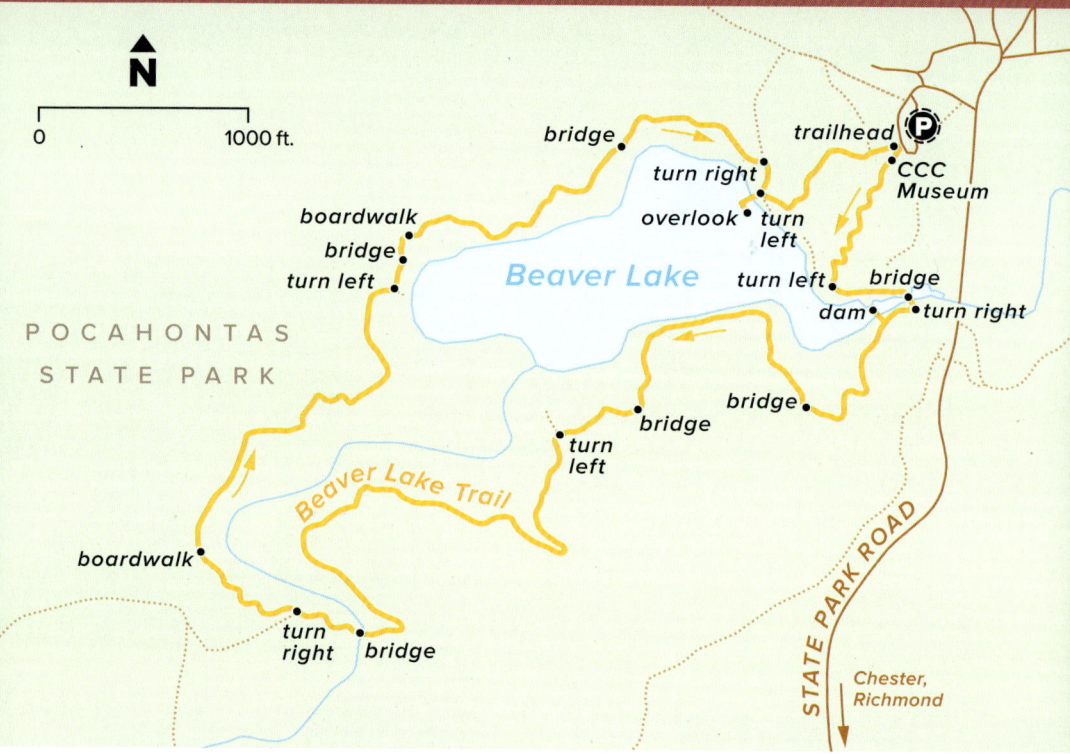

N

0   1000 ft.

bridge

turn right

trailhead

P

CCC Museum

boardwalk

bridge

turn left

overlook

turn left

Beaver Lake

turn left

bridge

dam

turn right

POCAHONTAS STATE PARK

bridge

bridge

turn left

Beaver Lake Trail

boardwalk

turn right

bridge

STATE PARK ROAD

Chester, Richmond

YOUR ADVENTURE

Adventurers, get ready to loop around a beautiful lake in Virginia's largest state park. You'll hike under large trees while crossing bridges and board-walks, getting close-up views of Beaver Lake. Begin on the paved path that starts to the left of the trail map kiosk. Pass the Civilian Conservation Corps (CCC) building on the left; today it houses a museum dedicated to the

Beaver Lake glistens in the sunlight →

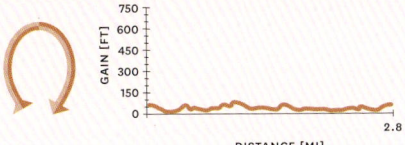

LENGTH 2.8-mile loop

ELEVATION GAIN 177 ft.

HIKE TIME + EXPLORE 1.5 hours

DIFFICULTY Moderate—combination of wide packed-earth and paved paths with mild elevation

SEASON Year-round; best in spring for blooms.

GET THERE From I-95 in Richmond, take VA-288 North for 6 miles and exit onto VA-10 / Iron Bridge Road. In 1.5 miles, turn right onto State Route 655 / Beach Road and follow 4 miles to turn right onto State Park Road. After 2 miles, turn left for parking at Beaver Lake Trailhead.

Google Maps: bit.ly/timberbeaverlake

RESTROOM At visitor center

FEE $7 per vehicle on weekdays; $10 weekends

TREAT YOURSELF Try a famous handcrafted s'mores bar from River City Chocolate, off Hull Street Road in Midlothian.

Pocahontas State Park
(804) 796-4255
Facebook @vasppocahontas

Depression-era workers who helped build the state park system. Pass the museum, then turn left onto the cobalt blue–blazed Beaver Lake Trail. Soon you'll see a large dam. Take the bridge over Beaver Lake. On the other side, turn right and reach a bench. This is a beautiful place to power up as you watch water rushing over the dam. Continue winding around the lake; pass over two wooden bridges before turning left and arriving at another bench. After more twists and turns, cross a bridge, then turn right at the fork. Pass over a long boardwalk. At the next fork, turn left and cross a wooden bridge, then hike along a boardwalk. Little explorers might especially like getting an up-close view of the lily pads on water's surface. Stay left over the next boardwalk, cross another bridge, then turn right—try birdwatching at this lookout! Take one more left turn, and you'll arrive back at the trailhead, completing your loop around the entire lake. There are many other activities at this park, including fishing, swimming, and camping, so consider staying for the whole weekend.

SCAVENGER HUNT

Beaver Lake Dam

This is a 17-foot-high gravity dam built for recreational purposes. Beaver Lake is part of the Swift Creek Reservoir system, and the water that spills over the dam eventually flows into the James River—Virginia's largest river. This is a beautiful place for a power-up. Take out your nature journal and sketch this beautiful dam and waterfall, or write down words to describe the sounds the water makes.

The dam was built in the 1930s

Eagle nest

Look for eagles' nests in the trees by the lake. Nesting season happens over six months each year—they may start nesting as early as late January and go until August. Eagles actually use the same nest year after year. The best time to spy eagle nests is in spring, before trees fill in with leaves. Use binoculars for a closer look!

Eagle nests can weigh 1,000–2,000 pounds

Water lily

Beaver Lake covers 24 acres, and a lot of that is vegetated with water lilies. They act like a filter, purifying the water where they float. This helps other aquatic plants that live nearby. They also provide shade and hiding spaces for fish in the lake. Can you spot any animals or other plants on, under, or next to a water lily?

***Nymphaeaceae* can grow year round on Beaver Lake**

Little heartleaf

Do you smell something fragrant? These plants have evergreen, heart-shaped leaves that grow only 4 inches off the ground and emit a scent when crushed. Their uniquely shaped flowers, which appear in early spring, resemble little brown jugs and are often buried under the leaves. Trace a heart-shaped leaf in your nature journal to make a valentine for your hiking buddy!

***Hexastylis minor* is sometimes called wild ginger**

33

WIND AROUND TASKINAS CREEK

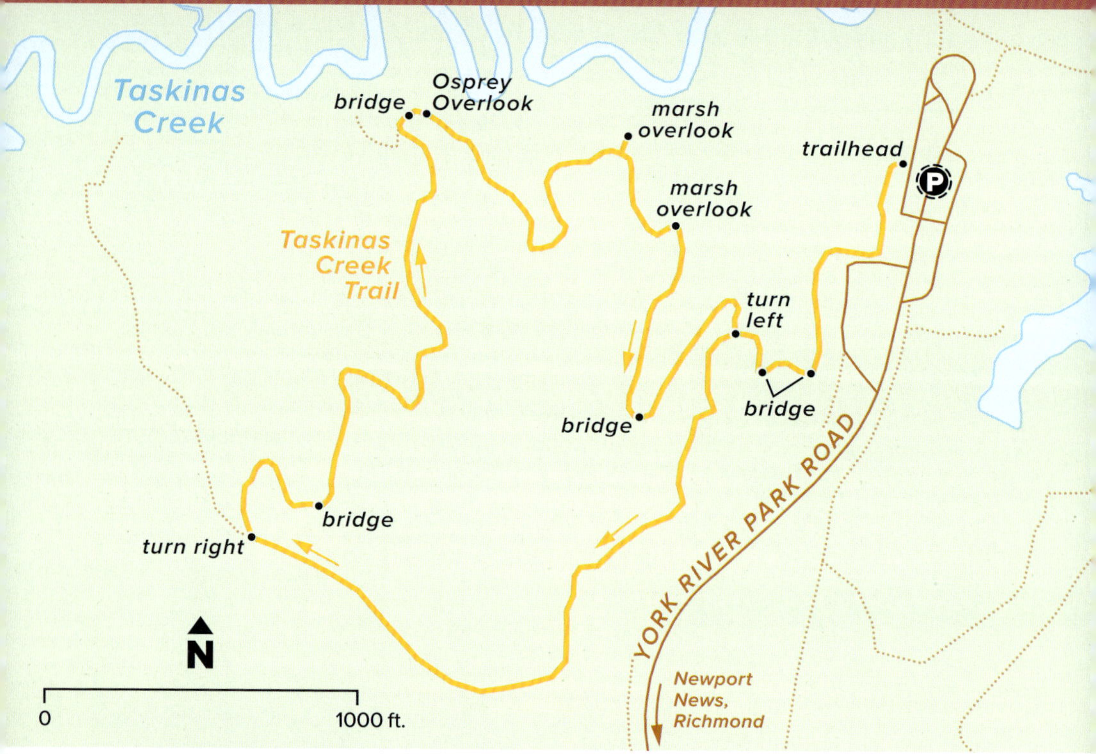

Taskinas Creek

bridge

Osprey Overlook

marsh overlook

trailhead

marsh overlook

Taskinas Creek Trail

turn left

bridge

bridge

bridge

turn right

N

0   1000 ft.

YORK RIVER PARK ROAD

Newport News, Richmond

YOUR ADVENTURE

Adventurers, welcome to the historical homelands of the Kiskiack. Taskinas Creek gets its name from their language, also known as Virginia Algonquin. This creek provided access to the York River, which led to the town Werowocomoco—the seat of power in the Chesapeake region. Chief Powhatan and his daughter Pocahontas lived in this area over four hundred

A view of the marshlands from the trail →

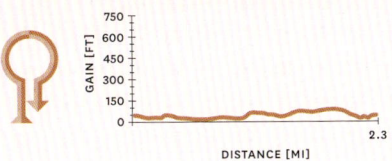

LENGTH 2.3-mile lollipop loop

ELEVATION GAIN 171 ft.

HIKE TIME + EXPLORE 1.5 hour

DIFFICULTY Moderate—combination of packed-earth and sand paths and boardwalks with mild elevation

SEASON Year-round. Best mid-spring through early fall for blue herons, red-winged blackbirds, and ospreys. Bald eagles nest here in January and February.

GET THERE From Richmond, take I-64 east to Exit 231-B for Route 607 toward Croaker. In 0.8 miles, turn right onto Moss Side Lane, then right again onto Riverview Road. Turn left onto York River Park Road and follow 2 miles to the parking lot.

Google Maps: bit.ly/timberyorkriver

RESTROOM At parking lot

FEE $5 per vehicle

TREAT YOURSELF Pick up some cocoa bombs at the Sipping Flea on Route 60.

York River State Park
(757) 566-3036
Facebook @vaspyorkriver

years ago. The red-blazed Taskinas Creek Trail begins across the parking lot as a short, paved walkway that quickly turns into a narrow, packed-earth path. Wind your way parallel to the creek and over two small wooden bridges. Turn left at the fork (you'll return on the other path) and walk until you reach a right turn. Go over another small wooden bridge and up stone steps. Continue by crossing another small wooden bridge before arriving at Osprey Overlook. Take your time here to see if you can spot any blue herons or ospreys in the marshland. Pass over another set of wood steps before arriving at two more overlooks, which provide views of the beautiful meadows below. Another small wooden bridge and more wood steps lead to a bench that's great for power-ups. Continue to wind around the marsh through an oak and hickory forest, then turn left to return to the original trail; retrace it to the trailhead. When you have completed the loop, if you have the energy, play at one of the two playgrounds.

SCAVENGER HUNT

Crown gall

Look up at some of the trees along the trail—do you notice knobby swellings (galls) on their trunks? This is called a crown gall, and it is caused by a bacterial disease of the stems and roots. The galls start out cream- or green-colored, then later turn brown or black. Take a few minutes to sketch or trace one in your nature journal.

Galls can grow to several centimeters in diameter

Leaves

See how many differently colored and shaped leaves you can find. Take pictures of them and use an app to help you identify the different trees they came from.

Colorful leaves found along the trail

Taskinas Creek

Taskinas Creek ranges from 8 to 15 feet deep during high tide and is about 60 feet wide. Animals you might see in or around the creek are muskrats, northern water snakes, snapping turtles, a variety of crabs, and fish (which sometimes jump out of the water!). Fiddler crabs dominate at low tide during warmer months. Do you see any animals or their tracks?

Taskinas Creek is a small tributary of the York River

Pine trees

As you hike through the forested part of the trail, you will be walking under a variety of pine trees. Depending on the time of year you visit, you may also see pine cones of different sizes and shapes. Gather a few from the ground and compare and contrast them. When you are done, please return them—we always want to leave nature the way we found it!

These belong to a family of plants from prehistoric times

Marsh overlook

These scenic overlooks are great spots to look for wildlife. Estuaries, along with the land and water that surround them, are a place of transition from land to sea and from freshwater to saltwater. Why do you think these areas are so important for the environment?

One of the scenic overlooks along the trail

34

BRAVE THE BOARDWALKS AT FIRST LANDING STATE PARK

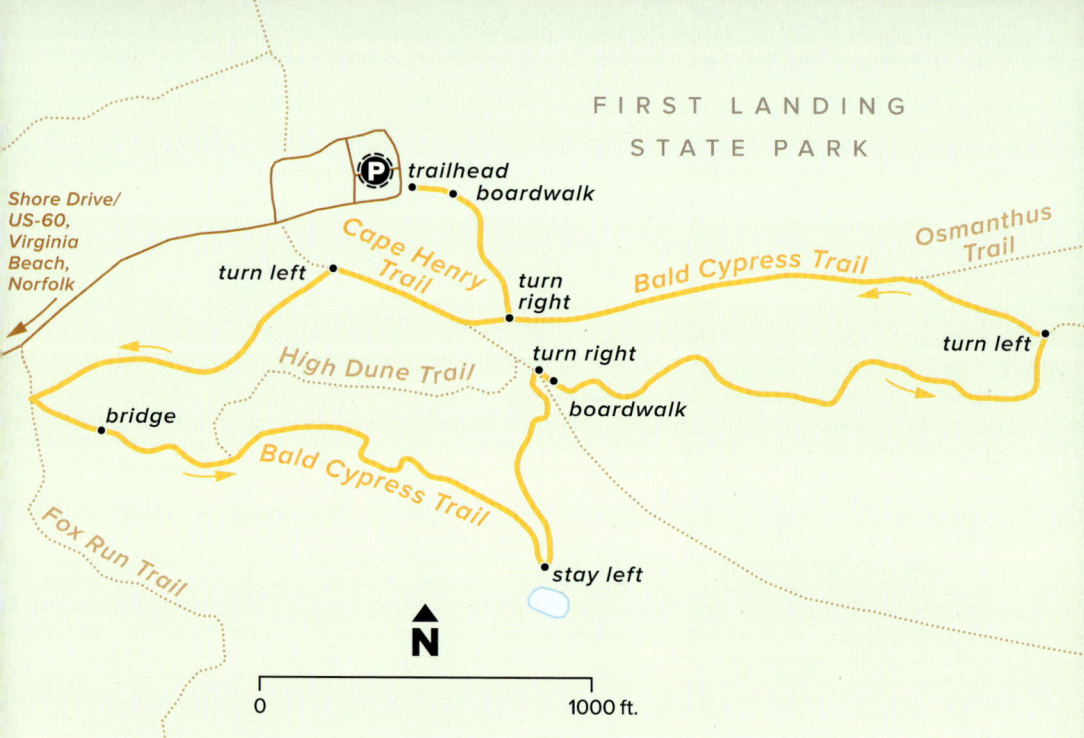

FIRST LANDING STATE PARK

Shore Drive/ US-60, Virginia Beach, Norfolk

trailhead
boardwalk
Cape Henry Trail
turn left
turn right
Bald Cypress Trail
Osmanthus Trail
turn right
turn left
High Dune Trail
boardwalk
bridge
Bald Cypress Trail
Fox Run Trail
stay left
N
0   1000 ft.

YOUR ADVENTURE

Adventurers, welcome to a swamp filled with mysterious bald cypress trees and knees! Today, you'll be near the historical homelands of the Lumbee and Chesapeake. The adventure begins just to the right of the trail center. Take the Bald Cypress Trail over a wooden bridge and onto a boardwalk across a freshwater cypress swamp. Turn right at the fork, onto the Cape

This area is known for the many bald cypress trees growing in the swamp →

GAIN [FT]

750
600
450
300
150
0

1.8

DISTANCE [MI]

LENGTH 1.8-mile lollipop loop

ELEVATION GAIN 30 ft.

HIKE TIME + EXPLORE 1 hour

DIFFICULTY Easy—flat, packed-earth and sand path, wooden bridges and boardwalks

SEASON Year-round; best in spring to avoid summer bugs.

GET THERE From I-64 in Virginia Beach, take US-13 / Northampton Boulevard toward Bridge-Tunnel / Chesapeake Bay 4.2 miles to US-60 East / Shore Drive. In 4.5 miles turn right onto Cypress Swamp Drive. Parking lot is by the trail center.

Google Maps: bit.ly/timberfirstlanding

RESTROOM At the trail center near the trailhead

FEE From April to October, $7 per vehicle on weekdays, $10 weekends; November to March, $7 daily

TREAT YOURSELF Enjoy some popcorn shrimp and Chesapeake crab dip at Hot Tuna, just down the road on Shore Drive.

First Landing State Park
(757) 412-2300
Facebook @vaspfirstlanding

Henry Trail, and then turn left onto the Bald Cypress Trail again. As you follow the path, admire the abundant bald cypress trees growing in the swamp. At the end of the boardwalk, cross the bridge and begin hiking on a packed-earth and sand path. Veer right, passing the High Dune Trail, and cross over a wooden bridge, then veer left to stay on the trail. At the 1-mile mark, you will arrive at a junction of trails. Stay straight on the Bald Cypress Trail, which will require you to go through a gate and turn right to cross over the Cape Henry Trail and then through another gate to return to the trail. After you cross the gated area, you'll find yourself back on a boardwalk that takes you over the water. Continue to wind around the path, but when you reach the Osmanthus Trail, turn left onto the Bald Cypress Trail again, then right to return to the original path and trailhead. Consider staying overnight at the state park campground so you can explore more amazing trails.

SCAVENGER HUNT

Cypress knee

See the knobby growths under the bald cypress trees? These "knees" are woody growths projecting up from the roots of bald cypress trees above the water line. Their exact function is not known, but some hypothesize that they might help the tree's roots breathe, assist in anchoring the tree in the soft, muddy soil, or create a barrier to catch sediment and reduce erosion. Which do you think seems right?

Taxodium distichum doesn't produce knees in dry climates

Eastern cottontail rabbit

Do you like to play tag? This mammal would be great at tag because it is able to hop up to 18 mph and zigs and zags in different directions to make it harder for predators to catch it. Play a game of bunny tag with your hiking mates—instead of running, hop!

Sylvilagus floridanus can twitch its nose 20 to 120 times a minute

Wild blueberry

Look for this small shrub's fruits from late July to early September. Wild blueberries are generally much smaller in size than cultivated blueberries you see in the grocery store. They also vary in color from various shades of blue to almost black. The shrub's lance-shaped leaves grow in an alternate pattern and turn red in fall.

Vaccinium angustifolium

Spanish moss

What's in a name, anyway? Spanish moss is not actually moss, and it's not from Spain! It's actually a bromeliad, a plant from the same family as pineapples! Indigenous peoples of this area call this plant *Itla-okla*, which means "tree hair." What name would you give this plant?

Tillandsia usneoides

35

GALLOP WITH FERAL PONIES ON CHINCOTEAGUE ISLAND

CHINCOTEAGUE
NATIONAL
WILDLIFE
REFUGE

N

VA-175, Chincoteague

0   1000 ft.

BEACH ROAD

• marsh viewpoint

Woodlawn Trail

Bivalve Trail

• beach

P

• trailhead

turn right

Tom's Cove

YOUR ADVENTURE

Adventurers, today you are headed to an island where wild ponies roam free! Chincoteague National Wildlife Refuge includes more than 14,000 acres of beach, dunes, marsh, and maritime forest on the historical homelands of the Chincoteague and Pocomoke-Assateague. Begin by turning right on the Woodland Trail, then follow a loop around the island's pine forest. Pass a

View of Tom's Cove →

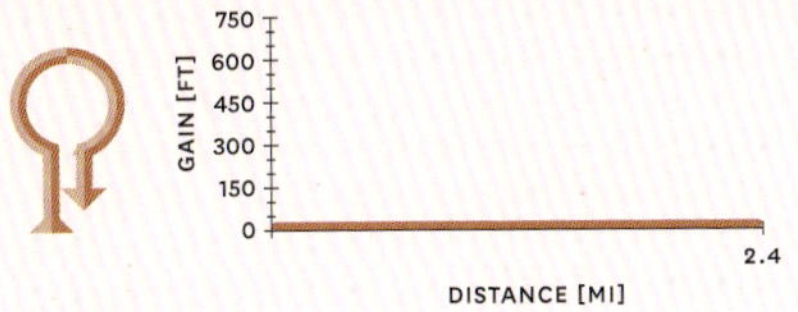

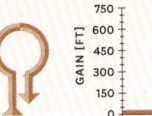

GAIN [FT]

750
600
450
300
150
0

2.4

DISTANCE [MI]

LENGTH 2.4-mile lollipop loop

ELEVATION GAIN 16 ft.

HIKE TIME + EXPLORE 1 hour

DIFFICULTY Easy—flat; a combination of paved path and boardwalk

SEASON Year-round; best in spring for shorebirds. Summer can be crowded and buggy.

GET THERE From Wattsville, take VA-175 / Chincoteague Road east until it becomes, first, Maddox Blvd., then, Beach Road. Follow signs for Woodland Trail parking.

Google Maps: bit.ly/timberchincoteague

RESTROOM At trailhead

FEE $10 per vehicle; free for pedestrians and cyclists

TREAT YOURSELF Head back up Maddox Blvd. to BYOC (Build Your Own Cookie) for one of their famous homemade sundaes.

Chincoteague National Wildlife Refuge
(757) 336-6122
Facebook @ChincoteagueNWR

bench, then turn right onto a boardwalk to an overlook of the salt marsh. Here you can admire the feral (wild) Chincoteague ponies who live here. Return to the trail and continue the loop around the island—with beautiful views all the way. Turn right onto the Bivalve Trail, which will lead you to a beach for a view of Tom's Cove. If you can linger, look for crabs, go clamming, or have a picnic here. Then retrace your steps back to the main path and turn right. Pass one more bench, then turn right to return to the trailhead. If you like, drive around the park to try and catch more glimpses of the beautiful feral ponies.

SCAVENGER HUNT

Feral Chincoteague ponies

While no one knows for certain how the feral ponies arrived at Chincoteague Island, one theory is that they are descendants of colonial horses brought to Assateague Island (the Maryland side of the island) in the seventeenth century by Eastern Shore planters when they could no longer let their livestock free roam elsewhere. Over generations, wild descendants of those small domestic horses have adapted to their environment. How many feral horses did you spot on your adventure today?

There are usually about 150 *Equus caballus* on Chincoteague Island

Soft-shell clam

This bivalve has two thin, chalky white oval shells that grow 3 to 4 inches long. If you see a coin-sized depression in the mud with water spurting out of a hole, you know there is a clam below! You might also find hard-shell or razor clams at Tom's Cove.

Mya arenaria can only move vertically

Marsh crab

This crustacean lives in burrows in the mud. All crabs have ten legs (two are claws, not used for walking), have a hard shell, and walk and swim sideways. Crabs have been around since the Jurassic Era, more than 200 million years

ago! Do a crab walk on the beach—hold your body off the ground with chest facing upward and knees bent, then move side to side.

Sesarma reticulatum at Tom's Cove

Common reeds

It's hard to miss these tall, slender plants along the trail. They grow 5 to 16 feet tall, with feathery flower clusters and stiff, smooth stems. The roots of this invasive species secrete a chemical that prevents other plants from growing nearby, and they grow so deep they are nearly impossible to pull out.

Phragmites australis along the trail

Piping plover

Try to spot these small shorebirds with sand-colored feathers on their backs and crown. They only breed in three geographic regions in North America, including the Atlantic Coast— lucky us! Due to habitat loss and human disturbance, they are classified as threatened under the Endangered Species Act. Can you think of one thing you could do to help this species?

Charadrius melodus eats insects, spiders, and crustaceans

36

MEANDER MOSSEY CREEK AT OCCONEECHEE STATE PARK

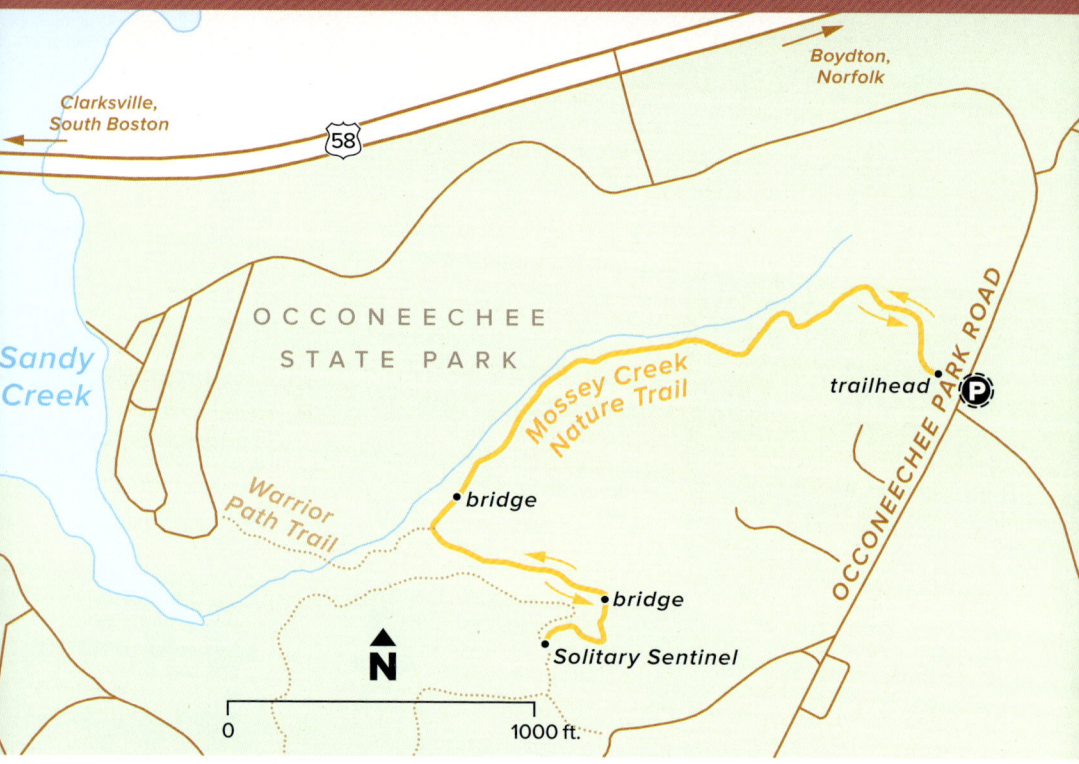

Boydton, Norfolk

Clarksville, South Boston

58

OCCONEECHEE STATE PARK

Sandy Creek

Mossey Creek Nature Trail

trailhead

OCCONEECHEE PARK ROAD

P

Warrior Path Trail

bridge

N

bridge

Solitary Sentinel

0   1000 ft.

YOUR ADVENTURE

Adventurers, welcome to Occoneechee State Park, on the shores of 48,000-acre Buggs Island Lake and the historical homeland of the Lumbee, Cheraw, Saponi, and Occaneechi. In 1839, William Townes built an impressive two-story, twenty-room mansion here, on his 3,000-acre tobacco plantation. It had at least three chimneys, along with horse stables,

Brick chimney ruins from the Occoneechee Plantation →

GAIN [FT]

750
600
450
300
150
0

1.4

DISTANCE [MI]

LENGTH 1.4 miles out and back

ELEVATION GAIN 112 ft.

HIKE TIME + EXPLORE 45 minutes

DIFFICULTY Easy—packed-earth trail; mild elevation gain

SEASON Year-round; best in spring for blooms.

GET THERE From US-58 in Clarksville, turn onto Occoneechee Park Road and follow 0.5 miles to the Mossy Creek Nature Trailhead on your right.

Google Maps: bit.ly/timbermosseycreek

RESTROOM None

FEE $7 per vehicle

TREAT YOURSELF Feast on some hot dogs and ice cream at the Cottage Barn just across the River in Clarksville.

Occoneechee State Park
(434) 374-2210
Facebook @vaspocconeechee

a smokehouse, servants quarters, and gardens. The house survived the Civil War, but burned down in 1898. Today you will begin on the blue-blazed Mossey Creek Trail. Walk through a forested area of ash, oak, sweet gum, and loblolly pine, then cross a wood bridge. Stay straight when the trail intersects with the Warrior Path Trail. Look up—can you spot birds in the trees? Walk along Mossey Creek and cross another wood bridge to reach the Solitary Sentinel, ruins from the plantation that once stood here. After taking in the history and powering up, retrace your steps back to the trailhead, staying right at the junction. To explore more of the park, stay overnight at the state park campground.

SCAVENGER HUNT

American sweetgum

"Sweetgum" refers to the brownish-yellow sap that leaks from the bark of these trees if they're injured. They have dark gray bark covered with scaly ridges and star-shaped leaves with five to seven lobes. Their fruit may be on the ground around you—do you see a spiny ball filled with seeds? Draw it in your nature journal to compare its shape with other trees' fruit, seeds, or nuts.

Liquidambar styraciflua can survive up to 400 years

Eastern gray squirrel

Look for this mammal out foraging for nuts and seeds. As winter approaches, they collect food and bury it in many locations. They hide more food than they will eat, so the buried nuts and seeds often sprout and begin to grow new trees the following spring—this makes squirrels important for seed dispersal and the survival of tree species.

Genus *Sciuridae* has an excellent sense of smell

Plantation ruins

Around 1839, William Townes moved to the Roanoke River and built his plantation here. It covered over 3,000 acres, including Occoneechee Island, and was practically a small town. You can still see some of the ruins of the main house and outbuildings. In 1865, at the end of the Civil War, the 160 enslaved people who were made to work here became legally free. What do you think it was like to live in this area over 180 years ago?

The old estate grew tobacco

Raccoon

Some of the most dexterous hands in nature belong to raccoons. In fact, the English word *rac-coon* comes from the Powhatan word *aroughcum*, which means "animal that scratches with its hands." Raccoons are very adaptable—some eat birds, insects, fruits, nuts, and seeds in the forests, but they also scavenge for food in human-populated areas at night and return to the woods during the day to sleep.

Procyon lotor is nocturnal, but you may see one during the day

Northern red oak

Look up and you might spot this deciduous tree with dark gray or brown bark and dark green leaves with seven to eleven sharp lobes. Their acorns are about an inch long with a reddish-brown cup on one end. Collect as many acorn caps as you can from the ground, cover your fingers with them, and have a puppet show with your hike mates.

Quercus rubra's fall leaf and acorn

37

DARE TO DESCEND TO DEVIL'S DEN

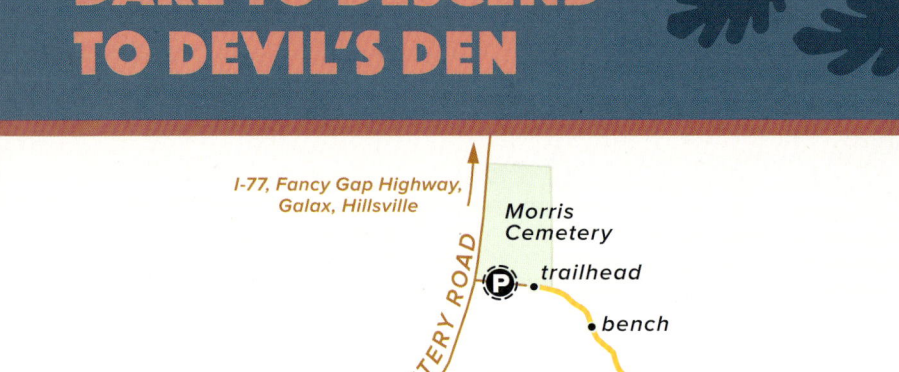

I-77, Fancy Gap Highway, Galax, Hillsville

Morris Cemetery

trailhead

bench

CEMETERY ROAD

Harris Mountain 2923ft.

bench

N

0   1000 ft.

bench   *Devil's Den*

YOUR ADVENTURE

Adventurers, grab your flashlights and get ready to hike to Devil's Den cave on the historical homelands of the Cheraw and Tutelo. This cave is millions of years old and is surrounded by almost 300 acres of hardwood forests and plateaus. Begin just past the Morris Cemetery and parking lot. The trail is narrow and steep at times as you descend through the forest. Please note

Devil's Den is a 600-million-year-old cave formation →

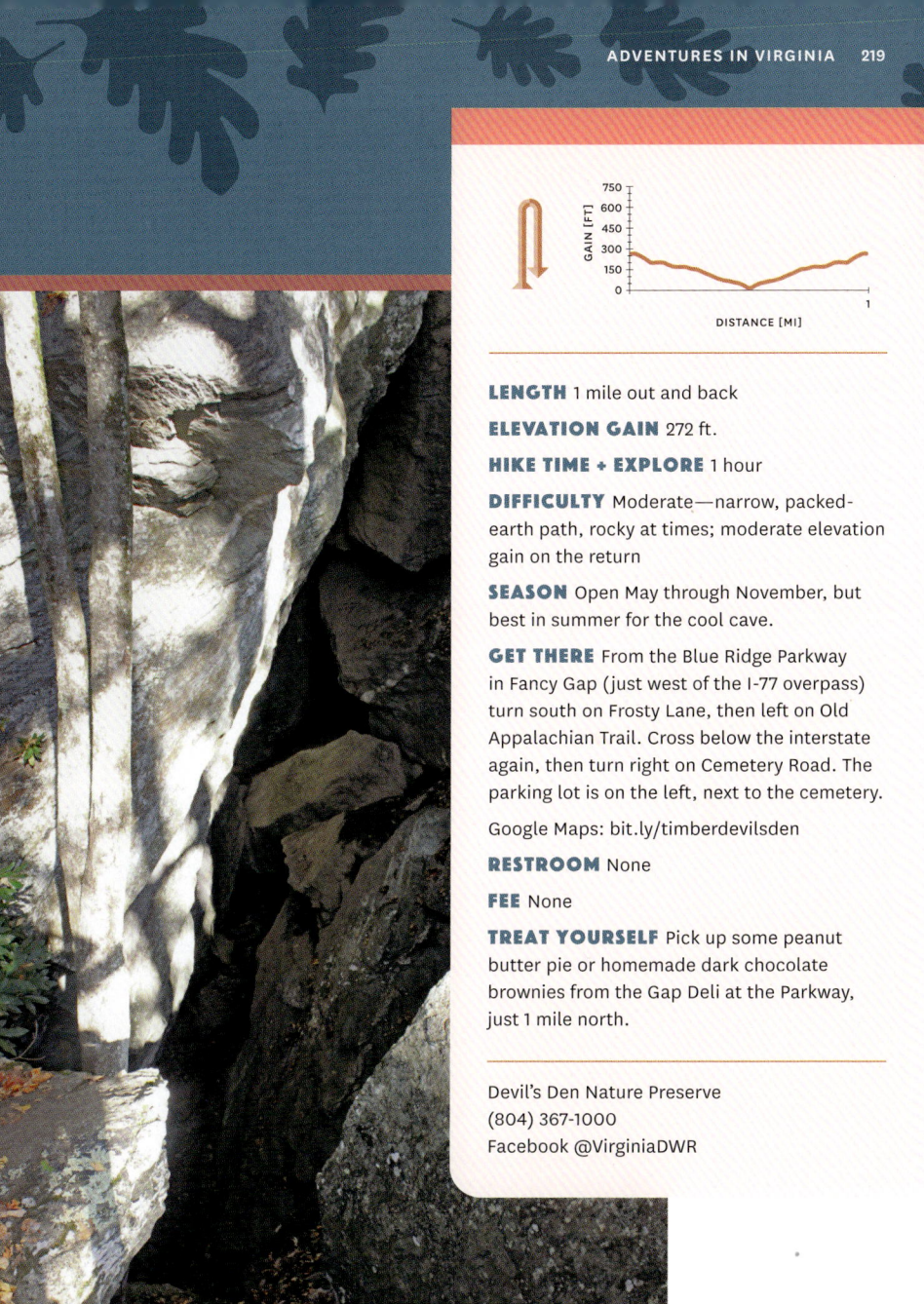

GAIN [FT]

750
600
450
300
150
0

DISTANCE [MI]

LENGTH 1 mile out and back

ELEVATION GAIN 272 ft.

HIKE TIME + EXPLORE 1 hour

DIFFICULTY Moderate—narrow, packed-earth path, rocky at times; moderate elevation gain on the return

SEASON Open May through November, but best in summer for the cool cave.

GET THERE From the Blue Ridge Parkway in Fancy Gap (just west of the I-77 overpass) turn south on Frosty Lane, then left on Old Appalachian Trail. Cross below the interstate again, then turn right on Cemetery Road. The parking lot is on the left, next to the cemetery.

Google Maps: bit.ly/timberdevilsden

RESTROOM None

FEE None

TREAT YOURSELF Pick up some peanut butter pie or homemade dark chocolate brownies from the Gap Deli at the Parkway, just 1 mile north.

Devil's Den Nature Preserve
(804) 367-1000
Facebook @VirginiaDWR

that while you are not walking right next to the edge, there is a significant drop-off to the left of the path—keep little explorers on the inside of the path. As you follow the arrows along the trail, pause and take in the views of the surrounding mountains and valleys, particularly the 2,923-foot-high Harris Mountain. As you near the cave, you will begin to see rock formations. A bench seems like it marks a dead end—go right, following the trail down through more rocks until you see the impressive cave. Some 40–50-foot-high rocks mark the entrance to Devil's Den. You can climb the rocks in front of the entry to the cave or walk around them to see what the cave looks like from above. Many little alcoves extend up and down for several hundred feet—explore as many as you like. You're allowed to go down into the cave, but don't enter the dark cave "rooms," as you might disturb wildlife living inside. When you're done exploring, retrace your steps back to the trailhead.

SCAVENGER HUNT

Devil's Den cave

The rocks of Devil's Den are 600 million years old; they formed many miles deep in the Earth and were pushed to the surface during the collision between North America and Africa. This is a "shelter cave," formed during a huge landslide on the mountainside. As a giant slab of rock slid down, it cracked apart to create the cave passages. Millions of years of erosion have now exposed them at the Earth's surface. The rocks are metamorphic schist and gneiss, which contain mica, pyrite, and veins of quartz. As you explore the cave, look for wrinkles and folds in the rock's metamorphic layering.

The cave rocks are part of the Appalachian Blue Ridge

Big brown bats

Look for these mammals flying around the area.
They are considered large for the genus, but still
only weigh about 1 ounce. They have brown or
glossy copper-colored fur, small, black, rounded
ears, and a broad nose. Would you like to live in
a cave?

Eptesicus fuscus can fly up to 40 mph

Common puffball

Can you spot these mushrooms, often found
in small groups or lines in grassy clearings?
They are a medium-sized puffball with a round,
off-white fruit body and a top covered in short
spiny bumps that can be easily rubbed off. When
mature, if the common puffball is compressed by raindrops or a passing
animal, it releases a smoke-like cloud of spores.

Lycoperdon perlatum, sometimes called a gem-studded puffball

Ruffed grouse

Did you hear something? While this bird's
grayish to reddish coloring camouflages it in
the woods, it's easy to hear, making a distinctive
drumming sound in spring. When you hear a
sound like an engine trying to start, you might
not realize it is coming from a bird. Can your
body make a noise like that?

Bonasa umbellus can digest toxic plants that many other
birds cannot eat

38

SCRAMBLE YOUR WAY TO STILES FALLS

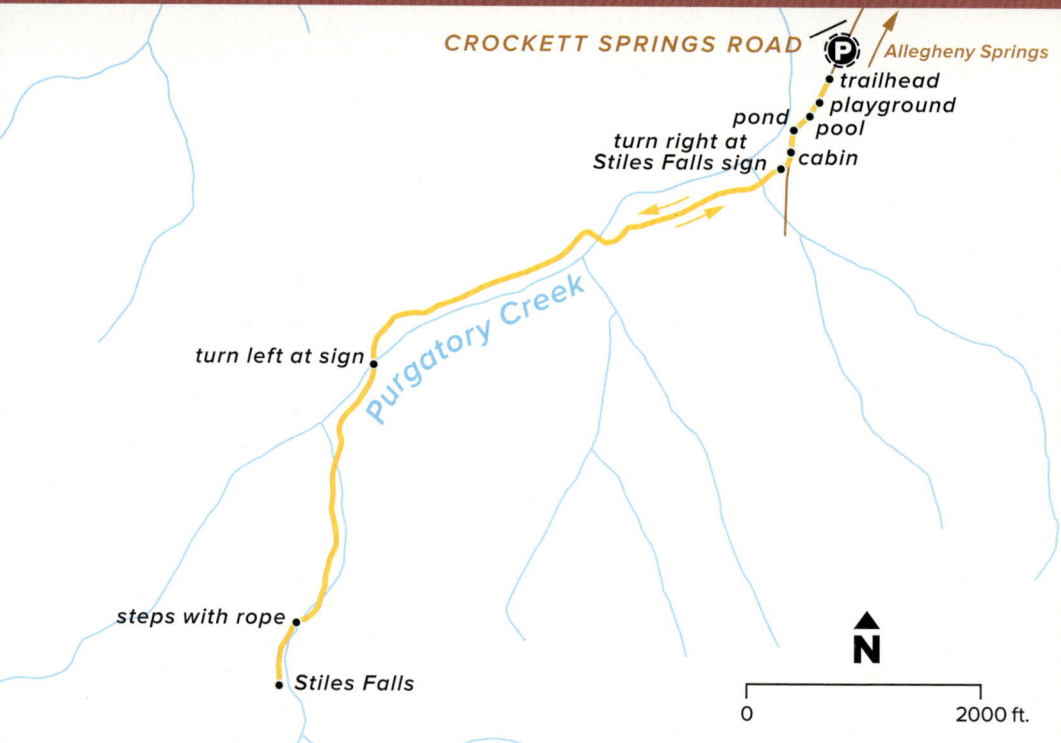

CROCKETT SPRINGS ROAD

Allegheny Springs

trailhead
playground
pool

pond

turn right at
Stiles Falls sign

cabin

Purgatory Creek

turn left at sign

steps with rope

Stiles Falls

N

0   2000 ft.

YOUR ADVENTURE

Adventurers, are you ready to scramble over a creek to find a hidden waterfall on the historical lands of the Tutelo? You will be exploring lands with rich history—used for hunting by Indigenous people, rural farming by European settlers, and later, during the Victorian Era, as a mountain resort and spa for the wealthy wanting to escape the heat of the coast. Begin hiking

The 40-foot drop of Stiles Falls is hidden in the woods →

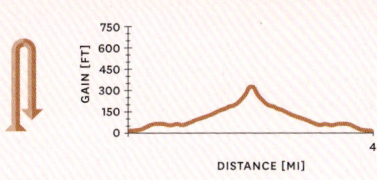

LENGTH 4 miles out and back

ELEVATION GAIN 348 ft.

HIKE TIME + EXPLORE 1.5 hours

DIFFICULTY Challenging—combination of wide gravel path and narrow packed-earth path with moderate elevation

SEASON Year-round; best during spring when the waterfall is rushing and flowers blooming.

GET THERE From I-81 in Salem, take Exit 132 at Dixie Caverns onto Route 11 / 460 toward Shawsville. In about 8 miles, turn left onto Alleghany Spring Road / Route 637. Camp Alta Mons is approximately 6 miles on the right.

Please note that you must drive onto private property owned by Alta Mons. They allow the public to park in their parking lot and hike to the falls for free (except during their summer and winter camp sessions, so check their website if you are planning to visit during these months).

Google Maps: bit.ly/timberstilesfalls

RESTROOM At trailhead

FEE None

TREAT YOURSELF Head west to Fatback Soul Shack in Christiansburg and get a Fatback burger basket.

Alta Mons
(540) 268-2409
Facebook @AltaMons

on the same gravel road you drove in on. Pass a playground and a pool and cabins, part of the summer camp, as well as a small pond with canoes. Turn right at the large sign for Stiles Falls. Take the walkway over the water and hike along a fenced-in field on the right, admiring the forested mountains beyond. Turn left at the next sign; the path narrows and turns to packed earth. Soon you will reach the first of three crossings over Purgatory Creek. After you scramble over rocks in the creek for the second time, the ascent becomes steeper. You will need to climb some steps that include a hand rope—use it to balance and help pull yourself up. Cross Purgatory Creek once more, and soon arrive at Stiles Falls. For a close view, scramble over the rocks. Find your preferred viewpoint, then have a power-up or picnic and take in the beauty of this hidden gem. Retrace your steps back to the trailhead. Alta Mons does allow hikers to camp here; they just ask that you pay through the information slot provided at the trailhead kiosk.

SCAVENGER HUNT

Red maple

Look for the leaves of this deciduous tree, which are three or five lobes with jagged edges. In spring, its fruit is enclosed at one end of a wing-like projectile called a samara. Many people call these fruits "helicopters" because the "wing" helps them catch breezes and spin through the air when falling from the tree. Have a helicopter race by dropping two (that you find on the ground) from the same height—which flies the farthest?

Acer rubrum gets its name from its red fall leaves

Purgatory Creek

You will walk next to and over Purgatory Creek for most of this hike. It's one of several creeks that empty into the South Fork of the Roanoke River. The South and North Forks of the Roanoke River join together, then flow through Roanoke all the way to North Carolina. In the 1890s, Crockett Springs Bottling Co. shipped half-gallon containers of spring water from this river around the country and to Europe.

This creek was once said to have healing powers

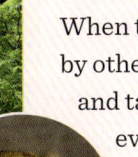

Eastern black walnut

When these deciduous trees are surrounded by other trees in the forest, they grow straight and tall and have few lower branches. However, when they grow in the open, they will branch out closer to the ground, developing a spreading shape. Look for their round, 2- to 3-inch nuts.

Juglans nigra's nuts are the size of a baseball

Rosebay rhododendrons

Can you spot this bush with glossy leaves and funnel or bell-shaped, fragrant flowers? The name *rhododendron* comes from the Greek words for "rose" (*rhodon*) and "tree" (*dendron*). Rosebay rhododendrons are evergreens, which means they keep their leaves all year. If you find a fallen leaf or blossom, trace it in your nature journal and make a bookmark by cutting it out when you get home.

Rhododendron maximum's peak bloom is in July

39

VENTURE THROUGH ROARING RUN

621

Woodland Trail

bridge

stone steps

small waterfall

Roaring Run Creek

Roaring Run Waterfall

Streamside Trail

bridge

bridge

JEFFERSON NATIONAL FOREST

Iron Ore Trail

bridge

Roaring Run Iron Furnace

turn left

N

0   1000 ft.

P

trailhead

SR-621, Strom, Roanoke, Covington

YOUR ADVENTURE

Adventurers, today we will see waterfalls, rock formations, and an old iron furnace on the historical homelands of the Shawnee. Follow the sign for the Roaring Run Falls Trail, diagonal from the trail kiosk. Start on the narrow Streamside Trail. Pass the Iron Ore Trail on your left but stay straight. Turn left to take the loop clockwise. Hike along Roaring Run Creek, over a wooden

Roaring Run is a 30-foot cascade of water →

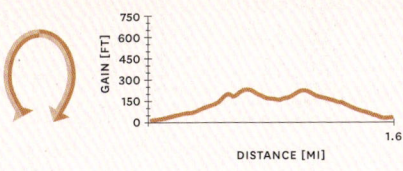

GAIN [FT]

750
600
450
300
150
0

DISTANCE [MI]

1.6

LENGTH 1.6-mile loop

ELEVATION GAIN 276 ft.

HIKE TIME + EXPLORE 1.5 hours

DIFFICULTY Easy—narrow, packed-earth and gravel path with mild elevation

SEASON Year-round; best in summer for playing on the natural waterslide.

GET THERE From US-220 / Botetourt Road in Eagle Rock, take SR-615 / Craig Creek Road 5.5 miles to turn right on SR-621. The Roaring Run entrance will be on the left in 1 mile.

Google Maps: bit.ly/timberroaringrun

RESTROOM At trailhead

FEE None

TREAT YOURSELF Pick up some hush puppies from Whitey's One Stop in Covington.

Jefferson National Forest
(540) 864-5195
Facebook @George-Wasington-and-Jefferson-National-Forests

bridge with an up-close view of a small waterfall. Cross back over the river on yet another bridge. The path is narrow and there is a drop-off—hold hands with the littlest explorers. Soon you'll see another small waterfall on the right. Admire it from a small clearing a few steps off the path. Cross a third bridge before climbing stone steps. At the Roaring Run waterfall, there are plenty of large rocks near the bottom where you can enjoy the scene and power up. Please don't climb to the top of the falls—the rocks are very slippery, and many people have gotten hurt. On your way back, don't cross back over the bridge—stay straight on the Woodland Trail. Loop around the forest and cross a small wood bridge to arrive at the Roaring Run Iron Furnace. After exploring, continue on the trail, then turn left and return to the trailhead.

SCAVENGER HUNT

Roaring Run Iron Furnace

This huge furnace was used to make iron in the mid-1800s for objects like nails and cannonballs. It took 1 acre's worth of lumber to make enough charcoal to fire the furnace for 24 hours! Step inside to get a sense of how big it is. What would *you* have made with its iron?

This iron furnace operated in pre–Civil War days

Slag

Slag is a glasslike waste product of iron blasting. It can be blue, black, or green. Search the ground near the furnace and see if you can find some slag—if you do, know that it was created over 180 years ago! Be sure to leave it where you found it for the next adventurer to find.

Slag found around the iron furnace

Limestone

Limestone is the most common mineral in the large rocks here. It creates a chemical reaction that removes impurities from the ore when placed in the furnace. Roaring Run was an ideal location for making iron in the 1800s, as all four ingredients needed—limestone, iron ore, trees, and running water—could be found here. Can you spot them all during your hike?

All four ingredients to make iron can be found at Roaring Run

Small falls

There are small waterfalls before you arrive at the Roaring Run waterfall. While it's not safe to swim at the main waterfall, swimming near the smaller falls is permitted. In summer, some daring adventurers will even slide down a natural rock waterslide. Take a few minutes to dip your foot or hand into the cold water.

Several small waterfalls pop up along the trail

Pink lady's slippers

In spring, look for this orchid that gets its name—lady's slipper—from its pouch. It's also sometimes called a moccasin flower. The deep pocket created when the flower closes shut makes a bee trap, so as the bee tries to wriggle out, it becomes covered in pollen. What name would you give this beautiful plant?

Cypripedium acaule flowers from May to July

40

JOURNEY TO CASCADES FALLS ON A NATIONAL RECREATION TRAIL

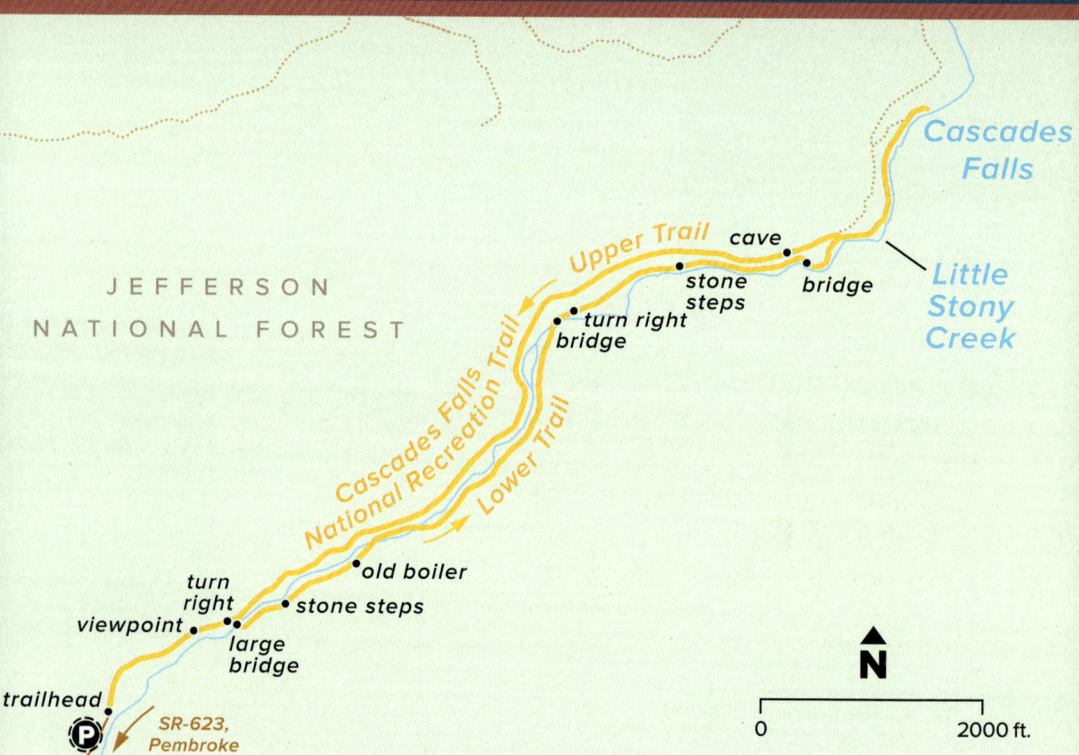

Cascades Falls

Upper Trail · cave
stone steps · bridge
turn right
bridge

Little Stony Creek

JEFFERSON NATIONAL FOREST

Cascades Falls National Recreation Trail

Lower Trail

old boiler
turn right · stone steps
viewpoint
large bridge
trailhead

SR-623, Pembroke

N

0   2000 ft.

YOUR ADVENTURE

Adventurers, today we will be taking a serious hike along Little Stony Creek as we make our way to Cascades Falls on the historical homelands of the Moneton, Yuchi, and Tutelo. Begin at the back of the parking lot. Take the Lower Trail toward the falls along Little Stony Creek. Soon you will see a short spur trail—a perch on the old stone steps offers a closer view of the

Cascades Falls drops 66 feet into a large rocky pool →

GAIN [FT]

750
600
450
300
150
0

5.1

DISTANCE [MI]

LENGTH 5.1-mile lollipop loop

ELEVATION GAIN 663 ft.

HIKE TIME + EXPLORE 2.5 hours

DIFFICULTY Challenging—packed-earth and rocky trails with high elevation gain and exposed edges

SEASON Year-round; best in late spring and summer to wade in the stream and pool.

GET THERE From US-460 in Pembroke, take Cascade Drive / SR-623 to the Cascades parking lot at the end of the road.

Google Maps: bit.ly/timbercascadefallsva

RESTROOM At trailhead

FEE $3 per vehicle

TREAT YOURSELF Stop by Cascades Café, on Cascade Drive, for some grilled cheese and French onion soup.

Jefferson National Forest
(540) 552-4641
Facebook @George-Washington-and-Jefferson-National-Forests

creek. After returning to the path, turn right to cross over a wide wood bridge. A little further down the path, you'll walk up natural stone steps; the path becomes narrower and rockier as you begin to ascend. Shortly you'll see the Old Boiler—step off the path a few steps to get a closer look. Hike on a flat man-made stone path alongside the creek; you'll see more cascades. Just after the 1-mile mark, the trail becomes very rocky and there are some rock scrambles. Cross over another large wooden bridge then turn right. Climb more stone steps that curve around the cascading creek, then walk over another bridge. When the trail turns right, Cascades Falls will come into view. Sit on logs at the bottom of the trail, or enjoy the viewing platform on the left. You can also choose to go to the second viewing area, about two to three stories above the water. To return, turn at the fork to take the Upper Trail, a much wider packed-earth path that is less rocky and requires no scrambling. Pass a large boulder and take in views of the creek far below. Return to the trailhead just before reaching the 5-mile mark. Congrats on a long adventure today!

SCAVENGER HUNT

Woodland salamander

These amphibians are lungless and breathe through their skin, which is covered in a protective mucus. They are cold-blooded, which means they cannot regulate their internal body temperature on their own, so they rely on external heat to get warm. What are some different ways you can make your body warm?

Plethodon species can regenerate lost limbs

Old boiler

This area was logged during the 1920s and 1930s by a small crew who used a portable sawmill along Little Stony Creek. This old boiler provided power to run the mill. Because it was so heavy, they had to use tracks and horses to move it here and no one ever took it back out.

Can you figure out how this boiler used to work?

Cave

You'll see many large sandstone boulders throughout this area—some you can view across the creek and some you'll walk right next to. These boulders are between 420 to 440 million years old! Look for this cave along the tail—can you see the small waterfall inside it?

What kind of animals do you think might call this cave home?

Little Stony Creek and stone steps

The Lower Trail will take you along picturesque Little Stony Creek for more than 2 miles. The trail includes numerous sections of path that are carved directly into existing rocks, as well as sections that include stone steps and walls. Can you imagine hiking to the falls without the help of the trail and man-made steps?

Stone steps along an exposed edge by the creek

41

GET TUNNEL VISION ON NEW RIVER TRAIL

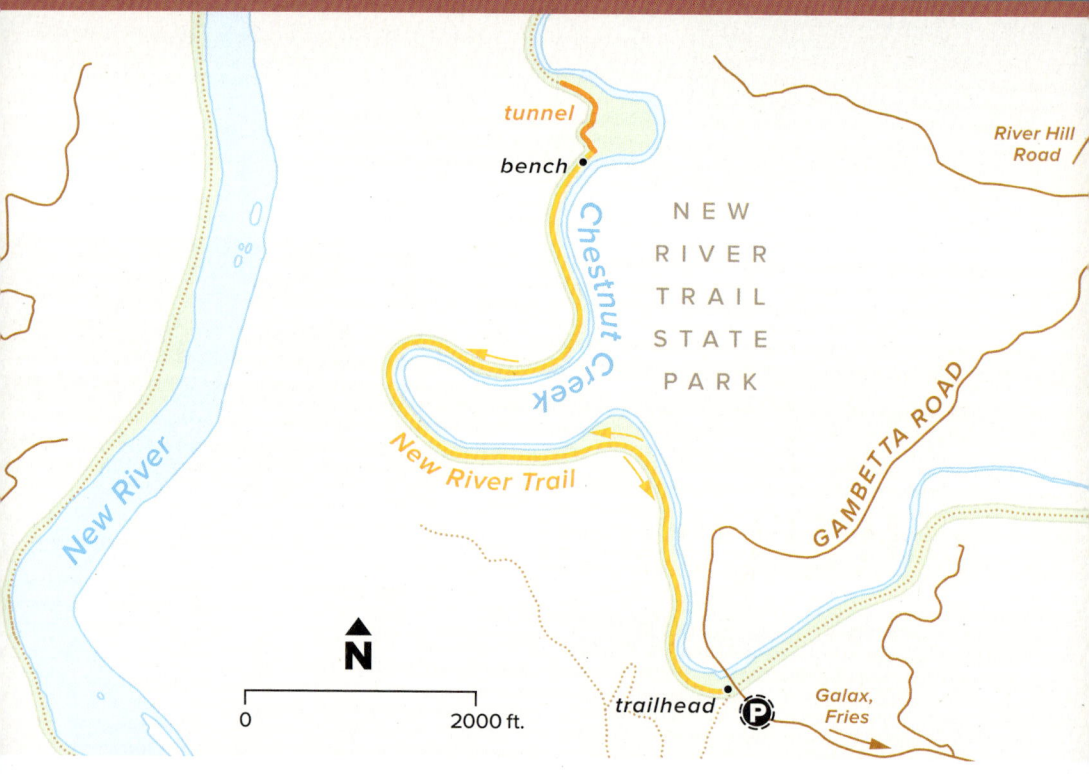

tunnel

bench

Chestnut Creek

NEW RIVER TRAIL STATE PARK

River Hill Road

New River Trail

New River

GAMBETTA ROAD

N

0 — 2000 ft.

trailhead Ⓟ

Galax, Fries

YOUR ADVENTURE

Adventurers, today we walk on one of America's premier rail-trails, on the historical homelands of the Moneton, Yuchi, Cheraw, and Tutelo. Our path is part of the abandoned N&W Railway that was called the Cripple Creek Extension; now it's just known as the New River Trail. Start behind the gate marker on a flat, wide gravel path. You'll hike first with the cascading

View of Chestnut Creek in fall →

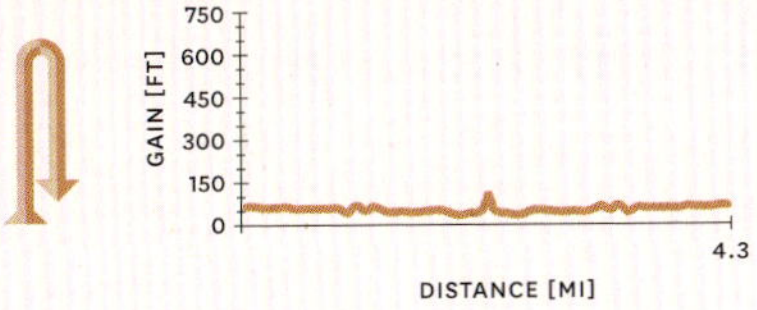

GAIN [FT]

750
600
450
300
150
0
4.3

DISTANCE [MI]

LENGTH 4.3 miles out and back

ELEVATION GAIN 223 ft.

HIKE TIME + EXPLORE 2 hours

DIFFICULTY Moderate—flat, wide gravel path with mild elevation

SEASON Year-round; best in fall for foliage.

GET THERE From I-77 in Woodlawn, take Coulson Church Road southeast for 2.5 miles. Turn right onto Mt. Zion Road. In 3.8 miles turn right onto State Road 635 and follow 2.3 miles to turn left on River Hill Road / State Road 736. Make a sharp left onto Gambetta Road. Parking will be on your right in about 2 miles.

Google Maps: bit.ly/timbernewriver

RESTROOM None

FEE $7 per vehicle

TREAT YOURSELF Stop by The Galax Cakery, on Main Street in Galax, for some fresh cookies.

New River Trail State Park
(276) 699-6778
Facebook @vaspnewrivertrail

Chestnut Creek to your right and forest and rock formations on your left. The path dips close to the creek at several points—enjoy these views! A little after the 2-mile mark, you will see a bench on the right side of the trail, and you will soon arrive at the abandoned Gambetta Tunnel. It is short, so you can see the opposite end as soon as you turn the corner inside. During the day you do not need a flashlight, but you would if hiking at dusk or dawn. Once through the tunnel, turn around. But if you haven't had enough, you can keep going—a mile farther on is a massive abandoned steel railway trestle over the river. After hiking back through the tunnel, consider having a power-up break at the bench you passed earlier, which gives you incredible views of Chestnut Creek! Walk down a little path right off the trail; it leads you to the water, where you can rock jump or skip stones. Then retrace your steps back to the trailhead. Want to explore more of the trail? Consider camping at one of the three primitive campgrounds at the state park, and explore the trails all weekend long.

SCAVENGER HUNT

Gambetta Tunnel
The Gambetta Tunnel was carved right through this cliff—and dug out without the use of explosives. The rough-cut edges you can still see show the grueling labor involved in the task! While inside, try to guess how long that job might have taken.

The tunnel is 195' tall

Bristly beard lichen

Lichens are a combination of algae and fungus that work symbiotically to support each other. This one looks like mini shrubs or tassels attached to the bark of tree trunks and branches. It's a pale gray-green, and sometimes produces disc-like fruit bodies. It prefers to live in the crowns of trees in shaded forests near bodies of water. Wildlife uses bristly beard lichen for food and nesting material. If you find a clump on the ground, make your own "beard," and have your hiking buddy take a photo of you.

Usnea hirta is fairly rare in the United States

Hornets

Did you know these stinging insects are a subset of the wasp family, and are considered gentler? Hornets generally only attack to defend their colony if they feel it is being threatened. Hornets are larger than wasps and love to snack on bees, due to their honey.

Always observe genus *Vespa* from a safe distance

Walking fern

You can most likely spot some walking ferns growing in clusters in moist, shady, rocky cliffs or rocks. These ferns are characterized by their narrow, triangle-shaped dark green blades. The common name "walking fern" refers to the way new plantlets sprout wherever the tips of the parent plant's arching leaves touch the ground, making the plant look as if it's spreading by walking along.

Asplenium myriophyllum is endangered in some states

42

FROLIC WITH FERAL PONIES ON THE GRAYSON HIGHLANDS

Appalachian Trail

boulder

go right

boulder

Appalachian Trail

Appalachian Spur Trail

turn right

Rhododendron Trail

Horse Trail North

Horse Trail East

N

0   1000 ft.

GRAYSON
HIGHLANDS
STATE PARK

Horse Trail East

wooden gate
backpacker camp sites

US-58,
Whitetop

trailhead   go
                   right

Massie Gap Trail

362

YOUR ADVENTURE

Adventurers, are you ready for a unique outing? Today we will roam over the Appalachian Mountains with feral ponies running free on the historical homelands of the East Cherokee, Moneton, and Yuchi! This 4,822-acre state park has beautiful views of mountain meadows along part of the Appalachian Trail. Begin at the Massie Gap parking area on

The sweeping views of the mountain meadows are often referred to as "balds" →

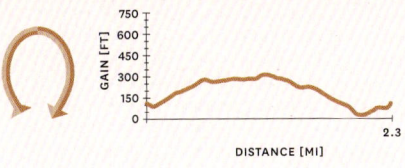

LENGTH 2.3-mile loop

ELEVATION GAIN 325 ft.

HIKE TIME + EXPLORE 1.5 hours

DIFFICULTY Moderate—combination of packed-earth, gravel, and at times rocky paths with moderate elevation

SEASON Year-round; best during fall foliage.

GET THERE Enter Grayson Highlands State Park from US-58, turning north onto VA-362. In about 3.5 miles, turn right into the Massie Gap parking area.

Google Maps: bit.ly/timbergraysonhighlands

RESTROOM At visitor center from May to October; a vault toilet at Massie Gap is open year round

FEE $7 per vehicle on weekdays, $10 weekends

TREAT YOURSELF West on US-58 in Whitetop, the Railroad Café & Market serves a caboose sandwich with homemade fries.

Grayson Highlands State Park
(276) 579-7092
Facebook @vaspgraysonhighlands

the Rhododendron Trail. While parts of the path have moderate elevation gains, the views of open ridges with mountains and trees that go on for miles are worth it! Soon, merge with the Horse Trail North. After half a mile, turn right at the trail marker to follow the Appalachian Trail northbound. The path becomes narrower, rockier, and steeper. When you reach two large boulders, take in views of the balds and alpine meadows. Loop around a wooden trail marker to the right for the blue-blazed Appalachian Spur Trail. Cross an open, grassy area and enter a hardwood forest. Be careful of the loose rocks and roots on the path here. Pass the Horse Trail East, going straight until you arrive at a wooden gate that you need to walk through. Cross over a small creek to an area designated for backpackers who want to camp overnight. Turn right at the trail marker for Massie Gap Trail; when you reach Massie Gap, turn left on your original trail and return to the trailhead. To see even more ponies, camp at the park and scout for them again tomorrow.

SCAVENGER HUNT

Feral Ponies

Watch for these famous feral ponies that roam the mountain terrain—there are approximately one hundred. They are categorized as "feral" rather than "wild" because they are the descendants of once-domesticated animals. Once a year, they are rounded up and given a veterinary exam. Then they are re-released, except for young stallions, who are auctioned off to control the population size. Keep count of how many ponies you spy!

Feral ponies are a common sight on this trail

Red spruce

Keep your eyes open for these evergreens—they thrive in cool, moist conditions and only grow at high elevations. They have a pyramidal growth shape and short, yummy-smelling needles. They are unique because each needle grows out of the branch from a strong, woody peg. How many of their rod-shaped pine cones can you count on one tree?

Picea rubens can grow to be more than 400 years old

Rhyolite boulders

There are several rock outcroppings along the top of this hike—they're rhyolite, an igneous rock formed in ancient volcanoes 750–755 million years ago. These special rocks are very hard and erode slowly, keeping Grayson Highlands higher than the surrounding land. There are not many other places in this area where you can see alpine-like peaks more than 5,000 feet high.

Large boulder along the path

Crisped pincushion moss

As you hike, it might be hard to take your eyes off the views of the balds, but look closely at some of the trees you pass, and you might notice this plant growing on the bark in tight mounds. It provides an ideal protective cover for many small invertebrates. Brush your hands gently across it—does it feel soft or hard? Look closely and try to see how many of its leaves you can count!

The foliage of *Ulota crispa* varies in color

43

TREK TO BIG FALLS

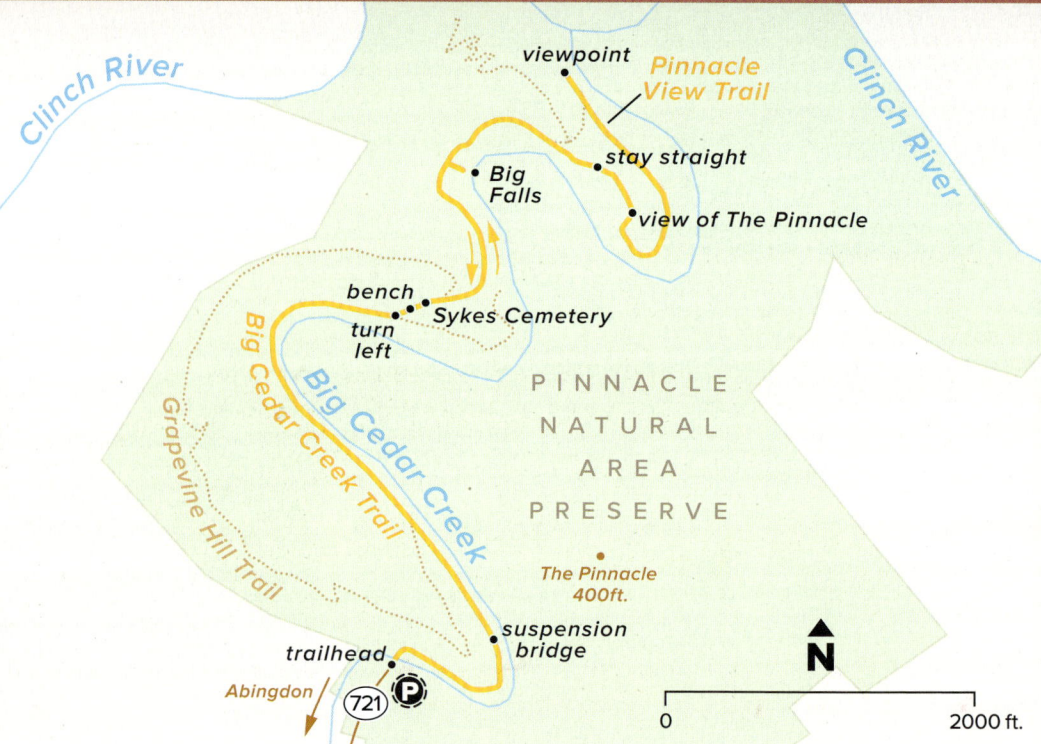

Clinch River

Clinch River

viewpoint

Pinnacle View Trail

stay straight

Big Falls

view of The Pinnacle

bench

Sykes Cemetery

turn left

Big Cedar Creek Trail

Big Cedar Creek

Grapevine Hill Trail

PINNACLE

NATURAL

AREA

PRESERVE

The Pinnacle 400ft.

suspension bridge

trailhead

Abingdon

721

N

0   2000 ft.

YOUR ADVENTURE

Adventurers, today we will wander through the forest to scenic overlooks, mystifying rock formations, tranquil rivers, and cascading waterfalls on the historical homelands of the East Cherokee and Yuchi. Begin by walking behind a yellow gate and climbing a series of steps onto a high suspension bridge and the Big Cedar Creek Trail—please note that this bridge is high

Big Falls reaches from bank to bank →

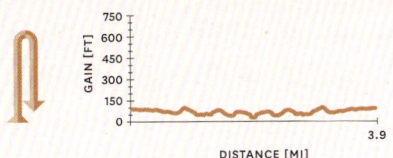

LENGTH 3.9 miles out and back

ELEVATION GAIN 308 ft.

HIKE TIME + EXPLORE 2 hours

DIFFICULTY Moderate—narrow packed-earth path; rocky at times with moderate elevation

SEASON Year-round; best in spring for rushing waterfall.

GET THERE From Abingdon, take US-19 north into Lebanon. Turn left onto VA-82 toward Cleveland. Turn right onto VA-640. Turn left onto VA-721 and follow it into the preserve. Follow the unpaved road 0.9 miles down to the parking lot on the left. Please note that there are limited parking spaces, which is intentional in order to preserve this natural area. If the lot is full, the preserve is full, so please return another time when it's less crowded. To avoid being turned away, consider arriving early.

Google Maps: bit.ly/timberbigfalls

RESTROOM At trailhead

FEE None

TREAT YOURSELF Grab a hot fudge cake from Honey Bea's Cafe & Ice Cream Parlor, off New Garden Road in Honaker.

Pinnacle Natural Area Preserve
(276) 676-5673
Facebook @VirginiaDCR

over the river below and does swing when you walk on it. There are several natural and man-made steps and big rocks before the trail turns left along the creek bank. Go up a small hill and pass a bench, which is a great place to have a power-up. You will come next to the overgrown Sykes Cemetery behind a split-rail fence. You can go off trail to get a closer look at the headstones of family members who lived here when this was private land. Then, just up ahead, you will see Big Falls. Take a right off the trail and down some stone steps to reach them. There is a stone-covered area just in front of the falls, perfect to linger on. After you're done exploring, return to the path and continue on the Big Cedar Creek Trail. At 1.5 miles, ascend a few stairs before reaching a four-way junction. Continue straight for the blue-blazed trail. Soon you will see a sign for The Pinnacle—look out and up, way past the path, to see this amazing natural wonder. The narrow path twists and turns with a few slight inclines until you reach the edge of the Clinch River. To return, retrace your steps back to the trailhead.

SCAVENGER HUNT

The Pinnacle

The Pinnacle is located near the confluence (a place where two rivers meet) of Clinch River and Big Cedar Creek. It rises 400 feet above you! This formation is composed of Copper Ridge dolomite and sandstone that was deposited over 400 million years ago, when this area was covered by a shallow inland sea. As the rocks decompose, they form calcium-rich soils that support many wildflowers. Do you see any shapes in the rock?

This rock has been weathered to create a spectacular formation

Suspension bridge

Your adventure begins high over Big Cedar Creek. Be prepared for the bridge to sway as you walk across it! If you are feeling brave, stop in the middle to take in the views of the rumbling river below.

This hike starts out swinging

Asian clam shells

Along the area below the falls, if you look closely, you will see many tiny shells. These are from the Asian clam, a nonnative, invasive species. Collect some of the shells and lay them on the ground to compare size, shape, and color, then return them to where you found them.

How many different shells can you find by Big Falls?

Orange jelly fungus

Keep your eyes open when walking through the woods and you might just see some bright orange jelly fungus. This uncommon fungus grows in groups on rotting trunks and the stumps of dead conifers. It can appear any time of year during wet weather but is most common in spring, summer, and fall. If you spot some, do your best jelly jiggle.

Dacrymyces palmatus dissolves into a wet mass as it ages

ADVENTURES IN
WEST VIRGINIA

Adventurers, you will quickly find out why West Virginia is known as the Mountain State. Unless you are traveling along a river valley, you'll be driving (and hiking) either uphill or down. In fact, the average elevation in West Virginia is higher than any other state east of the Mississippi River. Its borders are almost exclusively defined by natural features such as riverbeds and mountain ridges, giving this state one of the most irregular shapes in the union. You'll drive through its two main regions: the Appalachian Ridge and Valley region in the east and the Appalachian Plateau in the center and west. The Allegheny and Blue Ridge Mountain Ranges, which are part of the Appalachian Mountain range, run from the northeast to the southwest part of the state. These forested mountains are defined by their long, rugged ridges and the streams that run through the valleys that separate them. The Allegheny Front runs along the western edge of the mountains. This is where the more rugged mountains of the east converge with the rolling terrain of the Appalachian Plateau. Get ready to explore all that this wild and wonderful state has to offer. Begin your adventures in the southern corner of the state, climbing your way to the Hanging Rock Raptor Observatory before taking in some amazing views of the New River Gorge Bridge then hiking along the Appalachian Trail to a fire tower on top of Shenandoah Mountain. Your adventures will keep you heading north as you climb to the viewing platform on top of Seneca Rocks, hike to balanced rocks at Blackwater Falls, and explore the Tygart Valley River along the CSX train track. Your adventures will end on an island that was inhabited by settlers in the early 1800s on the state's lowest point, Harpers Ferry. While on your hiking adventures, adopt West Virginia's motto of "mountaineers are always free" and enjoy some wild and free moments on the trails. Keep that adventurous spirit alive beyond the trails and carry it with you wherever you go!

Young explorers taking in the views on an overlook at Seneca Rocks State Park

44

HANG OUT ON HANGING ROCK

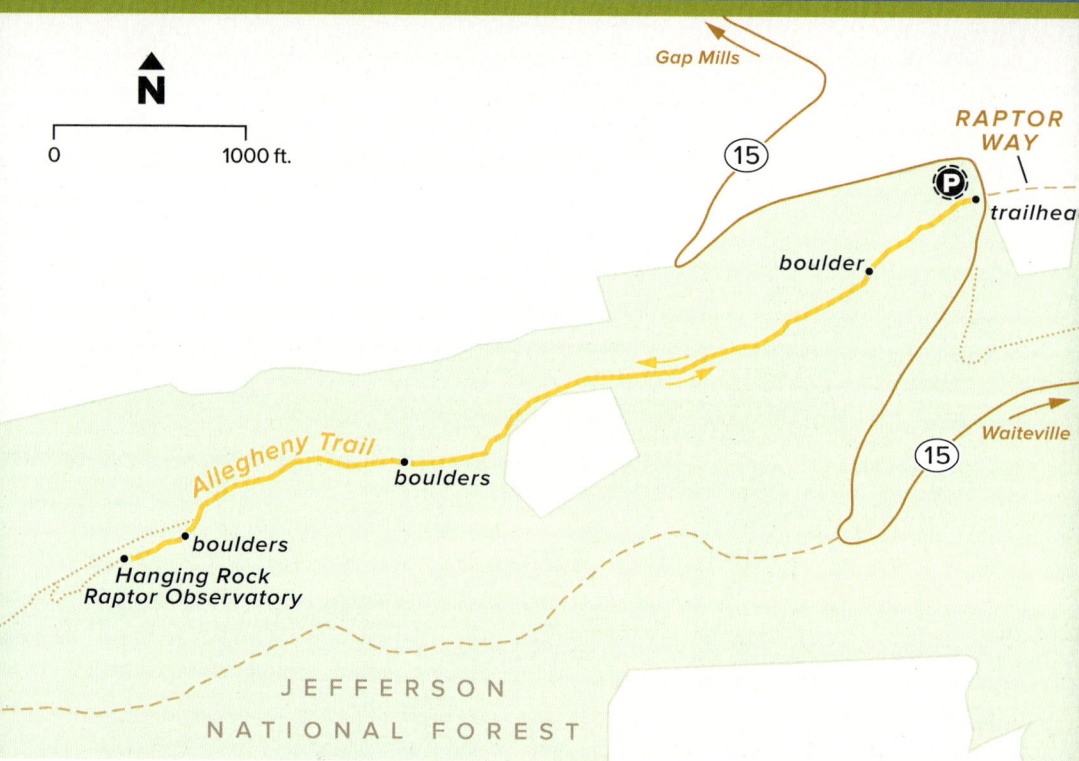

N

0   1000 ft.

Gap Mills

15

RAPTOR WAY

trailhea

boulder

Waiteville

15

Allegheny Trail

boulders

boulders

Hanging Rock
Raptor Observatory

JEFFERSON
NATIONAL FOREST

YOUR ADVENTURE

Adventurers, grab your binoculars because today we climb Peters Mountain. At the summit, you can watch for flying raptors at the Hanging Rock Raptor Observatory. This is the historical homelands of the Yuchi, Shawnee, and Tutelo. Start along the blue-blazed Allegheny Trail, a 330-mile-long trail from the Mason-Dixon Line to the Appalachian Trail. You will

The Hanging Rock Raptor Observatory sits atop rocks →

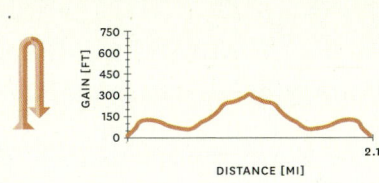

LENGTH 2.1 miles out and back

ELEVATION GAIN 436 feet

HIKE TIME + EXPLORE 1.5 hours

DIFFICULTY Moderate—a narrow path composed of packed earth and rocky terrain; moderate elevation

SEASON Year-round; best during fall for foliage and raptor migrations. Wear orange during hunting season.

GET THERE Travel south on US-219 from Lewisville. In Pickaway, turn left on Hillsdale Road. Follow 4.4 miles and turn left on Sweet Springs Valley Road / WV-3. Turn right onto Zenith Road, left onto Limestone Hill Road, and right into the parking lot.

Google Maps: bit.ly/timberhangingrock

RESTROOM At the peak, past the tower

FEE None

TREAT YOURSELF Grab a sandwich or a bag of candy 5 miles north at Cheese 'n' More.

Jefferson National Forest
(540) 265-5100
Facebook @JeffersonNationalForest

journey up the narrow and, at times, rocky path, ascending over 400 feet of elevation in just a mile. Wind up the mountain, passing several boulders. Turn left when you see a trail sign with a blue blaze. Climb the steep and rocky final ascent, passing large boulders that rise way above you. The observatory is located at over 3,800 feet, so the weather and temperature can be quite different from lower elevations— be prepared for changing conditions. Climb the steep steps and walk around the wrap-around porch to take in the view. Inside the observatory, birders record the birds they've seen each day. Admire the rock formations known as Hanging Rock along the top of the summit, which gave this mountain its name. When done exploring, retrace your steps back down the mountain.

SCAVENGER HUNT

Stinkhorns

Can you spot one of these unique-looking mushrooms? They are known for their intense stench—some say they smell like rotting meat, hence their name "stinkhorns." If you find one, will you be brave enough to smell it?

Phallus impudicus often grows on rotting wood

Calico aster

Look for these tiny white blossoms with yellow centers that later turn reddish-purple. Interestingly, the head of one of these flowers may include both colors at the same time, which gives them a multicolor, or "calico," appearance. Count how many petals are on one flower.

Symphyotrichum lateriflorum blooms from August to October

Hanging rocks

Numerous sandstone outcroppings along the crest of the 4,073-foot-tall Peters Mountain appear to be hanging off the summit. An outcrop is a visible exposure of bedrock on the surface of the Earth. In most places, bedrock is covered by soil and vegetation; however, in areas where the cover has eroded, the rock may be exposed or "cropped out." Take out your nature journal and, as you think about how layers came to be tilted, sketch these unique outcroppings.

The hanging rocks near the observatory

Golden eagle

Eagles are a kind of raptor—these birds of prey have strong legs, powerful grasping feet with sharp talons, and hooked bills. This raptor has golden feathers, and its wings make a V shape, the tips spread like fingers, as it soars high in the sky. Try "soaring" with your arms in a V and your fingers spread like a golden eagle.

Aquila chrysaetos is one of the largest raptors in North America

Hanging Rock Raptor Observatory

This observatory was originally an old fire tower. The tower and surrounding area were acquired by the US Forest Service in 1983. Today, the observatory provides 360-degree views of the surrounding areas and is one of the best places in the state to observe raptors. It sits along a popular southern migration path, so viewing is phenomenal during fall, especially in September. Fifteen species of raptors are associated with this observation area, including hawks, eagles, and ospreys.

The observatory sits 3,800 feet above sea level

45

TAKE IN THE VIEW ON LONG POINT TRAIL

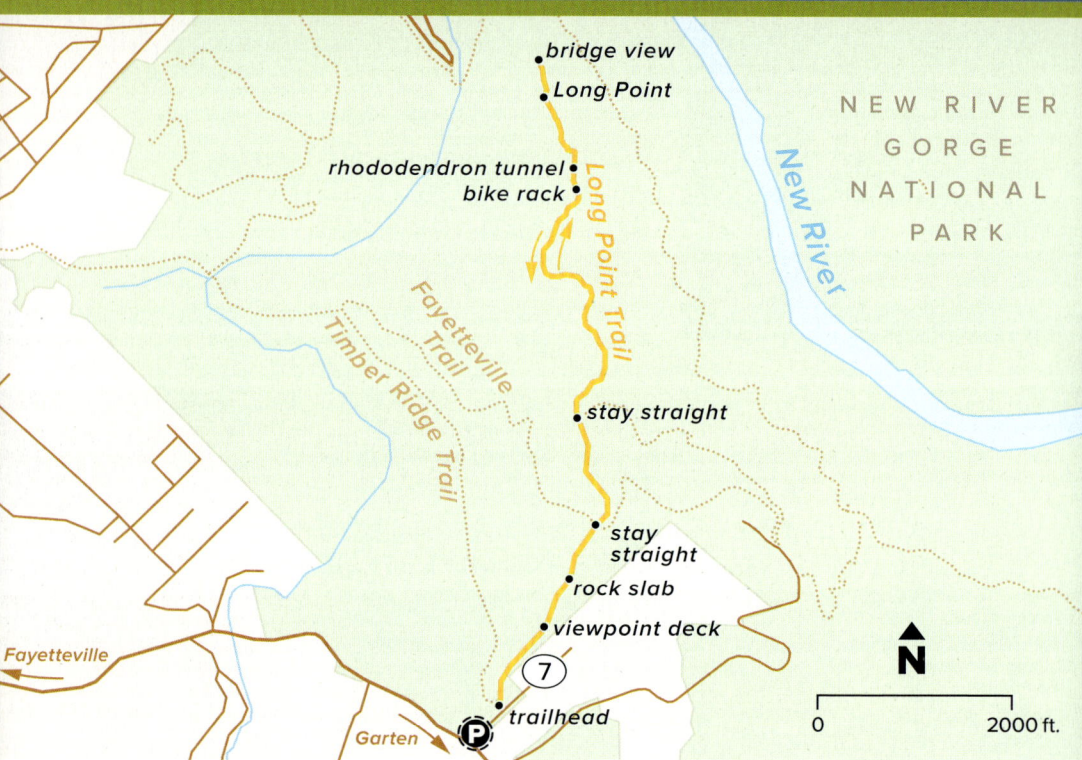

YOUR ADVENTURE

Adventurers, welcome to the historical homelands of the Moneton, Yuchi, Shawnee, and Tutelo, where we will be walking through a lush forest for a sweet view of the New River Gorge Bridge. Begin your trek on a flat, graveled pathway through the western edge of the Central Appalachian Mountains. Look at the great variety of greenery on either side of you, and be sure

At the end of the hike, you will see the 1,700-foot-long New River Gorge Bridge →

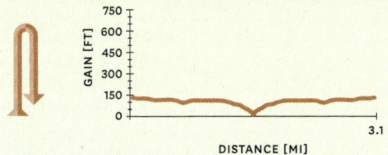

LENGTH 3.1 miles out and back

ELEVATION GAIN 141 ft.

HIKE TIME + EXPLORE 2 hours

DIFFICULTY Moderate—easy terrain during the first part, but the last portion is rocky and rooty; you'll need to carefully watch younger hikers out on the point, as it is exposed on three sides

SEASON Year-round; fall colors are incredible.

GET THERE From US-19 in Fayetteville, take Court Road 2.5 miles to turn left on Gatewood Road. In 1.8 miles you'll see a red barn on the right—turn left on Newton Road and the parking lot will be on your left.

Google Maps: bit.ly/timberlongpoint

RESTROOM At parking lot

FEE None

TREAT YOURSELF Grab a biscuit, any biscuit, at Tudor's Biscuit World on Court Street in Fayetteville.

New River Gorge National Park
(304) 465-0508
Facebook @NewRiverGorgeNPS

to stop at the first observation deck—how many species of birds do you see? What can you hear? Continue back on the trail and enter the deep forest. You'll come across a trail sign—stay straight on the Long Point Trail. Continue onward to another fork; stay straight. Finally you'll reach another fake fork—the right direction doesn't really go anywhere, so stay to the left. Here the trail narrows into a cool rhododendron tunnel—in spring this will smell amazing! Now the point emerges. Take in the view here (carefully) and try to imagine how long it took to construct the New River Gorge Bridge. Want to do the trail again? Consider renting a bike from a nearby rental center. Bikes shouldn't go out to the point, so lock it up at the bike rack on the trail. To stay longer, consider camping at Babcock State Park, across the river.

SCAVENGER HUNT

Tulip tree
Look for the bright green leaves of this deciduous tree that are the shape of a tulip flower. In your nature journal, trace a leaf you find on the ground and color it like an actual tulip. In summer, its flowers also look like tulips. Take a whiff if you happen upon one—they are fragrant!

Liriodendron tulipifera

Witch hazel cone gall aphid
These red spots are actually small aphids (sap-sucking insects) that force the witch hazel plant to grow a cone over them to protect them until they hatch. They look like little witches' hats. Draw in your nature journal what you think might be underneath the hats.

Hormaphis hamamelidis

Greenbrier

Look closely at the twining stems of this shrub but don't touch—they have spikes! Its white flowers come out in spring and summer. Can you make an acrostic poem, where each letter of the word goes down the page, B is for... R is for... I is for... E is for... R is for... and come up with an adjective for each letter that describes this cool plant?

Smilax rotundifolia

Fraser magnolia

Look for the beautiful bouquet of this small tree, named for botanist John Fraser. Large white flowers appear in spring—count the nine petals on each bloom. Carefully feel the warty bark on the trunk. If you were a botanist, what kind of plant would you like to have named after you?

Magnolia fraseri

Coralberry

These bright berries shine through their green oval leaves in fall. Can you count how many berries are in each cluster? They stick around through winter, providing much-needed food for birds and mammals. Can you spot anyone snacking on them today?

Symphoricarpos orbiculatus

46

DO A 360 ON HIGH KNOB TOWER

WEST VIRGINIA

VIRGINIA

High Knob Trail

Brandywine, Franklin

trailhead

33

Harrisonburg

Blue Ridge Mountains

Spruce Knob 4863ft.

GEORGE WASHINGTON NATIONAL FOREST

Shenandoah Mountain Trail

High Knob Tower

N

0   2000 ft.

YOUR ADVENTURE

Adventurers, are you ready for one of our most challenging hikes? You will skirt along the Virginia–West Virginia border as you climb to an old fire tower on the historical homelands of the Shawnee and Manahoac. Begin on the northern end of Shenandoah Mountain on a narrow path; walk around the parking lot guardrail on the eastern end of the parking area to a large

High Knob Tower sits on the state line between Virginia and West Virginia →

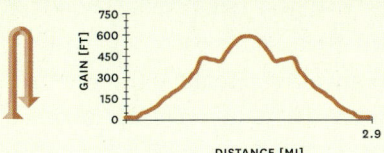

LENGTH 2.9 miles out and back

ELEVATION GAIN 689 ft.

HIKE TIME + EXPLORE 1.5 hours

DIFFICULTY Challenging—a combination of packed-earth paths and rocky terrain; steep elevation gain

SEASON Year-round; best during fall foliage.

GET THERE Take US-33 east from Brandywine. The parking lot is on your right, just before the state border. The trailhead is in the far corner of the lot, next to the road.

Google Maps: bit.ly/timberhighknob

RESTROOM None

FEE None

TREAT YOURSELF Grab some homemade sugar cookies from Sweet Dreams of Cakes and Things, on Sugar Grove Road in Brandywine.

George Washington National Forest
(540) 265-5100
Facebook @GeorgeWashingtonNationalForest

hiking sign. Immediately climb down big rocks on a steep, rocky decline on the yellow-blazed trail. In summer, you will pass a large section of wildflowers before the path levels out and becomes dirt. Fun fact: this part of the trail is part of the developing Great Eastern Trail, a new long-distance route that will eventually run west of the Appalachian Trail from New York to Alabama. The path continues at a steady climb and is rocky in patches. Turn left then right at the junctions to continue climbing to the summit. At the trail sign, turn left (do not turn right, as that is private property). When the trail becomes a dirt road, veer left out of the woods and into an open area. The path becomes wider and less rocky, but it's very steep, so go at your own pace! Walk into an open area and see the fire tower on your left. Climb to the top to see Spruce Knob to the west—the highest point in West Virginia at 4,863 feet—and the Blue Ridge Mountains and Shenandoah National Park to the east. Use a compass (maybe in an adult's phone) to verify which way is west and which east. The open flat area in front of the tower is perfect for a picnic. When ready, retrace your route back to the trailhead. To explore this area more, consider staying at the Brandywine Campground, just a 10-minute drive down the road.

SCAVENGER HUNT

Golden scalycaps

It is hard to miss these golden yellow-orange mushrooms with dark triangular scales. Look underneath and count the gills (what the mushroom uses to release spores so it can reproduce). Draw these mushrooms in your nature journal, so you can compare them with other mushrooms you see on your adventures.

The cap of *Pholiota adiposa* is always sticky

American asters

These wildflowers usually bloom around the autumn equinox and are some of the last species available for pollinating insects. In addition to being beautiful to look at, asters provide both habitat and food for pollinators into winter. Make like a bee and see how many American aster flowers you can find.

Symphyotrichum is part of the sunflower family

High Knob Tower

High Knob Tower was constructed between 1939 and 1940 using rocks from Shenandoah Mountain. It's the only stone fire tower in Virginia, and the only intact tower of its kind on natural forest lands east of the Mississippi River. If you feel comfortable, climb the tower to enjoy the views from the platforms.

View from the top of High Knob Tower on a foggy day

White dapperling

Can you spot these mushrooms? They might look different depending on how old they are—their caps start out convex (curved outward) but expand to become almost flat over time. The caps are usually smooth, but occasionally some are dotted with tiny flakes or scales. Draw the different shapes and textures in your nature journal.

Leucoagaricus leucothites can grow in forests or fields

47

BOULDER AROUND SENECA ROCKS

Petersburg

bench

wooden steps
with guardrail

North Bend River

rock
piles

observation platform
summit
Seneca Rocks
2421ft.

Harman

P trailhead

Seneca
Rocks
Trail
Bridge

Roy Gap Trail

Seneca Rocks
Discovery
Center

ROY GAP ROAD

N

0   1000 ft.

YOUR ADVENTURE

Adventurers, today we head to Monongahela National Forest, on the historical homeland of the Shawnee and Massawomeck, to climb Seneca Rocks—one of the best-known landmarks in West Virginia because they stand 9,000 feet above the valley! This trail follows the Potomac River and is known as a place where the Algonquin, Tuscarora, and Seneca tribes met

A view of Seneca Rocks from the valley, named for the Seneca peoples who fished, hunted, and traded here →

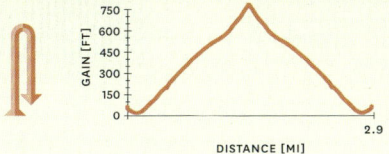

LENGTH 2.9 miles out and back

ELEVATION GAIN 758 ft.

HIKE TIME + EXPLORE 2 hours

DIFFICULTY Challenging—a combination of packed-earth and gravel paths; high elevation

SEASON Year-round; best during fall foliage.

GET THERE From US-33 in Seneca Rocks, take WV-28 / WV-55 north 0.2 miles to turn right onto FS-745A, which will take you to the parking lot and trailhead.

Google Maps: bit.ly/timbersenecarocks

RESTROOM At trailhead

FEE None

TREAT YOURSELF Just down the road on US-33, enjoy a treat from Harper's Old Country Store, built in 1902 and still serving snacks and fresh food.

Monongahela National Forest, Seneca Rocks National Recreational Area
(304) 636-1800
Facebook @MonongahelaNF

to trade. Begin on a packed-earth path next to an open field with a spectac-ular view of the mountain you are about to climb. You will quickly reach a bridge that crosses the North Fork River. Turn left at the fork, onto the Sen-eca Rocks Trail. Interpretive signs give information about the geology and trees along the trail. Continue past some rock piles, soon arriving at a row of wooden stairs, where the way gets steeper. Count how many switchbacks you climb. While it might be tempting to take a shortcut, please always stay on the trail to protect the landscape. Plus, switchbacks actually ease the difficulty of the elevation gain! Turn left and then loop right to arrive at a bench, a great place for a power-up. Loop left and right again to arrive at the summit. Enjoy the magnificent views from the platform looking over the side of the mountain. It is strongly discouraged that anyone but skilled climbers attempt scaling the nearby rock face, as it is extremely narrow with no railings. Consider having another power-up stop on the platform while you soak in the views. When ready, head back down the path the same way you came. Make a weekend of it and camp at the Seneca Shadows Campground overlooking Seneca Rocks and nestled into mountains.

SCAVENGER HUNT

Seneca Rocks Trail Bridge

The arched bridge at the beginning of the trail crosses over the 43.6-mile-long North Fork of the South Branch Potomac River. This river flows through West Virginia and eventually passes between Virginia and Maryland before it empties into Chesapeake Bay. Stop in the middle of the bridge to enjoy the amazing views both upstream and downstream.

Walking bridge along the trail

Scarlet elfcup

Look for this mushroom with very short stems and bright red, cup-shaped caps. They flatten to a shallower disk shape and get split edges as they age. The scarlet elfcup can be found growing on fallen branches and pieces of dead hardwood. They prefer shady, damp habitats with moss and leaf litter. They explosively release tiny spores to reproduce, making a loud "puff" noise when they do! Look closely—can you see its spores?

Sarcoscypha austriaca is one of the first mushrooms to appear in spring

Layered sandstone rocks

The layered sandstone rocks to the left of the path are made of very fine-grained sediment. They were deposited millions of years ago, in very still water. You can see where roots have grown down through cracks and along layers. This is one of the natural processes that breaks bedrock into small bits and eventually into soil.

Layered rocks along the trail

View from the summit

You will be rewarded for making it up the 10 percent grade to the summit by the spectacular views from the overlook! Look west to see the Potomac and Seneca Valleys, along with multiple 4,000-foot mountains. How many peaks can you spot? While on the platform, see if you can find your car in the parking lot. Isn't it amazing how tiny it looks from so high up?

Take in the views from 900 feet above sea level

48

JOURNEY TO THE BALANCED ROCK AT BLACKWATER FALLS

Blackwater River

Elakala Trail

trailhead

WV-32, Davis,
Courtland

CANAAN
LOOP ROAD

walking
bridge

stay
straight

Water Tank Trail

Yellow Birch Trail

Red Spruce Trail

Shay Trace Trail

Shay Trace Trail

Balanced Rock Trail

Red Spruce Trail

turn
left

bridge

BLACKWATER
FALLS
STATE PARK

rhododendron
tunnel

N

Balanced
Rock

0   2000 ft.

YOUR ADVENTURE

Adventurers, today you will journey to a hidden gem—two huge rocks balanced on top of each other! You'll be on the historical homelands of the Shawnee and Massawomeck. Begin at the Blackwater Lodge parking lot, following the Elakala Trail. Head into the forest and wind around until you reach a charming footbridge over Shays Run, a small creek cascading into Blackwater

Blackwater Falls cascades over a nearly a 60-foot drop →

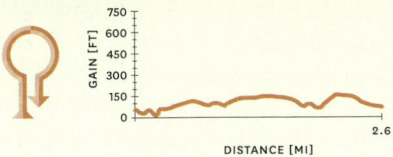

LENGTH 2.6-mile lollipop loop

ELEVATION GAIN 299 ft.

HIKE TIME + EXPLORE 1.5 hours

DIFFICULT Moderate—combination of packed-earth and gravel paths; moderate elevation gain

SEASON Year-round; best during fall foliage.

GET THERE Follow US-48 south from Thomas and bear right onto WV-32. In 0.4 miles, turn right onto Blackwater Falls Road. After 1.5 miles, turn left onto Canyon Point Road and take another left into the parking lot.

Google Maps: bit.ly/timberbalancedrock

RESTROOM In the snack shop that shares a parking lot with the trailhead

FEE None

TREAT YOURSELF Pick up some ice cream at the Blackwater Trading Company, in the same parking lot as the trailhead.

Blackwater Falls State Park
(304) 259-5216
Facebook @wvstateparks

Canyon. After crossing, turn around for a surprise—35-foot Elakala Falls under the bridge. Continue walking, crossing the street to continue on the orange-blazed Balanced Rock Trail. Be careful with little explorers. Continue straight past the intersection with the Shay-Trace Trail. At the fork, turn right to stay on the Balanced Rock Trail. Soon you will see a sign to Balanced Rock. Continue past dense rhododendrons that encroach on the path—then you'll arrive! After exploring and powering up, retrace your steps to the fork. Turn *right* on the Red Spruce Trail, then cross a bridge. At the next fork, turn left onto the Water Tank Trail. Cross the road again to return to the parking lot. After your post-hike snack at the trading post, consider walking down more than two hundred steps to see the park's namesake: Blackwater Falls. This 60-foot waterfall is darker than most because the needles from hemlocks and spruces surrounding it add tannic acid to the water, darkening it. If you are too tired to venture down today, consider spending the night at the park's campground and venturing here again tomorrow.

SCAVENGER HUNT

Balanced Rock

Balanced Rock is a 15-foot-high table rock composed of layers of sandstone and conglomerate. Look closely to see little "jelly bean" pebbles within the rock—these are actually little pieces of quartz. This formation is over 300 million years old and was created by a phenomenon called "differential weathering." Over time, rocks erode at different rates, creating unique formations. Here, the top rock has withstood the elements better than the bottom; therefore, a "table rock" remains. Draw this amazing natural occurrence in your nature journal.

A large sandstone table rock in an uncanny position

Elakala Falls

The 35-foot waterfall gushing under the foot-bridge is one of four cascades making up Elakala Falls. Like the larger Blackwater Falls, Elakala is known for its colored water, dyed dark amber by tannins from nearby hemlocks. When the needles fall in, they dye the water. There are many legends about where the falls' name came from, including a princess and a warrior named Elakala. Come up with your own legend for how these falls were named!

Elakala Falls pours under the footbridge

Apple tree

Did you know there are more than 7,500 different varieties of apples? Wild apple trees can grow to be over 29 feet tall. They bloom with bright white flowers for a short time between April and May, then produce fruit in late summer and early fall. What is your favorite type of apple?

Malus domestica

Bridge

Look down at the water from the bridges today, noting which direction the water flows and how fast it's going. What factors might influence how much water is in the stream or river? Drop in a leaf or twig and envision it flowing all the way to Chesapeake Bay!

There are several small wooden footbridges along the trail

49

GO WILD AT VALLEY FALLS

YOUR ADVENTURE

Adventurers, today we will explore the historical land of the Monongahela, Calicuas, Osage, Shawnee, and Massawomeck. This later became the site of a lumber mill and grist mill in the 1850s. Ruins of the mills can still be seen today next to the water. Start on the wide, packed-earth Rhododendron Trail at the end of the parking lot. On the left side of the path, you will see

Waterfalls on the Tygart Valley River →

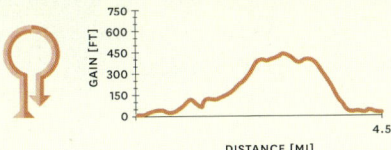

GAIN [FT]
750
600
450
300
150
0
                                    4.5
DISTANCE [MI]

LENGTH 4.5-mile lollipop loop

ELEVATION GAIN 548 ft.

HIKE TIME + EXPLORE 2 hours

DIFFICULTY Challenging—combination of wide, packed-earth paths and a narrow rocky paths; moderate elevation gain

SEASON Year-round; best in spring for blooms.

GET THERE From I-79 in Fairmont, take Exit 137 to WV-310 south for 7 miles. Turn right at the Valley Falls State Park sign. Go 2 miles to the park entrance. You will pass a small parking lot by the park office, where you can get maps and information. The main parking lot is at the bottom of the hill as you continue down Valley Falls Road.

Google Maps: bit.ly/timbervalleyfalls

RESTROOM At trailhead

FEE None

TREAT YOURSELF Pick up a famous pepperoni roll from the Country Club Bakery in Fairmont.

Valley Falls State Park
(304) 367-2719
Facebook @wvstateparks

CSX train tracks—they are still in use today. In fact, if you time your adventure correctly, you might even get to see a train with full coal cars drive by! Running parallel to the train track and the path is the Tygart Valley River, 135 miles long. After hiking along the river and tracks, turn right to stay on the trail. Next, stay straight, passing the Rocky Trail (you will return that way). Continue on the path, then turn right to stay on the trail. A huge boulder on the right side of the path makes a fun power-up point. Turn right to leave the Rhododendron Trail onto the Rocky Trail. Turn right again to stay on the Rocky Trail. You'll arrive at an area with several huge boulders that you can play on. It is worth taking the time to stop here and really explore and play in this magical spot. Return to the path, which becomes rocky and starts a sharp decline. Turn left onto the Rhododendron Trail again and retrace your steps. After returning to the trailhead, walk across the parking lot and over the walking bridge to relax on the rocks by the gorgeous waterfall that gives the park its name.

SCAVENGER HUNT

Boulders

Run in between these large rock formations, and if you feel comfortable, climb on top of them. They have broken apart on fractures called "joints," which are usually very straight and meet at angles. The joints formed while the rocks were still under the Earth's surface. Some-

times joint boulders trick us into thinking people must have carved them because they're so square, but it is an entirely natural phenomenon.

These huge boulders are a perfect spot to rest or explore

Leucoagaricus

This amazing mushroom is white when young and turns pinkish or maroon as it ages. The cap is round at first, then becomes flat with age. They grow in small groups on stumps, wood chips, sawdust piles, or on the ground in summer and fall. How many can you find?

Leucoagaricus americanus changes colors when damaged

B&O Railroad

Traders built a lumber mill and grist mill on this land in the 1830s and 1840s, but it was the completion of the Baltimore & Ohio railroad line from Grafton to Wheeling in 1853 that helped this community flourish. Imagine what it was like back then to see a huge train coming through the forest toward your small town.

The train tracks, completed in 1853, are still used today

American giant millipede

Watch for this arthropod—it's only 4 inches long but has fifty pairs of legs! Observe its long wormlike body, which is deep maroon to black, as it inches along. It's commonly found in or under decaying logs from March to October. When it feels threatened, it curls up in a spiral. Gently lift up some logs and see if you can find one!

Narceus americanus

TAKE A WALK BACK IN TIME AT HARPERS FERRY

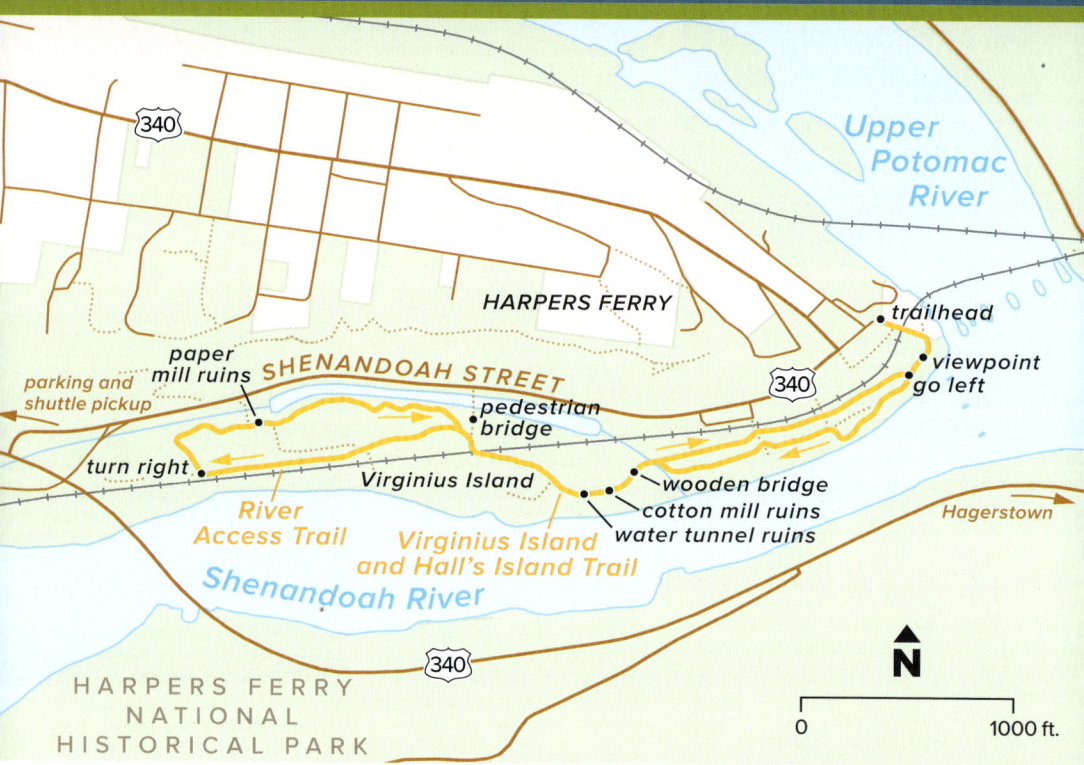

Upper Potomac River

340

HARPERS FERRY

. trailhead

paper mill ruins
parking and shuttle pickup

SHENANDOAH STREET

. viewpoint
go left

340

pedestrian bridge

turn right .

Virginius Island

wooden bridge
cotton mill ruins
water tunnel ruins

River Access Trail

Virginius Island and Hall's Island Trail

Shenandoah River

Hagerstown

340

N

HARPERS FERRY NATIONAL HISTORICAL PARK

0   1000 ft.

YOUR ADVENTURE

Adventurers, take a walk back in time on Virginius Island, on the historical homelands of the Shawnee and Massawomeck. The island was created by the Shenandoah Canal and was constructed by the Patowmack Company starting in 1806. Begin in Lower Town, where you will have spectacular views of the Appalachian Trail Bridge, an active railroad bridge adjacent

The original railroad bridge over the Potomac River in Harpers Ferry →

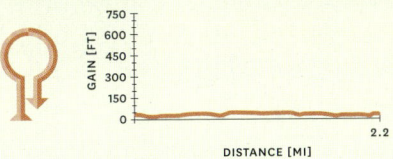

LENGTH 2.2-mile lollipop loop

ELEVATION GAIN 72 feet

HIKE TIME + EXPLORE 1 hour

DIFFICULTY Easy—compacted earth, sand, and gravel paths; little elevation

SEASON Year-round; best during fall foliage.

GET THERE From US-340 in Harpers Ferry, follow Shoreline Drive south to the park entrance. After paying your fee, park in the visitor center lot and ride the park shuttle into Lower Town. The shuttle runs every 15 minutes and is free (cost is included in the park entrance fee).

Google Maps: bit.ly/harpersferryparkinglot

RESTROOM In Lower Town, next to the bookshop and train station

FEE $20 per vehicle

TREAT YOURSELF Before you take the shuttle back to your car, cool off with some delicious soft-serve at Creamy Creations on Potomac Street.

Harpers Ferry National Historical Park
(304) 535-6029
Facebook @harpersferrynps

to the Goodloe E. Byron Memorial Footbridge, which allows Appalachian Trail hikers and regular pedestrians to cross the Potomac River. Go down some steps and turn left to hike along the Shenandoah River—we'll come back via the other trail. Cross the wooden footbridge to Virginius Island and start on the Virginius Island Trail. Ruins of the cotton mill and the water tunnel soon appear. Imagine what it was like to live in this small community two hundred years ago. Stay straight before turning right to cross the train tracks. Turn left onto the River Access Trail, weaving into the forest, around the water, and next to train tracks. Stop along the water to look for wildflowers, birds, and river wildlife. At the fork, turn right and wind your way through the paper mill ruins before hiking along Lake Quigley and passing the historical pedestrian bridge. Cross the tracks again, then stay straight to retrace your steps back to the trailhead. Consider exploring the small town of Harpers Ferry or walking or driving to other parts of this national historical park. Or make a weekend of it and camp at Harpers Ferry Campground.

SCAVENGER HUNT

Shenandoah pulp factory

You will walk beside the towering walls of an old pulp mill. This factory was built to provide wood pulp for the paper industry. Take a few minutes off the path to explore these ruins. Do you know how wood becomes paper?

Pulp is wood ground into tiny pieces and mixed with water

Great blue heron

Can you spot the most common and largest of North American herons? These birds can live in both freshwater and saltwater habitats. They are known to eat anything within striking distance, including fish, frogs, salamanders, turtles, snakes, insects, rodents, and other birds. Their necks are shaped like an S, which allows them to dart it out quickly, like a spring. If you cannot spot a great blue heron, can you spot something it might like to eat?

Ardea herodias is the size of a goose—or bigger

Pedestrian bridge

Imagine what it was like for island residents in the nineteenth century to walk these same paths. Massive flooding in 1852, 1870, 1924, and 1936 destroyed or damaged many of Virginius Island's structures and made it uninhabitable. Ultimately, these events allowed the island to return to a more natural state.

This bridge crosses the Shenandoah Canal to Virginius Island

Cotton mill and water tunnels

When it was built, the four-story brick factory cotton mill was the largest building on Virginius Island. It was equipped with gas lighting and steam heat and furnished with the latest cotton-milling machinery. Water tunnels near the mill increased power by controlling the flow of water to the mills.

Are you wearing any cotton today? During the Civil War, the building served as a Union hospital. After the war, it was converted into a flour mill.

The cotton mill was built in 1848

ACKNOWLEDGMENTS

There is nothing more reaffirming that we live in a world full of caring people than when hard-working rangers, parents, conservationists, biologists, geologists, and hikers call me back or respond to my emails, helping me get that species identification just right, or helping me verify the year a major discovery happened on the trail.

Special thanks to Philip Prince, geologist; Matthew S. Baker, superintendent at Blackwater Falls State Park; Haley Rodgers, Virginia Department of Conservation and Recreation; Kara Asboth, Virginia Department of Conservation and Recreation; Jennifer Legates, Woodlawn Manor Cultural Park; Meredith Petty, Alta Mons; Martin Callahan, Wye Island Natural Resources Management Area; Bradley Thomas, York River State Park; James Dayton, Bear Creek Lake State Park; Leah Taber, Harpers Ferry National Historical Park; Marceia Holland, Grayson Highlands State Park; Iris Allen, Department of Natural Resources; Jack Perdue, Department of Natural Resources; Jeff Simcoe, Department of Natural Resources; Michael Dixon, Chincoteague National Wildlife Refuge; Evelyn Shotwell, Chincoteague Chamber of Commerce; Emi Endo, Virginia Department of Conservation and Recreation; Shauna McVey, Delaware State Parks; Richard Julian, Cape Henlopen State Park; Will Koth, Trap Pond State Park; Alta Mons; Felicia M. Graves, Patapsco Valley State Park.

Huge thanks to Stacee Lawrence, Cobi Lawson, Mike Dempsey, Sarah Milhollin, Andrew Beckman, David Deis, Melina Hughes, Kathryn Jeurgens, and the entire Timber Press family for believing in a new volume to help reach mid-Atlantic families!

Having a strong family supporting you makes adventure possible.

To Wendy's family—Thanks to Gail, Xavier, and Jaedon Moore for being my trusty guinea pigs. To my father, Alan, for being an amazing driver and hiker. To my husband, Garrison, for being head GPS tracker and cheerleader and chef. And to my mother, Ginny, for her research skills.

To Alison's family—Thanks to my husband, Ronnie, who was our fearless navigator and driver to every hike and whose continuous support made this book possible. To our four amazing children, Teagen, Willow, Weston, and Stone, who bravely completed every single hike, and who were immensely helpful in every aspect of creating this book. To my parents, Stephen and Lucia, who taught me at an early age to always believe in myself and follow my dreams. And in memory of my older sister Stephanie who taught me to live life to the fullest. This book is about getting outside and spending quality time together as a family, and we truly hope it inspires you to prioritize outdoor family adventures.

And thank you to all the families reading this and getting outside with each other! We can't wait to see the adventures you go on.

PHOTO CREDITS

All photos by the authors unless noted below.

MerlinTuttle.org, 135 middle, 181 top
NPS.gov Collection, 183

Dreamstime
Adina Munteanu, 193 top
Ahkenahmed, 168
Bob Grabowski, 241 top
Brian Lasenby, 115 middle, 169 male tanager, 277 top
Brianguest, 153 top
Bwylezich, 212 bottom
Carlos Aranguiz, 193 bottom
Chris Dale, 229 bottom
Christian Weiß, 224 inset
Cvandyke, 240
Dennis Donohue, 165 top
Fascinadora, 110 inset?
Gerald D. Tang, 102 top main, 209 top inset, 209 middle
Harold Stiver, 169 female tanager
Ianhainsworth, 153 bottom
Iulian Gherghel, 106
Jon Bilous, 167
Joseph Morelli, 209 bottom
K Quinn Ferris, 197 middle main
Karel Bock, 164 bottom
Kazakovmaksim, 131 top
Kenneth Keifer, 184 bottom main
Kristof Lauwers, 185 bottom main
Larry Metayer, 184 top, 257 middle

Lianem, 66

Lukas Blazek, 91 bottom

Mikelane45, 253 middle

Ncristian, 74

Ondřej Prosický, 87 bottom

Rob Lumen Captum, 173 top

Simona Pavan, 225 middle main

Steve Byland, 78, 209 top main, 213 bottom

Tetiana Zbrodko, 149 middle inset

Tomasztc, 130 bottom

Vadim Startsev, 115 top

Victoria Moloman, 110

Vrabelpeter1, 256 top inset

William Wise, 221 top

Wirestock, 221 bottom

Flickr

Gilles Gonthier, 185 top

iStock

Kazakovmaksim, 56

Shutterstock

Wirestock Creators, 191

Wikimedia

Don Loarie, 139 middle, 217 middle

Paul Hurtado, 143 bottom

US Coast Guard, 87 middle

USCapitol, 164 top

William Hole (engraver, d. 1624), 49

INDEX

ABOUT YOUR LEAD ADVENTURERS

MEGAN RIGDON

ALISON holds a master's degree in clinical psychology and is a college professor and licensed psychotherapist in private practice. With her background in psychology and early childhood education, she has made a career of helping individuals and families improve their quality of life and has spoken at several national conventions on the topics of mental health and education. Alison homeschools her four young children, with an emphasis on hands-on, child-led learning and unstructured time in nature. She and her family believe in making the world their classroom. As part-time travelers and full-time adventurers, they opted to run their own businesses so they would have more time to go on adventures, travel, and chase sunsets. In addition to taking road trips and exploring nature with her family, Alison enjoys running, reading, photography, and writing. Follow her family's adventures on Instagram @raisingmavericks and email *alison@raisingmavericks.com*.

BOONE RODRIGUEZ

WENDY holds a master's degree in learning technologies and is a former classroom teacher. As part of her quest to bring science education alive, she has worked as a National Geographic Fellow in Australia researching Tasmanian devils, a PolarTREC teacher researcher in archaeology in Alaska, an Earthwatch teacher fellow in the Bahamas and New Orleans, and a GoNorth! teacher explorer studying climate change via dogsled in Finland, Norway, and Sweden. Today, she is a global education consultant who has traveled to more than fifty countries to design programs, build communities, and inspire other educators to do the same. She enjoys mountain biking, rock climbing, kayaking, backpacking, yoga, photography, traveling, writing, and hanging out with her family and nephews. Follow her on social media @50hikeswithkids and email *wendy@50hikeswithkids.com*.